TEACHERS AS LEADERS

PERSPECTIVES ON
THE PROFESSIONAL
DEVELOPMENT
OF TEACHERS

**Edited by
Donovan R.Walling**

Phi Delta Kappa Educational Foundation
Bloomington, Indiana

Cover design
by
Victoria Voelker

Library of Congress Catalog Card Number 94-66516
ISBN 0-87367-468-5
Copyright © 1994 by the Phi Delta Kappa Educational Foundation
Bloomington, Indiana

To Katy,
a teacher

TABLE OF CONTENTS

INTRODUCTION

Teachers must be — and often are — leaders in the education profession. *Teachers as Leaders* gives voice to the issues surrounding the recruitment, retention, and development of quality teachers. The authors of these diverse essays offer analyses of critical problems and pose both theoretical and practical solutions. Together, the various viewpoints converge on the key belief that teachers must be at the center of improvement and reform.

Many forces came together during the 1980s to give impetus to the current school reform movement. But it was the publication of *A Nation at Risk* in 1983 that focused public attention on education and subsequently subjected schools to microscopic examinations that they had not undergone since the late 1950s and early 1960s. Unfortunately, among the flaws in that document was the glaring omission of teachers as leaders either in the education profession or in school reform.

A Nation at Risk enumerated the ills of teaching. It even suggested that "master teachers should be involved in designing teacher preparation programs and in supervising teachers during their probationary years" (National Commission on Excellence in Education 1983, p. 31). But when it addressed the idea of leadership, it spoke only to principals and superintendents (p. 32).

Since that publication, educators at all levels have worked to put teachers back in the center of education, which is where they must be if any reform or revitalization of education is to occur. In the recently published *Roots of Reform: Challenging the Assumptions that Control Change in Education*, Astuto, Clark, and their co-authors write,

> The hope of authentic reform rests in empowerment that generates action at the site of responsibility by encouraging people to assume responsibility for themselves. When self-control replaces bureaucratic control, people are free to work at the edge of their competence and, consequently, to develop in ways that expand the limits of their expertise. (Astuto et al. 1994, pp. 89-90)

The current reform movement is a mix of the bureaucratic and the anti-bureaucratic. However, in large measure, those efforts at moving teachers to the center of reform that are most successful tend to be least bureaucratic. Now, more than a decade after *A Nation at Risk*, reform efforts more often draw from a renascent Progressivism than from the global-competition model that was espoused as the leading response to the "unilateral educational disarmament" with which the reform movement began.

The parallels between today's reforms and the Progressive Movement in education (1876-1957) are more than merely striking. Thirty-three years ago, Lawrence Cremin (1961) wrote a history of the movement that characterized Progressivism in this way:

> [I]t revolted against formalism and sought to extend the functions of the school . . . to delineate those things that the school needed to do because if the school did not do them they would not get done. (p. 352)

That same characterization can be applied to much of today's reform movement, perhaps with even greater accuracy. But the same caveat that Cremin offered for the Progressive Movement must be advanced for the current reform movement, which is that it has been "marked from the very beginning by a pluralistic, frequently contradictory, character" (p. x).

The most telling remark comes in the last sentences of Cremin's book, when he describes the demise of the Progressive Movement, which he marks by the dissolution of the Progressive Education Association in 1955 and the end of its journal, *Progressive Education*, in 1957. He says:

> [T]he authentic progressive vision remained strangely pertinent to the problems of mid-century America. Perhaps it only awaited the reformulation and resuscitation that would ultimately derive from a larger resurgence of reform in American life and thought. (p. 353)

Now, at the end of the century, that progressive vision is still pertinent. And perhaps that larger resurgence has begun. Certainly, many of the authors of the essays in this volume might agree.

This book provides diverse perspectives on the professional development of teachers. These perspectives are offered by individuals who have engaged in many facets of the education enterprise, from classroom teachers, principals, and superintendents to college and university educators to policy makers, organization leaders, and pundits.

When, on behalf of Phi Delta Kappa, I invited these authors to contribute to this volume, I posed the topic of teacher leadership and professional development in broad terms, hoping to encourage diverse and thought-provoking responses. I was not disappointed. I suggested four potential themes: 1) attracting the "brightest and best" to a teaching career, 2) inducting teachers into the profession of education, 3) empowering teachers through professional development, and 4) nurturing and empowering teacher leadership in schools. I recognized that many of the writers not only would combine these themes but also might roam afield to draw in related issues and ideas. The resulting collection of essays is a powerful combination of thoughtful, illuminating, persuasive, sometimes contradictory viewpoints.

In arranging these 20 essays, I have attempted to retain the original themes as categories. To these four categories, I have added a fifth — teachers and the improvement of schools — because several writers made specific ties between teacher professional development and school improvement. But I must acknowledge that the resulting sections are only loosely cohesive. Indeed, some of the essays are sufficiently wide-ranging that they might have been placed in any or all of the sections.

Part I centers on teacher recruitment and begins with James Hutto's essay, "Attracting the Best and Brightest to the Teaching Profession." Hutto, a high school principal in Meadville, Mississippi, looks at how to encourage talented students to consider a future in teaching. Rita Greer, a personnel specialist in the Jefferson County Public Schools in Louisville, Kentucky, narrows the focus to African-American students. And Katherine Green, a professor of psychology at Millersville University in Pennsylvania, draws attention to the teacher's role in recruiting the "brightest and best" in her "grassroots approach" essay.

Part II examines how teachers are — or might be — inducted into the profession. The section starts with Carnegie Foundation Senior Fellow Gene Maeroff's essay, "On Matters of Body and Mind: Overcoming Disincentives to a Teaching Career." My own essay on "Induction, Retention, and Collegiality" follows, summarizing recent strategies that seem to hold great promise. Ted Sanders and Nancy Ann Eberhart contribute "Teaching as Learning." Sanders, who is Ohio state superintendent, and Eberhart, who is a director in the Ohio Department of Education, discuss how teachers are transformed by continuous learning. The section concludes with "Celebrating Education as a Profession" by Marlin Tanck, director of teacher development at Marian College in Wisconsin.

Part III focuses on teacher empowerment. This central theme is aptly addressed in William Webster's essay, "Teacher Empowerment in a Time of Great Change," which begins the section. Webster is a professor of educational administration at California State University in Bakersfield. Mary Hatwood Futrell, who directs the Institute for Curriculum, Standards, and Technology at George Washington University, offers another perspective in her essay, "Empowering Teachers as Learners and Leaders." The section ends with Michael Schmoker and Richard Wilson's essay on "redefining results." Schmoker is a research analyst in the Amphitheater Schools in Tucson, Arizona, where Wilson is the superintendent.

Part IV offers specific connections between teacher development, leadership, and school improvement. "Can Teachers Be Educated to Save Students in a Violent Society?" announces the central theme of the opening essay by Martin Haberman, a distinguished professor at the University of Wisconsin-Milwaukee. David Hopkins and Mel West at Cambridge University provide a British perspective in their description of the Improving the Quality of Education for All (IQEA) Project. Peter Burke, who directs the licensing bureau at the Wisconsin Department of Public Instruction, contributes a view of teacher leadership in professional development. Ralph Fessler and Antoinette Ungaretti at Johns Hopkins University offer a treatment of how to expand opportunities for teacher leadership. And Sam Yarger and Okhee Lee at the University of Miami focus on instructional leadership opportunities. These last two essays make a convenient bridge to Part V.

Part V provides essays that look in-depth at teacher leadership, beginning with Michael Fullan's "Teacher Leadership: A Failure to Conceptualize." Fullan is dean of the Faculty of Education at the University of Toronto. Daniel Duke, a professor of education at the University of Virginia, offers his perspective in "Drift, Detachment, and the Need for Teacher Leadership." Vivian Troen and Katherine Boles contribute a teacher viewpoint in their aptly titled, "Two Teachers Examine the Power of Teacher Leadership." This essay is followed by Daniel Heller's "The Problem with Power." Heller is supervisor of instruction at Brattleboro Union High School in Vermont. The concluding essay of the section and of the book is by James Kelly, president of the National Board for Professional Teaching Standards, which looks "Toward a Community of Teacher Leaders."

In these 20 essays, the authors tackle the important issues that surround teacher recruitment, induction, and development. They address, in varied ways and from varied perspectives, the central themes of professional leadership and school improvement and reform. If one can draw from these essays a key concern, it is for educational excellence, which cannot be achieved without attention to all facets of the professional development of teachers. The authors of these essays offer thoughtful analyses, raise important questions, probe questionable assumptions, pose possible solutions, and urge specific actions in order to address this concern.

References

Astuto, T.A.; Clark, D.L.; Read, A.-M.; McGree, K.; and Fernandez, L.deK.P. *Roots of Reform: Challenging the Assumptions that Control Change in Education*. Bloomington, Ind.: Phi Delta Kappa Educational Foundation, 1994.

Cremin, Lawrence A. *The Transformation of the School*. New York: Alfred A. Knopf, 1961.

National Commission on Excellence in Education. *A Nation at Risk: The Imperative for Educational Reform*. Washington, D.C.: U.S. Government Printing Office, 1983.

PART I
ATTRACTING THE "BRIGHTEST AND BEST" TO A TEACHING CAREER

ATTRACTING THE BEST AND BRIGHTEST TO THE TEACHING PROFESSION

BY JAMES R. HUTTO

James R. Hutto is principal of Franklin High School in Meadville, Mississippi.

During the first grading period of the 1993-94 school year, seven students in our high school achieved the highest honors by making all A's. As their principal, I thought it would be interesting to discuss their future plans over an informal luncheon. To say the least, this luncheon provided some insights into how a small group of our "best and brightest" view their future and some of their thoughts about the teaching profession.

A luncheon of sandwiches on whole wheat bread (trying to teach nutrition) was provided. As the seven young women (no boys made all A's) began to eat, I told them that I wanted to elicit their opinions about certain issues. At this time, I did not tell them that I was writing an essay on attracting the best and brightest to the teaching profession.

"What career do you plan to pursue?" I asked.

Lakecha, a junior cheerleader who has never had any grade below A on her report card, responded, "I plan to major in medicine — really, pediatrics."

"Why did you choose that profession?"

"I went on a field trip and saw babies who had been born deformed," she said. "Because of that experience, I want to help children."

"My mother's a nurse, and I have thought about going into medicine," said Jennifer. "But, I don't want to be in a profession that will be so time-consuming."

Janna, Jennifer's identical twin sister, agreed that the medical profession may be for her. "My grandmother had brain surgery. It was an experience that made me appreciate the work of medical personnel."

"Chemical engineer," said Tasha. "I have an uncle who is a chemical engineer. He has encouraged me."

"But, Tasha, aren't both of your parents teachers?" I asked, knowing the answer.

Tasha smiled and admitted that her parents are teachers. "My parents come home from school and tell me, 'You don't want to teach'."

"Why would they say that?" I inquired.

"You know — the discipline problems, the stress. It's just too much."

"Have any of you thought about teaching?" I asked.

"There is nothing about teaching that interests me," Lakecha emphatically stated. "The children can be so bad and cause a nervous breakdown." Everyone laughed.

The twins joined in. "Yeah, we all have had students in some of our classes who don't care. They cause problems in class. I wish we could have classes that were for students who want to learn."

"We don't look at teaching as being successful," Tasha said. "We all want to be successful. They must start teaching that teaching is a successful profession."

"It's the 'routine-ness' of it," said Lakecha. "You can only do so much with students who don't care about learning. But I could see the rewards of having a positive influence on someone's life."

"Yeah, we have all had teachers who have cared about us. They have given a lot to help others," said Tasha.

Later that afternoon, I reflected on the statements of these young women. Although far from a scientific survey, several significant conclusions may be drawn from their remarks.

We all would agree that improved salaries for teachers should attract more of our best and brightest to the profession. However, none of these high school honor students mentioned limited financial rewards as a factor in their decision to not pursue a career in education. In fact, none of them mentioned money as the driving force in their choice of careers. Instead, they talked about helping people and other humanitarian concerns. Although admitting basing your career choice on financial considerations (unless you are an athlete) is not socially acceptable, I had thought that the "money issue" might have arisen during our informal luncheon. Since it did not, let us for the sake of argument assume that, though important, low salaries may not be the factor that deters our best and brightest from the profession.

These honor students repeatedly alluded to unmotivated students as a deterrent to choosing teaching as a profession. There seems to be a perception, not only among these students but in the population as a whole, that students in our schools are not motivated to learn and that this lack of motivation creates unbearable working conditions. On what is this perception based? Media reports of violence in our schools, falling test scores, an overall lack of concern among American public school students? In the case of these honor students, their perception was based on personal experiences with classmates who do not value education.

There seems to be a vicious cycle at work here. Until we attract the best and brightest to the profession, our students will suffer from sub-par teaching that contributes to low motivation. Therefore, our brightest students will attend classes with unmotivated students who disrupt learning and cause students like Jennifer to say, "I don't want to work with students who do not care about themselves or others."

For any profession to offer its clients the very best service, there must be a nucleus of bright, highly motivated practitioners continuously entering the profession. Although we must concede that a teaching career is not for everyone, how can we ensure that our profession will entice a rightful share of the best and brightest? What can be done to increase our ability to attract highly motivated, intelligent young people into the profession?

First, increased financial rewards *will* attract more of our top young people to the teaching profession. Numerous articles and essays document relatively low teachers' salaries. Athletes make millions of dollars, yet teachers continue to perform perhaps the most important job of all for a "mere pittance." There are waiting lists to get into medical schools, law schools, and engineering schools — all of which promise their graduates high-salary jobs.

Even though great men and women have altruistically served their fellow human beings, our society seems to worship at the altar of financial benefits. "Success" equals a high salary. This seems to be the formula that causes a student such as Tasha to say, "We don't look at teaching as being successful."

People repeatedly have stated in surveys that they are willing to support increased taxes to upgrade their schools and pay teachers better wages. Yet the "vicious cycle" also strikes here. Until we attract better-qualified people to the teaching profession, the public will deal with educators who are not the best and brightest. Even worse, they may find unqualified individuals in their schools who were hired because top graduates were not available. Consequently, the teaching profession may remain negative in many people's eyes.

Beyond the obvious attraction of greater financial rewards, four nonfinancial "need to do's" may assist in attracting our top students to the profession. I readily concede that all of these "need to do's" may be expensive, but they do not involve direct teacher compensation.

"Need to do" number one is to have a national campaign, perhaps under the auspices of the national principals organizations, to establish clubs in every school that promote an early awareness and commitment to teaching as a career. Students need to hear about the positive opportunities and rewards associated with teaching. Too often, our young people hear about the negative aspects of teaching. I have been told by several teachers that they would never encourage any of their students to choose teaching as a career. It is no wonder that many intelligent young people are turned off to the teaching profession.

Clubs and organizations that have as their mission the promotion of teaching as a career should be established in all schools. Teachers of Tomorrow and Future Educators of America are two organizations that attempt to attract the best and brightest to an education career. Although both of these organizations have worthy goals, they are not well known. I had heard that some schools established such clubs. But when I contacted our state department of education and received the information on these two organizations, I was appalled to learn of their relative obscurity. In fact, even though I am a veteran of 25 years in public education, I had never before received information about Teachers of Tomorrow or Future Educators of America.

This is not an indictment of these organizations; it does point to the need for a concerted dissemination of information about them to school leaders. Teachers of Tomorrow and Future Educators of America could, through cooperative efforts with the National Association of Elementary School Principals and the National Association of Secondary School Principals, disseminate much-needed information about these clubs to school leaders. Perhaps, these principals organizations will see that administrators can be only as good as the people they lead and commit not only to disseminating the information but to making the establishment of future teachers clubs a reality in every school.

"Need to do" number two is the establishment and adequate funding of the teacher corps concept on the national level. At present, several states, including my home state of Mississippi, have ongoing programs that are designed to use alternative certification to attract bright liberal arts graduates to the teaching profession. I will give a brief overview of the Mississippi Teacher Corps and relate one success story from the project.

The Mississippi Teacher Corps, operating since 1990 with recruits from such universities as Harvard, Stanford, and the University of Chicago, is designed to provide a structured entry into the teaching profession for talented liberal arts graduates with strong backgrounds in such areas as foreign language, natural science, and mathematics. At the same time, these young, talented graduates are routed to districts with teacher shortages. Since its inception, the Mississippi Teacher Corps has provided numerous hard-to-find teachers for districts throughout the state.

Jeff Seinfeld, a 1990 graduate of Stanford University, came to Mississippi in the summer of that year to participate in the first year of the Mississippi Teacher Corps. His strong background in the natural sciences made him a natural to pursue certification in that area. He eventually was matched with a small rural school in Vaiden, Mississippi (population 600) and agreed to teach chemistry and physics, giving Vaiden High School a chance to offer a physics course for the first time in five years.

After arriving at his teaching assignment, Jeff discovered that the school needed a Spanish teacher in order to offer its students a foreign language. Being truly one of the best and brightest, he earned alternate certification in Spanish and taught Spanish along with his science classes. Not only did he provide access to physics, chemistry, and Spanish to some rural kids in Mississippi for that school year, but he brought experiences to these students of untold value. Because of his love for these kids and his love of teaching, Jeff taught an extra year, thereby sharing his knowledge and dedication with even more students.

Albeit a short-term, short-range approach to attracting the best and brightest to the teaching profession, the teacher corps approach has attracted some bright young people. And, who knows, others like Jeff may stay on for many years in a profession they grow to love.

This alternate entry route also may be used to attract other bright — not necessarily young — people to the profession. Although many educators oppose the idea of using alternative certification to attract people to the profession, there is merit in what I will call "reverse entry."

During my tenure as a high school principal, I have worked with two teachers who "burned out" in their engineering jobs. These bright individuals met the standards for alternative certification in the area of mathematics and were willing to take pay cuts to work in teaching. How many others in such diverse professions as medicine, law, accounting, or engineering are burned out? How many want to revitalize their careers by moving into teaching? These professionals could benefit themselves and the profession by this "reverse entry" into teaching.

The military provides a means for its retirees to enter the teaching profession as Junior Reserve Officer Training Corps (JROTC) instructors at the end of their active military duty. Perhaps this process might serve as a model for other professions whose recent retirees yet may have much to offer in America's classrooms. It is common to find doctors and lawyers teaching on the college level. These and other professions may provide an untapped resource of individuals who are looking for an opportunity to give something back to their community through teaching, especially in the areas of mathematics and science. Attracting some of these outstanding individuals to teaching, even briefly, may be a worthy endeavor.

For "reverse entry" to work, an alternate-route certification program must be in place. However, this alternate-route certification process need not be watered down to test only subject matter knowledge. Instead, this process should include authentic assessment of pedagogical and human relations skills. Each alternately certified teacher then might be provided a mentor, a master teacher who has been trained to provide mentoring.

Finally, an awareness campaign would be needed to convey information about the process. The military's system of promoting teaching positions for their retirees through public school JROTC programs offers an example. By providing information about these teaching positions to active-duty personnel, the military works closely with public schools to provide a cadre of eager, qualified individuals to fill teaching positions. Using a similar system, we might call on other professions to disseminate information about teaching to their members.

When we consider that most people change careers several times, we in education may be the beneficiaries if we can attract bright, motivated people from other professions to an alternate career in teaching. At the beginning of the 1993-94 school year, our school employed as a math teacher a man who had originally taught math then made a career change to work for a large oil company. After 20 years with that company, he chose early retirement and returned to the teaching profession. His math class is immersed in hands-on, "real life" learning, and this teacher can draw on his personal experience to answer the common student question: "How are we going to use this algebra in the real world?"

On the subject of changing professions, let us also consider the college students who change majors. Many young people choose certain college majors because they are drawn to promises of future wealth and prestige. But after a time, they decide that a career choice based on financial gain is unfulfilling. Or the career is not what they thought it would be, or the college preparation is not to their liking. For whatever reason, many decide to change majors. We need a safety net to catch these bright young people and guide them to the teaching profession.

Consider the following true-life scenario. Janice, a bright, articulate, minority student, is the child of two first-generation teachers. She was salutatorian of her high school class and scored in the top percentiles on all standardized tests. Everyone expected her to pursue a career in medicine, law, or some other highly esteemed profession. Janice received many scholarship offers and finally decided to major in chemical engineering. As everyone expected, Janice made excellent grades in college and seemed to be on her way to a rewarding career in chemical engineering. Notwithstanding all her college successes, Janice began to question her decision to seek a degree in engineering. She learned more about her chosen field and considered her needs and personality. Out of this introspection came a decision to change her college major and to pursue a career that better matched her needs. But what career path would she now follow?

Janice was almost ashamed to admit that her heart was leading her to teach English. She always had loved the study of the language and felt that she would be an excellent teacher. But what would others think? She was considering leaving a prestigious college major in order to enter the study for a career field that many people view as less than a profession. Additionally, her choice would cost her untold future dollars.

Janice chose to follow her heart and pursue a teaching degree in English. Today, she is happily employed as a high school English teacher. She likes her career choice and is glad that she made the decision to change college majors. But how many others stay in a major that they do not enjoy? Janice was fortunate to be guided by two understanding parents who were teachers. They supported her decision to enter teaching and offered her guidance and love. How many other young people have the help they need to make these tough decisions?

That brings me back to the idea of providing a safety net. Most high schools do follow-up work with their graduates. Such follow-up usually consists of tracking students in order to make needed curriculum changes to better serve future graduates. Very little of this follow-up has anything to do with providing services for graduates. Although many former graduates face monumental decisions that require guidance, practically none is provided by the school system where these students have spent thirteen years of their lives. Granted that public school counselors, teachers, and administrators are overwhelmed with their current duties and are reluctant to take on additional responsibilities; however, to attract the best and brightest, we may need to include counseling high school graduates who are considering a career change. Each high school might be encouraged to follow up on the career choices of their top graduates. This follow-up could include surveys, telephone contacts, and visits to the college by high school personnel.

I am aware of one high school that invites graduates back to the school just before Christmas break. Since most colleges dismiss for Christmas break before the public schools, this is a convenient time. When these graduates come back, small- and large-group meetings can be planned in order to gather information and to provide a safety net for those considering a change of college major. And it follows that at least some of these changes might draw some of our best and brightest to the teaching profession.

Although a national teacher corps program, "reverse entry," and a safety net to catch students who change college majors may be controversial and in need of refinement, these and other creative methods must be pursued to ensure that the teaching profession will garner more of the best and brightest. Many details must be worked out, but let us be open to any new recruitment idea.

"Need to do" number three is to continue to provide and enhance award programs that recognize excellent teaching. Numerous teacher award programs recognize excellence in the teaching of various disciplines. The primary goal of most of these awards is peer recognition. Notwithstanding the excellence of this goal, we must see the role that these awards can play in changing the public perception of teaching. Significant awards that rate media coverage can help to elevate teaching to a higher status in our society. The award program that comes closest to achieving this goal is the Disney Channel's annual teacher awards program.

The Disney Teacher Awards Program resembles the popular Academy Awards. With a format that shows video clips of the five teachers nominated for the "Best Teacher Award" in each subject area and a presentation of the nominees by famous actors and well-known public figures, the awards program is a fast-paced media event. Unfortunately, the program is available only to cable subscribers. How helpful it would be to let all America see such a program. Hearing famous individuals commenting on teachers who touched their lives made me proud to be an educator.

As young people watch such an awards program, they can see the rewards of a career in teaching. I know that many of our best and brightest — students such as Janice — are drawn to teaching but do not see the success associated with a teaching career. I also know that if they saw and felt what I felt as I watched this awards program, they would catch a vision of teaching that could inspire a commitment to the profession.

"Need to do" number four is to allow teachers to police their own profession. Although a complex task that often is mired in politics, a licensing board that is self-governing and whose majority members are teachers will be a move toward professionalizing teaching. And any move toward professionalizing teaching potentially will attract more able students to the profession. Since the late 1980s, the National Board for Professional Teaching Standards, a self-governing, nongovernmental board whose majority members are teachers, has moved toward the goal of setting rigorous standards for professional teachers. Taking its cue from other professions, the National Board for Professional Teaching Standards is committed to enriching the preparation and development of teachers.

More bright, young people will be attracted to a profession that not only provides preparation and continuing development for its members, but also oversees the profession under the aegis of current members. Under the direction of a licensing board directed and controlled by their peers, medical doctors have achieved a status in our society that bestows power, prestige, and lucrative financial opportunities. Doctors would shudder at the idea of any other group controlling the licensing of their members. Conversely, the teachers currently are licensed through systems that often lack consistency and professional input. The National Board's voluntary certification process may be a first step in allowing teachers to police their own profession and, thereby, aid in attracting the best and brightest to the profession.

My conversations with the honor students point to the need to improve our schools. Many schools are using contextual teaching and authentic assessment to provide more relevant learning experiences

17

and to increase students' motivation to learn. As schools move in this direction, we are less likely to hear comments such as those made by the honor students about unmotivated, disruptive students. Such improvements in current practice will increase our chances of attracting to teaching our share of these motivated, articulate students.

Likewise, improving teacher salaries will provide an incentive for students to look seriously at teaching as a career.

The four "need to do's" also might accomplish much. A national recruitment campaign with future teacher clubs in every school; a nationwide teacher corps to help young people experience teaching, to bring seasoned professionals into teaching through "reverse entry," and to provide a safety net for college students who want to change majors; high-profile awards programs that enhance teachers' feelings about themselves and raise the status of the profession in the eyes of the public; and allowing teachers to police their own profession are all important ideas that can help us to recruit the best and brightest.

Since I started writing this essay, I have encouraged several young people to think about a teaching career. I also plan to discuss these issues with my faculty. We, as educators, must take a personal role in attracting our best students to our profession. We must glimpse the future. Although "vision" has become a catchword, it is real and necessary. And we must act on this vision in order to improve education.

ATTRACTING TALENTED AFRICAN-AMERICAN HIGH SCHOOL STUDENTS TO CAREERS IN EDUCATION

BY RITA G. GREER

Rita G. Greer is a personnel specialist and data management coordinator for the Jefferson County Public Schools in Louisville, Kentucky.

"Who will teach America's youth in the year 2000?" is a question being pondered across this nation. Not only are professional educators concerned about the fate of the teaching profession, but government officials, the business community, and the nation's parents are anxious about the quality and quantity of future teachers. Will there be enough teachers in the pipeline to meet the demands of increasing enrollments and teacher retirements? Will these individuals possess the necessary characteristics for success? These are the issues at hand.

Projections about the size of the turn-of-the-century teacher pool vary. While an overall teacher shortage predicted for the mid-1990s may not materialize, "spot shortages" or subject-area shortages have been the norm for the past ten years. Exceptional education, bilingual, mathematics, and science teachers have proven to be the most difficult to obtain; and these fields continue to lead the list of areas where fully certified personnel are unavailable (Akin 1986; ASCUS 1993). Those who monitor teacher numbers feel certain that this phenomenon will continue into the year 2000.

The issue of teacher quality also is a source of controversy. What are the indicators of high-quality teachers? How should quality be measured? Should there be standards that all teachers must meet before being certified? Should teachers be prepared to teach fewer grade levels but with more depth? Should teachers be specialists or generalists? Should access to teaching be reserved for those who are considered the best and brightest? (Schlechty and Vance 1983; Mercer 1982; Pipho 1986). Discussion of such questions brings a variety of answers, as demonstrated by the array of reform movements across

19

the nation, each touted as the way to address the quality issue. Professional standards boards are a part of many of these reform movements.

While the debate over the quality and quantity of the turn-of-the-century teaching force continues, there is agreement on one aspect: The severe decline in the number of African-American teachers during the 1990s will continue into the next century unless dramatic action is taken to reverse the trend. Additionally, observers believe that the need for teachers of color will peak in the late 1990s and early 2000s as those who entered teaching in the mid- to late-1960s leave the profession at a time when the number of children of color entering public school systems across the nation will be rapidly increasing (Darling-Hammond 1987; Hodgkinson 1985; RNT 1993).

This essay will discuss lessons learned over the past decade about how we might interest African-American youth in general and academically talented African-American youth in particular to consider careers in education. It is based on research begun in 1985 with the Jefferson County Kentucky Public Schools' Minority Teacher Recruitment Project that has continued to the present. Furthermore, data have been collected informally from high school and college students across the nation as part of the process to improve minority recruitment efforts. The focus is directed to high school students because of the current emphasis being placed on "catch them while they're young" efforts that are being supported by federal and state governments and private foundations.

It is the intent of this essay to shed some light on how we might glean some insight from our past experiences and available data to help us utilize available resources to create effective recruitment programs that appeal to talented African-American students. Patricia Graham (1987) points out:

> If the general demand for able, well-prepared compassionate teachers is great, then the demand for able, well-prepared compassionate black teachers is acute. Blacks are declining rapidly as a percentage of the teaching force, even as black enrollment is rising. For blacks and non-blacks alike, it is important that we find and encourage blacks to become the able, well-prepared compassionate teachers who will instruct our young for the benefit of us all. (p. 605)

A Historical Perspective

Teaching has been a cornerstone of professionalism in the African-American community ever since there was an African-American community. When other occupations were closed to blacks seeking professional opportunities, the ministry, nursing, and teaching were the accessible avenues that provided stable employment, income, and professional status. Historically, predominantly black colleges and universities supplied the talent pool for these professions. Over the years, teaching came to be dominant as these colleges produced more than half of the African-American teachers in the nation's classrooms (Williams et al. 1991).

The near demise of teacher education programs at historically black colleges and universities still remains a secret to many alumni of those institutions and, to a great extent, to the African-American community at large. For many who remember the large numbers of education majors in the halls of the Knoxville, Tuskeegee Institute, Bethune-Cookman, and their sister institutions, it is difficult to comprehend the dramatic changes that have occurred as teacher training has been relegated to a low-priority status, based on the number of African-American graduates being produced.

An early indication of the trend away from education as a primary career choice was recognized by Lyson (1983), who examined the curriculum emphasis of black students attending both predominantly black and predominantly white land grant colleges between 1967 and 1977. Lyson reported a significant decline in the percentage of students in black land grant colleges who were awarded degrees in education: 18.5% over the 10-year period. However, for those attending white land grant colleges, the percentage of education degrees awarded was virtually unchanged. These data become significant in light of the prominent role that teacher education had played in black institutions. Teacher preparation had been their "bread-and-butter" foundation.

Trent's findings (1984) also shed light on this developing scenario. He reported that of the degrees awarded in 1975-1976 to black males, 14.5% were in education. The percentage had dropped to 10.5% by 1981-1982. Similarly, the degrees in education awarded to black females during the same times declined nearly 13% from 31.7% to 19%.

Several explanations have been put forth to account for the waning interest in teaching as a career among African-Americans. Among the explanations, expanding employment opportunities for women and minorities, teacher testing, low status of the teaching profession, and the overall decline in enrollment of African-Americans in four-year colleges are generally accepted as representative of the national perspective.

Nearly 30 years of changes brought about by the civil rights movement, affirmative action policies, the women's movement, and direct government interventions have expanded career opportunities for women and minorities. The barriers that limited access and advancement in male-dominated, traditionally white occupations have been somewhat removed. Although there are now rumblings that America is returning to the pre-1960s era in terms of integration and affirmative action, one still notes that society has invited women and minorities to pursue academic options that improve their marketability and that prepare them for a broader range of careers. Expanded employment opportunity undoubtedly is a primary factor in the waning interest in teaching as a career among African-Americans.

Increasing demands on those who would become teachers is another factor. The National Teacher Exam, the primary test used for teacher certification, is not the lone barrier. Admissions tests, certification tests, recertification tests, and performance assessments are all part of the testing arena. Admissions and certification tests have proven to be the most challenging to African-Americans (Smith 1987). While accusations of test bias still are being explored, the fact is that increasing standards for entry into and exit from teacher education programs have not been matched by similar improvements in teacher salaries and working conditions. Indeed, the hoops have been made more difficult while the rewards have remain unchanged; and the rewards appear mediocre when compared to the salary benefits and perks offered by other professions.

The status of the teaching profession is another factor in the declining interest of African-Americans in teaching. The academic ability of those who choose to teach versus the ability of those who enter other university departments still is characterized by the old saying, "Those who can, do; those who can't, teach." The hierarchy of departments within the university is based on the perceived academic ability required of the students in each department. The higher the perceived academic ability needed, the more rigorous — and therefore the more prestigious — the department (Vance and Schlechty 1982).

When considered independently, any one of the these factors might influence the career decisions of high school students. But when one combines the perception that the least capable students are the education majors, that anybody and everybody can teach, and that teaching is a female-dominated occupation that will command lower compensation than male-dominated occupations, then the self-esteem of teachers already in the profession also is affected. Thus when teachers, the primary professional role models for African-American youth, are bombarded with these perceptions, the impact of these negative messages cannot be prevented from carrying over into the everyday life of teachers and influencing the career choices of their students (Greer 1989).

With this historical backdrop in place, let us turn our attention to the data collected and the lessons learned over the past decade regarding attracting academically talented African-American high school students to careers in teaching.

Career Choices of High School Students

"What do you want to be when you grow up?" How often this question is asked of elementary children, and how often the answer is "doctor," "teacher," "fireman," "basketball player," and so on. On any given day, some youngster will say, "I want to be like Ms. Jones, my teacher." However, ask an African-American high school junior or senior the question, and you rarely will find teaching included in their list of career choices. Teaching simply is not popular. Its lack of popularity evokes several questions or concerns, since the primary professional role models of high school-aged students are teachers. Why business or medicine, law or sports, rather than education?

When high school students are asked to tell why they selected a particular career as their first choice, they give a number of reasons. As one might suspect, pay/salary is a major factor. However, for black males, good benefits and advancement opportunities also are important. For black females, pay/salary, though a major factor, is not as important as for black males. Black females also seek job availability and advancement opportunities and consider their future need for the career as major reasons for a career choice. Important to note here is what students tell us about career selection. The following comments reflect the perceptions of many black male high school students:

> It's so scary when you think about the future. Teachers and counselors don't tell black men [students] anything about careers.

$$* \quad * \quad *$$

> They [teacher/counselors] are so busy telling us that we have to make up our minds because we are young adults that they forget that we still need help and want them to give us some direction.

Our teachers don't talk to us about careers, they talk to girls.

* * *

We are smart, but we [black men] aren't expected to do anything anyway, so nobody really talks to us about teaching or any other career.

The influence of significant others in helping students make career choices is important to the development of effective recruitment efforts. But for black high school students, parents play a key role in making the selection. Figure 1 shows students' opinions of who influences their career choices. The opinions of black and white students are included to show the contrast between the two groups.

Comparing the responses of the black and white groups, blacks indicate that teachers have more influence on career decisions than counselors, others, or friends. By contrast, whites indicate that others and friends have a greater impact than teachers or counselors. For both groups, parents are most influential.

Effective recruitment of African-American students to a career in education must come from parents and teachers, the two groups most influential in their career choices. Thus teachers can play an important role in shaping the career decisions of blacks by working collaboratively with parents.

A high school teacher underscores the possible importance of teachers as active recruiters of future teachers. The teacher asked one of her students if she knew any of her friends who wanted to be a teacher. The student responded, "Mrs. Harlan, I want to be a teacher." Mrs. Harlan said, "But Jane, you've already registered to enter engineering school next fall." The young lady replied, "Yes, but the people from engineering school asked me to be an engineer and also the people from medical school asked me if I wanted to be a doctor. But no one has ever asked me if I want to be a teacher."

Can teachers saying to black students, "I think that you will make a great teacher," prove to be an important recruitment tool?

Table 1 highlights some of the opinions, beliefs, and perceptions about teaching and teachers that often are quoted as reasons why black high school students do not consider teaching as a viable career choice. Socioeconomic status (SES), grade level, and sex of the students provide an interesting overview to consider.

Cross-referencing these three categories yields some strong results. For example, high-SES males in grade 12 feel strongly that teachers

Figure 1. Influence of most significant other on career choice.

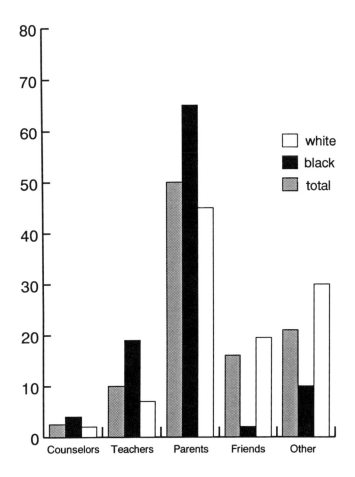

Source: Attitudes of Academically Talented Black High School Students Toward Teaching as a Career

Cross-referencing these three categories yields some strong results. For example, high-SES males in grade 12 feel strongly that teachers do not make enough money. Black females are strong in their belief that "computers will not replace teachers" and that teaching should not be considered as "women's work." Low- and mid-SES respondents strongly disagree with the notion that teaching is a job for those who cannot do anything else. High SES (61.8%), males (56.1%),

do. If you don't pay people for what they do, then people must not think you're doing very much. I guess teachers are at the bottom of the barrel because, God knows, they're always talking about not getting paid enough!

*   *   *

Basically, teachers are middle class, so I guess the status of teaching is middle status.

*   *   *

The status of teaching or of any job depends on how much education you must have to get the job. If a job doesn't require much education, then it is low status. If it requires a college degree, then it is high status. Now some jobs require more than one college degree, so they have even higher status. Well, teachers who have their master's have higher status than teachers who don't!

*   *   *

Status of teaching is like status of anything else. For example, status of where you live. The status of teaching is how teaching is as an occupation compared with other occupations. Teaching as a job is all right, but the status of teaching is low.

*   *   *

Teaching has low status because teachers are mostly women and women are still thought to be unequal to men in our society today.

*   *   *

Teaching may be high or low status. If you're talking about what a teacher makes, then teaching is low status. If you're talking about what teachers do, then teaching is high status.

*   *

Teaching doesn't have status now, according to my mom. But, it used to have [status] back in the Fifties and Sixties when blacks couldn't do anything else.

*   *

The status of teaching is fair. Most parents don't see teachers as being important or having good status or they would make their children behave in school. The students in Honors see teaching as having good status. We treat our teachers right or

28

our parents will be on us. Still, they [parents] don't want us
to be teachers.

*   *

The status of teaching is how the community respects teachers.
This community usually treats teachers with respect. . . . Our
teachers haven't had to strike like in some other places. And
our teachers are always getting awards and gifts. Remember,
we have a teacher who was the National Teacher of the Year!

*   *

Teaching changes from high to low depending on what your
parents do for a living. My dad is a teacher, so teaching is high
status for me. I respect my dad and his profession. But I guess
my dad would say the status of teaching is low because so many
other students don't respect him or other teachers in general.

The following statement seems to capture the essence of respondents' views of the status of teaching:

Your place in society is status. The status of teaching is how
other members of the community or society treat you; whether
or not they honor you or give you grief. It also depends on how
teachers carry themselves. You look at some teachers and they
represent high standards. You look at others and you wonder
how they ever got to be teachers. They make teaching low status.
But you must think teaching is high status or you wouldn't
wonder how they got to be teachers. In any case, the status of
teaching is based on how people respect teachers and, I guess,
teaching compared to other jobs.

The status of teaching may be an illusive concept, but the comments made by these students are illuminating.

A final piece of significant information is the impact of testing requirements on career choice. How will reducing test requirements affect decisions to become a teacher? According to many academically talented black high school students, reducing test requirements will not affect their decision to become (or not become) a teacher. Only black males (both low and high SES) see reducing test requirements as having some importance in career choice.

Programmatic Recommendations

The previous discussion provides a number of considerations for those who are serious about the recruitment of talented African-

American high school students into teaching careers. Specific recruitment strategies that target academically talented African-American students must be developed. Following are suggested recruitment strategies; but they must be tailored to the socioeconomic status, grade level, and sex of the targeted subgroup:

1. Develop information campaigns for current teachers, targeted students, parents, and the community at large.
2. Provide early intervention programs that take targeted students to visit college campuses early in their school careers, perhaps during middle school but absolutely no later than ninth grade.
3. Create early test readiness programs for subgroups who are uneasy about testing, particularly low-SES and high-SES black males.
4. Identify black male role models within the local community who are willing to interact with the targeted group. Establish an ongoing program where students, especially black males, can have contact with black male professionals.
5. Since black male teachers generally are few in number in most school districts, develop ways to use them as role models for black male students, for example, by using alternative scheduling approaches where outstanding and respected black male teachers might spend part of their day teaching their usual subject or grade and then might spend the remainder of the day in a quasi-counseling role, working with groups of black male students on career guidance.
6. Target specific groups of students for a variety of career guidance programs. Include specific plans to address varying student needs as part of the overall school guidance plan.
7. Develop a high school course, possibly "Career Exploration in Teaching," that may be taught by a master teacher. Offer the course for elective credit during the junior year.
8. Develop an Introduction to Education course offered at the high school level for college credit during the senior year.
9. Work with professional education organizations so that they are represented at career fairs and other career-related events.
10. Advertise yearly themes and produce information leaflets and other advertisements to be distributed throughout the community, including distribution to current teachers.
11. Encourage teachers and other professionals to identify students who are prospective teachers, just as they identify prospective engineers, doctors, and other professionals.

12. Bring the university faculty to the school campus, where feasible, to teach education courses at the local school, so that the university becomes a familiar possibility rather than a foreign concept, especially for black males.
13. Develop mentoring programs between schools and colleges of education in which students have opportunities to work with university professors, as well as with high school teachers, on special projects or research in education.
14. Work with the state and community organizations to establish special scholarship programs for prospective teachers who are in the top 25% of their graduating class, rather than for only those in the top 5% to 10%.
15. Target individual students early and "court" them as other professions court their future professionals.
16. Host periodic "parent nights" and invite parents to participate in recruitment.
17. Offer professional development on teaching across the curriculum to encourage all teachers to incorporate information about teaching in their everyday lessons and curriculum design.
18. Extend an invitation to students to consider teaching as a secondary career choice, if not their primary choice. Promote teaching as an "extension" career that adds to their career flexibility.

We must set about to develop deliberate, systematic programs that nurture and support individuals based on their needs and perceptions. Knowing how one's students view teaching and teachers is critical to the process of program development and delivery. Being responsive to this population means exercising flexibility within structure.

We can and must attract more of the talented African-American high school students into the profession. For those of us who are seasoned, we might begin by expanding our vision of the profession. We may want to begin looking at teaching as simply one career within the education profession and marketing the profession as such.

Additionally, collaborative recruitment efforts involving the total community — the school district, the university, the state department of education, and organizations within the community — must be initiated if we are to muster the resources, skills, and talents needed to attract talented black high school students to join the education profession.

Finally, we must remember that this problem did not occur overnight, and we should not expect to see immediate results. What we can hope to see is a change in attitudes and, therefore, more consideration and thought given to careers in the education profession. We must always remember that "academically talented" implies that the targeted population can read between the lines. Thus vestiges of tokenism must be removed from our recruitment repertoire. Our African-American students must be recruited for their talents, skills, abilities, and gifts, not simply because they are black.

References

Akin, J.A. *Teacher Supply/Demand in the U.S.* Madison, Wis.: Association for School, College, and University Staffing, 1986.

Association for School, College, and University Staffing (ASCUS). *Teacher Supply and Demand in the United States, 1993 Report.* Evanston, Ill., 1993.

Darling-Hammond, L. *Career Choice for Minorities: Who Will Teach?* Washington, D.C.: National Education Association and Council of State School Officers, 1987.

Graham, P.A. "Black Teachers: A Drastically Scarce Resource." *Phi Delta Kappan* 68 (April 1987): 598-605.

Greer, R.G. "A Study of the Attitudes of Academically Talented Black High School Students Toward Teaching as a Career." Doctoral dissertation. University of Louisville, 1989.

Hodgkinson, H. *All One System: Demographics of Education, Kindergarten Through Graduate School.* Washington, D.C.: Institution for Educational Leadership, 1985.

Lyson, T. "The Changing Curriculum Orientations of Students at Black Land Grant Colleges: A Shift-Share Approach." *Research in Higher Education* 18, no. 4 (1983): 485-94.

Mercer, W. "Future Florida Black Teachers: A Vanishing Breed." *Negro Education Review* 33 (July 1982): 135-39.

Pipho, C. "Quantity vs. Quality: States Aim to Improve Teaching and Teachers." *Phi Delta Kappan* 67 (January 1986): 333-34.

Recruiting New Teachers (RNT). *State Policies to Improve the Teacher Workforce: Shaping the Profession that Shapes America's Future.* Denver, Colo., 1993.

Schlechty, P., and Vance, V. "Recruitment, Selection and Retention: The Shape of the Teaching Force." *Elementary School Journal* 83 (March 1983): 470-87.

Smith, G.P. *The Effects of Competency Testing on the Supply of Minority Teachers.* A report prepared for the National Education Association and the Council of Chief State School Officers. Jacksonville, Fla.: University of North Florida, December 1987.

Trent, W.T. "Equity Considerations in Higher Education: Race and Sex Differences in Degree Attainment and Major Field of Study 1976 through 1981." *American Journal of Education* 93 (May 1984): 280-305.

Vance, V.S., and Schlechty, P.C. "The Distribution of Academic Ability in the Teaching Force: Policy Implications." *Phi Delta Kappan* 64 (September 1982): 22-27.

Williams, J.B., et al. *Improving Teaching in the South*. BellSouth Foundation Task Force Report. Atlanta, March 1991.

A GRASSROOTS APPROACH TO THE RECRUITMENT OF POTENTIALLY TALENTED TEACHERS

BY KATHERINE GREEN

Katherine Green is a professor in the Department of Psychology at Millersville University in Pennsylvania.

It has been suggested that for sustained teacher satisfaction, several needs must be met: challenging work, a comfortable psychological environment, informative feedback, and coaching (Murphy and Hart 1986). These needs usually go unmet in the teaching profession, which points to the sense of isolation, abandonment, and loneliness many teachers experience working within a school system.

For too many the system does not provide adequate psychological and professional support even among colleagues. Maintaining strong commitment to the profession of teaching in this dissociated state is difficult for most and impossible for some. Added to this, teachers report that they are concerned about low salaries, low status, and seemingly impossible demands from the system (Feistritzer 1983). A negative public image and lack of recognition and rewards for accomplishments within the profession contribute to the low morale of teachers. Bell and Steinmiller (1989) state that 20 years ago 60% of teachers reported that they would again embark on a teaching career if they were starting over. Today, however, only 21% of teachers respond affirmatively to that question. And only 10 years ago, 75% of parents would have been pleased to see their child become a teacher; today that number has dropped below 50%.

Is it any wonder that we are now faced with significant teacher shortages? And who can we attract to this profession of teaching if we ourselves are engaged in a struggle for professional survival? As a response to these questions, this essay will argue in favor of a grassroots recruitment strategy that places the burden of teacher recruitment squarely on the shoulders of teachers. But in so doing, a sense of renewal and increased interest in the profession of teaching and both professional and personal development may be attained. The target population of this recruitment effort is children and youth. While it is true that this population will not actually enter the profession for several years — an immediate solution is not possible using this recruitment strategy — ongoing and immediate benefits to students, teachers, and the profession will be apparent; and a long-term solution will be possible.

Targeting Children and Youth

A recent survey of high school students indicated that the strongest influence for freshman and seniors concerning their postsecondary plans were their parents' attitudes (Pennsylvania Association of Colleges and Universities 1984). Similarly, another study indicated that families were the most helpful factor, along with interesting high school classes, in planning for a career; but teachers also rated as highly influential in this process (Noeth, Engen, and Noeth 1984). In fact, the classroom experience was critical. These findings are consistent with those of a survey of 128 high school students who were accepted into the Pennsylvania Governor's School for Teaching (PGST) during the summers of 1990 and 1991 (Klinedinst and Green 1992). More than one-third of these talented and gifted students reported that their families greatly influenced their choice of a teaching career. Fully half of these students credited their teachers with having a great deal of influence on their choice. Clearly, both teachers and parents influence students' career decisions.

This knowledge carries with it certain responsibilities, because our actions as teachers shape the lives of our students. If we wish to attract the best and brightest to our own profession, then we have to model self-respect and respect for teaching, promote our discipline, demonstrate effective teaching and best practice, and invest our time and commitment in our students as potential teachers. While we may feel powerless to locate funds, to tap a reservoir of energy, or to find the time to launch district or statewide recruitment programs, what is within our control is our "selves" as a resource. We do make a difference in the career paths of our students, and it is within our reach to engender a grassroots recruitment movement.

Recognizing Potentially Talented Teachers

Some people are born to teach. Cox (1981) suggests that this gift often emerges and is recognizable as early as the primary years. These are the children who offer to help other children. They teach through coaching athletics, assisting a fellow student who is grappling with a difficult concept, volunteering for youth projects, and the like. These are the youth who surround themselves with children and are sensitive to the struggles inherent in learning.

Careful observation can reveal the potentially talented teacher to us; but it may not be through high grades, an expressed appreciation for academics, or an affinity for us as teachers. It is most often potential for the "art" of teaching that is revealed to us, even though we seem to pay more attention to potential for the "science" of teaching. While both art and science can be learned, it is the artful nature of teaching that is more innate. Thus some of us are "born" to teach. These are the children and youth we must recognize so that we may cultivate their gift.

Who are these students that might want to teach and what do they think about the teaching profession? The results of the survey of 128 high school students who attended the PGST suggest that they are intrinsically motivated to teach. A majority of these students indicated that the desire to help others, their interest in the subject matter, and their motivation to share ideas with others greatly influenced their decision to become teachers. Their general affective response toward teaching was very positive. They viewed teaching as a legitimate discipline and reported a high level of respect and commitment for the profession of teaching.

Extrinsic factors had less to do with this career decision. These same students reported that job security and work hours only moderately influenced their decision and that status and salary had relatively little to do with their decision. The majority of the PGST students only moderately believed that teaching is a high-status profession and that it could provide them with personal satisfaction.

These students also revealed good self-awareness about issues related to teaching. They believed strongly that they could handle discipline problems in the schools and felt that they would be able to influence what they could teach students. The PGST students saw themselves as team members where knowledge of personal style was important. They only moderately believed that they understood their own personal style or the field of education and its complexities.

After the PGST experience, students perceived the profession of teaching as a higher-status profession than when they entered the program. They also reported a much greater understanding of the field of teaching. In other words, students entered the PGST with very positive beliefs and attitudes about the profession of education but with less knowledge of the specifics of teaching or its complexities. These same students became increasingly sophisticated about the profession as they gained more information through participation in the PGST experience. Despite this added realism, their beliefs and attitudes remained strong and positive.

Recruitment Efforts

In recent years recruitment efforts have not been limited to undergraduate students in colleges and universities but have shifted to high school and even junior high and elementary school students. Guidera (1987) discusses a Teaching Assistant Program aimed at attracting talented high school students to the teaching profession through offering them a course on teaching, including field experiences. Other high school students have been hired as tutors for middle school students in order to test their beliefs about teaching and their commitment to a possible teaching career (Nicklin 1991). Still other programs incorporate experiences such as peer tutoring and membership in clubs and organizations such as the Future Teachers of America, which aim at acclimating students to the teaching profession. Some states have provided financial incentives in the form of university scholarships for those who major in education, such as a Washington, D.C., program that guarantees college financial aid to certain students who agree to teach at least three years in the District of Columbia (Sanchez 1988).

Max Weiner, dean of Fordham's Graduate School of Education, suggests that junior high school is not too early to start students thinking about a career in education (Rhodes and Garibaldi 1990). Rhodes and Garibaldi describe one such university consortium program that recruits promising young minority students for teaching careers. Eight colleges and universities target 700 students a year (100 students each in grades 6 to 12) to participate in lectures on education topics and to give mini-lessons to their peers.

A Grassroots Recruitment Strategy

First, we need to develop a strategy that can be carried out by individual teachers with few available resources, psychological or otherwise. This strategy must benefit teachers by providing them with a sense of renewal, excitement, and concern about the profession through their ability to cultivate potentially talented new teachers.

Second, this strategy must identify students who possess a strong inclination to serve others and must reinforce this intrinsic motivation. Recognizing talent and giving it expression through hands-on experience is of paramount importance so that the art of teaching can be explored.

Third, this strategy must encourage students to view themselves as capable and competent in a subject matter of interest to them, and in this manner encourage them to explore more fully the science of teaching.

Fourth, this strategy must increase students' and teachers' understanding of the field of teaching. Knowledge of its organization, struggles, and complexities must be gained along with an appreciation of the value and importance of education in our society.

This strategy can be implemented using a grassroots, three-stage, developmental approach, in which children from second grade through high school and individual teachers may participate. This model consists of three levels of skill building, which are geared to the interests and cognitive abilities of students at three points in their development.

Level I: Teaching Skill/Relationship Building presents structured field experiences that develop skills and content knowledge, such as in math and reading, and fosters the desire to help others through the facilitation of learning. At Level I, students are provided with opportunities to serve as cross-age peer tutors, to participate in cooperative learning groups, to teach and learn as the teacher, and to measure, manage, and provide corrective feedback as part of instruction. Students receive reinforcement for altruistic behaviors and successes in both learning and in teaching. In this manner, academic time, competence, and confidence are maximized.

Level II: Metacognitive Skill Building incorporates the use of metacognitive activities, that is, studying and observing what and why we do what we do in teaching. Several activities designed to increase awareness of the teaching process are utilized. These activities include: 1) working in a cooperative group to detail the oral history of the school by interviewing present and former teachers, administrators, custodians, etc.; 2) keeping a journal of the personal responses to peer tutoring and other teaching activities; 3) analyzing what goes on in teaching by observing various teachers and discussing those observations; 4) making a classroom map of the rhythm of teaching; 5) thinking about and sharing critical education moments such as the student's favorite/least favorite teacher/educational moment and why; and 6) participating in focus groups to discuss what is learned, how it is learned, and why.

Level III: Formal Pedagogical Skill Building presents an introduction to formal knowledge about pedagogy and the blending of science and art through seminars and coursework on teaching. At this level, teaching mentors are assigned to students, and the scope of volunteer teaching activities is broadened. Education issues, such as the reform movement, status, salary, isolation, systems, and organizations, are discussed and debated. Mentors and students self-disclose on a more personal level about the profession of teaching, and club activities (such as Future Teachers of America) and attendance at conferences are supported. Those students who develop a particular penchant or talent for teaching, as the profession is revealed to them, will continue to take part in the more structured teaching forum and will develop a relationship with a mentor teacher. Other students may opt not to pursue this more formal component of the teaching awareness activities.

This three-level model for the recruitment of teachers among children and youth is developmental in that the young child, as early as second grade, shows the ability to explain a concept to others, begins to understand other perspectives, and is capable of developing and maintaining empathic and altruistic relationships (Eisenberg and Miller 1987; Bryant 1982). Level I activities enable the young child to teach and to build teaching relationships.

Level II activities are introduced around grade four, when children begin to be able to monitor their own behavior (Zimmermann 1990) and metacognition becomes more comprehensive involving knowledge of strategies and task variables (Wellman 1985). According to Selman (1976), children at this age also are able to adopt a self-reflective perspective, which allows them to view their own thoughts, feelings, and behaviors from other perspectives and to recognize that others can do the same.

Since Level III activities concern more abstract concepts and hypothesis-testing about issues in the field of education, these activities are introduced during eighth grade, when students are in Piaget's formal operational stage of cognitive development (Berk 1994). Consideration of education issues at this level also requires the ability to adopt multiple perspectives, including that of society, which begin to emerge at around this grade (Selman 1976).

This three-level progression of teaching awareness moves from the development of knowledge to thinking about this knowledge in terms of what we know, how we know it, how we convey it, how we make decisions about it, and how each decision we make leads to another. It is important for each teacher to motivate each student to think about education and to try her or his hand at it. Through fostering our students' thinking about teaching and what is positive in it, we ourselves think about our chosen profession. Introspection can result in renewal; and if it is one that is undertaken with the support of other teachers, at least in one sense our isolation may be diminished.

And what about those students who show little or no desire in teaching as a profession whom we have required to think about the process of education? Do we lose them? Perhaps to the profession of teaching, but not to the process of education itself. They may have children whom they will need to teach in their role as parents, and they may become more effective "teachers as parents" as a result of our "failed" recruitment efforts. Then again, their children will soon be ours to teach. And, it is hoped, these children will come to us valuing education and its complexities because we shared the art of our profession with their parents. This process should well serve those of us who teach yet another generation.

References

Bell, D., and Steinmiller, G. "Avoiding the Teacher Shortage." Paper presented at the Annual Meeting of the Southeastern Regional Association of Teacher Educators, San Antonio, Texas, November 1989.

Berk, L.E. *Child Development*. Needham Heights, Mass.: Allyn and Bacon, 1994.

Bryant, B.K. "An Index of Empathy for Children and Adolescents." *Child Development* 53, no. 2 (1982): 413-25.

Cox, D.L. "The Board's Responsibility for Attracting and Landing the Best Teaching Staff." 1981. ERIC Document ED 207142.

Eisenberg, N., and Miller, P.A. "The Relation of Empathy to Prosocial and Related Behaviors." *Psychological Bulletin* 101, no. 1 (1987): 91-119.

Feistritzer, C.E. *The Condition of Teaching: A Sate by State Analysis*. Carnegie Foundation for the Advancement of Teaching Technical Report. Lawrenceville, N.J.: Princeton University Press, 1983.

Guidera, B. "Teaching as a Career: The Teaching Assistant Program." 1987. ERIC Document ED 292757.

Klinedinst, M.R., and Green, K. *Teachers for Tomorrow: The Pennsylvania Governor's School for Teachers*. Fastback 337. Bloomington, Ind.: Phi Delta Kappa Educational Foundation, 1992.

Murphy, M.J., and Hart, A.W. "Career Ladder Reforms." *Teacher Education Quarterly* 13 (Autumn 1986): 51-59.

Nicklin, J. "Enrichment Program for Middle-School Students Helps Potential Teachers Make Career Choices." *Chronicle of Higher Education*, 11 September 1991, pp. A37, A40.

Noeth, R.J.; Engen, H.B.; and Noeth, P.E. "Making Career Decisions: A Self-Report of Factors that Help High School Students." *Vocational Guidance Quarterly* 32 (June 1984): 240-48.

Pennsylvania Association of Colleges and Universities. *Parents, Programs and Pennsylvania Students' Plans: A Study of 1983-84 Freshman and Senior Plans for After Graduation from High School.* Harrisburg, Pa., 1984.

Rhodes, E.M., and Garibaldi, A.M. "Teacher Cadets Answer the Call." *Momentum* 21 (November 1990): 36-38.

Sanchez, R. "Instilling Students with a Love for Teaching: New D.C. School Program Lays Foundation for Classroom Careers." *Washington Post*, 17 October 1988, pp. A1, A4.

Selman, R.L. "Social-Cognitive Understanding: A Guide to Educational and Clinical Practice." In *Moral Development and Behavior: Theory, Research, and Social Issues*, edited by T. Lickona. New York: Holt, Rinehart and Winston, 1976.

Wellman, H.M. "The Child's Theory of Mind: The Development of Conceptions of Cognition." In *The Growth of Reflection in Children*, edited by S.R. Yussen. Orlando, Fla.: Academic Press, 1985.

Zimmermann, B.I. "Self-Regulation Learning and Academic Achievement: An Overview." *Educational Psychologist* 25, no. 1 (1990): 318.

PART II

INDUCTING TEACHERS INTO THE PROFESSION OF TEACHING

ON MATTERS OF BODY AND MIND: OVERCOMING DISINCENTIVES TO A TEACHING CAREER

BY GENE I. MAEROFF

Gene I. Maeroff is Senior Fellow at the Carnegie Foundation for the Advancement of Teaching in Princeton, New Jersey.

Derek Bok, the former president of Harvard University, has written of the disparities in the earnings of educated people who pursue careers in different fields, disparities that in recent years have grown ever wider. He wondered whether the gaps in compensation levels redound to the disadvantage of the nation, since highly talented people are dissuaded from entering such vital fields as teaching and public service. "Schools can hardly begin to meet our expectations unless they muster a corps of teachers that is at least equal in ability to the college student population as a whole," Bok wrote in 1993 (p. 179).

No doubt more lavish salaries would add to the appeal of school teaching. Historically, teachers were perceived as akin to the clergy, people of a "calling," who served the children in their classrooms much as pastors might minister to their congregations. Both groups, school teachers and clergy, wore self-denial as a badge. Nonetheless, elementary and secondary schools had for generations a ready supply of talent in women, both whites and blacks, who were blocked from other fields by social custom and discrimination. Their early employment possibilities were mostly in teaching, nursing, and clerical work. Underscoring the monastic nature of school teaching was the expectation that women who taught would not wed, as if they were nuns who had taken a vow of chastity. In later years, when they were permitted to marry, female teachers were dismissed at the first sign of pregnancy, a practice not ended until the U.S. Supreme Court declared in 1974 that teachers had a right to maternity leave (Maeroff 1982, p. 160).

So ingrained were the societal attitudes that kept women out of most occupational areas that it was taken for granted as recently as

45

the 1960s that the newspaper classified advertising pages acted properly in listing jobs under headings of "male" or "female." The women
of that generation became the mothers and grandmothers of today's
female lawyers, physicians, engineers, and corporate executives.
When, finally, mores changed and opportunities opened, the talent
pool was drained of many of the kind of women who formerly went
into teaching. Increasingly, those − female and male − who em-
barked on classroom careers tended to be among the undergraduates
with the lowest college entrance scores. Students intending to make
careers in school teaching have combined SAT scores 47 points below
the national average (College Board 1993, p. 8).

The question at this juncture is how to draw more of the best and
brightest into teaching. They are needed desperately. Public schools
struggle to provide education to youngsters who, for a host of reasons,
sometimes seem almost impervious to schooling. The challenges confronting today's teachers are more daunting than in years past. It is
surely more difficult to be a teacher today than it used to be. However, the schools are not staffed by enough men and women of the
sort who can meet the new challenges. That bodes poorly for the
students. To paraphrase Bok, schools cannot rise above mediocrity
on the backs of mediocre teachers. A steady stream of outstanding
newcomers is needed to enrich the spent talent pool and to provide
the potential leaders of tomorrow's teaching corps.

It is not that candidates for teaching positions are in short supply,
even if they are not necessarily the best that the college graduating
classes have to offer. Many of the more than 15,000 school systems
turn away job applicants by the droves. The lure of presiding over
a classroom, after all, still includes features that help offset the contents
of the pay envelope. Few other careers offer so lavish a vacation
schedule. Long-term job security is excellent, though not the perfect aegis from unemployment that it once was. Good health coverage generally is tied to the job, and retirement benefits tend to be
better than those available to most non-governmental workers. Altogether, this package of perquisites ensures an availability of
candidates.

But the measure of the excellence of the nation's teaching corps
must be based on more than the cumulative temperature of the warm
bodies at the front of classrooms. Vacations and retirement benefits
are fine, but they alone will not induce the ablest young people to
teach unless the American economy were to take a dire downturn
and the market for the high-paying professions contracted drastical-

ly. It was just such a turn of events in another era — the Great Depression — that forced legions of outstanding people into teaching and other public-sector employment. But another economic disaster would be a severe price for the country to pay so that it might secure for the schools the services of more of the ablest college graduates. So it is clear that teaching cannot and almost certainly will not be able to vie for the best and the brightest on the basis of compensation.

On the other hand, the salaries of teachers are not as penurious as they often are made out to be. Most college graduates in this country — not just those who teach — do not receive incomes equal to those of physicians, lawyers, and chief executive officers. The average teacher in the United States in 1992-93 was paid an annual salary of $35,104, according to a survey by the American Federation of Teachers. This is an amount about the same as the $33,864 that the U.S. Department of Commerce said was received in 1992 by the average American worker with a master's degree in any occupation, a credential, incidentally, possessed by only half the teachers. Many school systems pay experienced teachers $50,000 to $60,000 or more a year.

But some of the other fields in which salaries are roughly equal to those in school teaching — college teaching and journalism, for example — have little difficulty attracting more capable candidates than those who enter school teaching. In fact, talented newcomers are beating down the doors in both of these fields and are willing to work for a pittance to gain a foothold. Their perseverance comes in the face of financial disparities every bit as great as those confronting teachers in elementary and secondary schools. Thus a compelling case can be made for the idea that obstacles besides noncompetitive compensation stand in the way of recruiting talented teachers.

Just what are those other barriers? The most important of them, I think, have much to do with disincentives in the areas that I propose to call *matters of the body* and *matters of the mind*. On the one hand, public schools can be demeaning and even physically dangerous places to work. On the other hand, schools can be mentally stifling places, where the mind seems to stagnate. Together, adverse circumstances in both spheres create and sustain a culture for those who work in schools that makes teaching less than attractive. Addressing these matters would go a long way toward enabling public schools to attract and retain more of the highly able people for whom Bok and others say they are not now able to compete. Let me turn now to the circumstances I have cited.

47

First, matters of the body, which derive mainly from societal and financial pressures so familiar that they are often regarded as the *sine qua non* of school employment. Matters of the body that affect teachers negatively range from the difficulty of being able to make a phone call during the working day to the threat of attack by insolent teenagers. Eleven percent of all teachers have been victims of violence in or near their schools, according to a survey released at the end of 1993 (Metropolitan Life 1993, p. 104).

The indignities affecting what I call matters of the body take many forms. Teachers, by and large, have no private space they can call their own. Sometimes they cannot take a break even to go to the lavatory. These are college graduates who supervise toilets, cafeterias, and hallways. They are assigned to search for smokers in the stairwells and speeders in the parking lots. Making photocopies is a big deal because access to the copying machine is restricted. At one middle school I visited, the Xerox machine was in the principal's office so that potentially profligate teachers could be monitored as they used it.

Supplies are so inadequate that 44% of teachers say they end up spending more than $400 a year out of their own pockets for materials (Carnegie Foundation 1990, p. 47). Clerical help is seldom available, and teachers have to be their own secretaries. The "clients" with whom a teacher deals — especially at the secondary level — are an involuntary audience that does not necessarily want to be there, somewhat like inmates in a prison. The litany of adversities is endless, and the school setting bears little semblance to what a young person would encounter if he or she were to enlist with an investment banking house, a law firm, or a major business corporation. Clearly, these conditions detract from the satisfactions one may find in teaching.

With a little ingenuity, some measures might be implemented to alleviate the most egregious of the matters of the body so that the school milieu could be more pleasant and rewarding. For example, society might want to consider how long it is willing to continue to tolerate the small number of high school students who make life miserable for their fellow students and for the teachers. The time may be at hand to banish such students to separate settings — if they truly want to continue work toward a diploma — so that teaching and learning can be pursued productively by everyone else. Any number of such initiatives might be considered so that the physical circumstances of work in schools could improve.

So much for matters of the body that impinge adversely on school teaching and render it an unattractive career option. These matters are worth an entire discussion in their own right, but that will have to wait for another occasion. Much of the remainder of this discourse will be devoted to the other circumstances, matters of the mind, that in their negative form obstruct prospects for satisfaction and effectiveness. This area may be the more difficult to address because, to a great degree, matters of the mind are largely internal to the teachers. Unlike matters of the body, which are largely a function of external circumstances, matters of the mind are tied to the attitudes of teachers.

If one word best captures the essence of what must change so as to reinforce the positive aspects of matters of the mind, it is that school teaching ought to become a more "intellectual" pursuit. Not intellectual in the egghead sense, but in regard to those who teach doing more thinking about their work, keeping up with the field, and knowing enough about theory, practice, and research to improve their own classrooms and the schools of which they are part. "The first requirement is jobs that will challenge and reward the best minds now in teaching, and that will attract others just as good," stated the Holmes Group (1986, p. 8), an organization of deans of education colleges.

The professional life of school teachers must be enhanced if the field is to compete for and retain more of the best people, those who could be among teaching's future leaders. Young men and women considering careers in the classrooms of elementary and secondary schools should be assured that these are places where the intellectual growth of adults is valued and where they will be in the company of colleagues who share their interest in matters of the mind.

This is not to say that some first-rate teachers are not already working in school classrooms. Among the nation's 2.4 million school teachers are people who read good books, delve into educational theory, understand the pedagogy attendant to particular disciplines, and possess curious, inquiring minds. Some are masters in motivating and engaging youngsters and in nurturing the fragile sparks of learning that they ignite in students. They are able to fashion strategies to overcome both in-school factors and out-of-school factors that conspire to limit learning. But such teachers are a distinct minority. Moreover, little occurs in most schools to reinforce the interests or the intellectual inclinations of such teachers and to promote their professional growth. One who visits schools invariably encounters large numbers of teachers who seldom read subjects in or out of education, people who are essentially blue-collar workers with chalky hands. To make this observation is not to disparage people who work with their hands, but to assert that an orientation of this sort is inappropriate for those whose careers are supposed to revolve around matters of the mind.

One illustration of the penchant of many teachers not to stretch themselves in even the most cursory fashion is their failure to keep up with what is happening in education generally. Admittedly, outside reading takes extra time; and all too many teachers tend to be the victims of schedules that make them feel like laborers on an assembly line. Nonetheless, many of those in other occupations that exact heavy demands on time somehow keep abreast of their vocations. *Education Week*, a fine, comprehensive journal that covers ideas and trends in elementary and secondary education, has never − despite its merit − been able to build a substantial audience of readers among classroom teachers. Its circulation has had to rely disproportionately on administrators and others in non-classroom positions. The question here is not whether teachers are conscientious; teachers overwhelmingly care about the duties of their jobs. But for too many teachers, it is solely that: a job, not a profession. And little occurs in the average school building to lift the faculty to new intellectual heights.

Some deficiencies in matters of the mind were highlighted for me when I had the chance to compare American teachers with their counterparts in England (Maeroff n.d.). In a general sense, teachers in England are simply better educated than teachers in the United States. It is this very issue, the adequacy of the intellectual preparation of teachers, that Arthur E. Wise, the president of the National Council for the Accreditation of Teacher Education, seemed to have in mind in his effort to compel institutions of higher education, as the price of accreditation, to ensure that future teachers have "a full liberal education so that they may gain the full range of intellectual development associated with it" (Wise 1993, p. 9).

Another difference between teachers in the United States and their counterparts in England has to do with professional colleagueship. The collegiality that tends to prevail in schools in England undergirds a professional aura that all too often is absent in American schools. I refer in this regard to much more than mere social climate. It is fine if teachers who work together in a building get along well and enjoy talking about their families and what they did on the weekend; but such interaction, however warm, is not predicated on matters of the mind. Sociability should not be confused with professional collegiality. Therefore, employment in America's elementary

50

and secondary schools has to be seen in a new light if it is to appeal to more of the kind of people that Bok and others maintain are needed to transcend the ordinary.

How might such a school look? First of all, it would be a place where teachers are not shackled by schedules that presume that they do nothing of importance except spend time teaching students. Such a school would certainly be a site of substantive conversation about teaching, where people would wonder aloud about the methods and content of their teaching. Colleagues would share ideas, observe each other's teaching, and invite constructive comment on their work. Reflection on practice would be a source of continual growth. The day-to-day activities of teachers would provide fodder for research projects that they themselves would conduct. Teachers would read and contribute to journals. Professors at institutions of higher education would be potential collaborators in all pursuits. Such a school would be an exciting and fulfilling place in which to work. When matters of the mind occupy teachers in this manner, school teaching just might possess sufficient appeal to attract and hold more of the men and women who now bypass careers in precollegiate education.

One small example of how some such elements may enhance the appeal of school teaching can be seen in the impact of the Yale-New Haven Teachers Institute. This is an ambitious program to enable those who work in the schools of the city in which Yale University is situated to collaborate with professors at Yale University in formulating curriculum units. Some teachers in the New Haven Public Schools say that the chance to participate in the institute has kept them from seeking jobs in other school districts or from leaving teaching altogether. Another illustration of how outside influences on matters of the mind can promote the professional development of teachers is the system of academic alliances that was created, discipline by discipline, working out of headquarters at the University of Pennsylvania, to establish forums in which school teachers could gather with college and university professors from their own fields. Such ventures represent only a portion of what has to happen to create a climate in which matters of the mind start to loom large among the concerns and interests of school teachers.

A reformulation of the professional lives of teachers could, at the very least, provide opportunities for rebirth for some of the teachers who now feel stuck in a professional cul de sac. The term "burnout" has probably been overused when it comes to teachers; nonetheless, it is a real condition that can prove debilitating to teachers. Under the proper circumstances, though, more classroom teachers might be happy and productive. Implicit here is the idea that people who are more knowledgeable, more capable, and more motivated are apt to evince greater enthusiasm for teaching. More of them are likely to realize their potential for leadership. As a result, the schooling of children could improve; and, after all, such improvement ought to be the aim of professional development.

Does this vision contain seeds that, once planted, could sprout into a panacea? I doubt it. I would like to be able to say that a more professional teaching force is all that is needed as an antidote to what ails elementary and secondary schools, but I doubt that this is the case. Even the ablest teachers are not magicians. Society and the family exert a powerful hold over America's children. The best of teachers are reduced to playing Sisyphus when society inculcates twisted values in kids and when the dysfunctionality of families robs children of proper guidance and nurturing. But so long as the doors of American schoolhouses are going to swing open each morning, children ought to have the best teachers possible.

The school reform movement in its various iterations was supposed do something about the shortcomings of elementary and secondary education. Reform was meant to address shortcomings so that obstacles that thwart students might be breached. However, anyone who has watched that movement inch along since its inception in 1983 will realize that the accomplishments have been modest. Teaching has changed hardly at all, and advances in teaching and learning are not on a scale to cause any degree of jubilation. Despite the protests of the revisionists, America's schools are not educating all young people to the extent that they are capable of being educated.

One difficulty has been the Harry Houdini syndrome, the assumption that waving the magic wand of regulation and uttering a few abracadabras would bring change to the classroom. This has not been the case. Teachers have been largely omitted from the equation. Not enough consideration has been given to the role of teachers as agents of change. Finally, professional development now is beginning to receive unprecedented attention. This new-found interest in upgrading teachers might well be the vehicle for altering careers in ways that add to the profession in the eyes of talented college students. Such a change is needed. One study of high school students who participated in programs that allowed them to explore careers in teaching warned in 1993 that such programs too often "fail to introduce prospective teachers to compelling new ideas; in doing so, the programs may fail to engage the interest of a brighter, more risk-taking cohort of future professionals" (Recruiting New Teachers 1993, p. 46).

Much is afoot to strengthen the education of future teachers. The Holmes Group has propounded a vision of good preparation for a career in the classroom. As already mentioned, the National Council for the Accreditation of Teacher Education, under the leadership of Arthur Wise, has been battling to force higher standards in the institutions that educate teachers. The concept of the professional development school is emerging. Collectively, these various initiatives may help upgrade the preparation of those who pursue careers in the classroom and demonstrate that school teaching is an option for people who like to use their minds. Yet, despite the role of teacher education in laying a foundation for a profession of higher caliber, an equally crucial factor in enhancing school teaching for newcomers is apt to be the quality of the working life — matters of the body and especially matters of the mind — that are a teacher's lot on the job, day in and day out. School teaching must be neither a physically nor a mentally inhibiting way of earning a living.

This means, in part, that those who teach in elementary and secondary schools should not have to endure professional isolation. School teaching will inevitably continue to reduce itself to the most familiar of transactions: one teacher and a group of students. The teacher, as solo guide, will continue to help students negotiate the arduous journey along a route crisscrossed by rudimentary paths that meander in one direction or another, tempting curious learners to blaze new trails of their own choosing. This is the nature of the activity known as teaching. However, just because teaching calls largely for working on one's own, the result need not be professional isolation.

Even if most of their work with students continues to keep school teachers separate from one another, professional isolation could be dispelled. Professional isolation is, after all, as much a state of mind as a state of being. Attention to matters of the mind could help teachers construct intellectual bridges to colleagues. What I am talking about here is the kind of collegiality now found in only the most exceptional elementary and secondary schools. People who work in classrooms need opportunities to spend more of the time when they are outside the classroom interacting professionally with each other.

A change of this kind would require fundamental readjustments in the ways that schools operate. As matters now stand, the organizational structure of schools discourages and impedes professional contact between and among teachers. This is a reason why it is so difficult to alter educational practices. Breaking down isolation and strengthening collegiality depend on teachers being afforded more occasions for "meetings" of the mind. Intellectual liaisons of this sort may be brought about by more frequent gatherings of the entire faculty, but − more practically − it could be accomplished by making it possible for teachers to interact as members of teams. A team is a more manageable unit for interaction than an entire faculty. Possibilities for building teams are manifold. A team can consist of teachers who work with the same group of students, teachers who work at the same grade level, teachers who are members of the same department, teachers who share an interest in a subject, or teachers bound together by their common exploration of a pedagogy such as cooperative learning (Maeroff 1993, pp. 34-39).

The basis for building such teams excludes some of the motivations that have brought together groups of school teachers in the past. The kinds of teams that I propose are not predicated on shared interests in flower arranging or in bowling. Social bonding among school teachers is fine, but it cannot be counted on to produce intellectual growth. Team members may engage socially, but social activities should not be the *raison d'etre*. Peter Senge (1990) imagines teams as one of the possible units within the "learning organization" that he says a place of employment ought to be. If any workplace is suitable to be a learning organization, it most certainly should be an elementary or secondary school.

Teaching amounts to less than it might when matters of the mind are not accorded prominence and when teachers do not interact from a professional vantage. Where collegiality is circumscribed, the teacher becomes a trumpeter trying to play while wearing mittens. Teachers need free reign to create more of the beautiful sounds that inspire students to fulfill their potential. Dispensing information is an important function of the teacher, but it cannot be allowed to be the sum and substance of teaching.

Teachers need the intellectual wherewithal to make teaching more learner-centered and less didactic so that learners can exercise greater initiative. Teachers need to know how to work more like coaches who prompt and encourage students in the quest for knowledge. Teachers should learn to hurl questions like projectiles that prod learners to take risks. Without pedagogical content knowledge, a teacher lacks sufficient insight to adjust lessons to the needs of learners. Without a grasp of how to teach for understanding, a teacher usually falls back on trying to squeeze the "right" answers out of students. Without a background in alternative methods of assessment, a teacher is less able to meld curriculum and assessment into the unified whole that they ought to be.

Teachers should be empowered to rise above what has been the norm for many of them. This is how the field can be made more appealing. "Empowerment" is spoken of frequently in conversations about teachers. Some observers assume that empowering teachers simply means giving them greater authority to make decisions. That is a part of empowerment, but more must be involved. It is difficult to imagine teachers exercising power wisely unless matters of the mind loom larger in their day-to-day working lives. The sort of empowerment that can make a difference in teaching and learning depends on teachers being knowledgeable. Empowerment rests, like a tripod, on three legs: knowledge, status, and access to decision making (Maeroff 1988). Each of the three components of empowerment complements the others.

A teacher who is knowledgeable achieves greater status, in her own eyes and in the eyes of others. Her knowledge also can give her entry to decision making. But access to decision making without a concomitant progression in knowledge raises the possibility that the decisions teachers help make will not be as sagacious as they might be. Thus a school system truly committed to empowering teachers by giving them access to decision making must be prepared to foster a new professional culture in the schools, a culture that accords high priority to matters of the mind. Teachers ready to move in this direction should be permitted to take the lead in doing so. Teams of like-minded colleagues should be able to invite fellow teachers to join them as they move ahead by trial and error to transform themselves as professionals.

Such schools are apt to be places in which able young people want to work. School districts have the latitude to establish such settings so as to make employment in elementary and secondary schools a more inviting prospect. However, school boards and administrators frequently seem either unwilling or unable to alter the climate in schools to allow empowerment to flourish so that matters of the mind may take precedence. And sometimes teachers themselves are at blame, reluctant to tolerate change if they perceive a threat to the status quo. I know, for instance, of one high school in particular that turned down an invitation to apply for a large corporate grant for restructuring that the school almost certainly would have received.

The school's teachers were apprehensive in the face of the unknown. They felt more comfortable clinging to the familiar, rationalizing shortcomings by criticizing students, parents, administrators, and the school board.

Some schools are so averse to change that they have grown downright sclerotic, as stagnant as a fetid pool deprived of fresh water. These are not settings amenable to talented newcomers. Veteran faculties that are set in their ways grow stale without transfusions of new blood. The situation may be exacerbated by hiring policies that are unduly bureaucratic or even geared to patronage. One group of researchers concluded that "salary increases, by themselves, will not enable some districts to attract better teachers, because inefficient and inappropriate personnel procedures hinder the recruitment of strong candidates for teaching positions" (Murname et. al. 1991, p. 50).

Thus the cultivation of future leadership in the teaching ranks is imperiled not only by salary levels, but also by hiring practices. I am reminded of the case of Ara Berberian, whom I interviewed after he graduated in 1993 from Trenton State College, one of the most highly regarded institutions of higher education in New Jersey. He got his bachelor's degree with honors and was certified to teach social studies in any grade from seventh through twelfth. Berberian, who went into the Navy after high school and spent four years on the staff of the Chief of U.S. Naval Operations, completed college in four years after his military discharge and won membership in an international society for history majors. He made the dean's list several times and earned a 3.57 grade point average out of a possible 4.0. He did one term of practice teaching in an inner-city high school and another at a suburban high school.

Berberian sent 136 job applications to school districts in seven states, garnering only one offer of an interview. Forty-seven of his inquiries were in direct response to positions that had been advertised as available. Unable to attain a teaching position, this mature young man of 25 put his freshly minted degree in a drawer and accepted a security job at a county youth detention center, hoping that any employment that kept him in proximity to young people would add to his credentials. Then, just before school opened in the fall of 1993, Berberian was hired by a high school as a social studies teacher, finally obtaining the job for which he had specifically primed himself.

The enthusiasm and energy of teacher candidates such as Berberian can be a source of regeneration for schools. Collectively, young people of this sort are a human reservoir that can be tapped for future leadership. Because salaries are not competitive, the imperative is that much greater for schools to respect matters of the body and matters of the mind in ways that show future teachers that schools are places where they will not suffer indignities and where their intellect will be valued.

References

Bok, Derek. *The Cost of Talent: How Executives and Professionals Are Paid and How It Affects America*. New York: Free Press, 1993.

Carnegie Foundation for the Advancement of Teaching. *The Condition of Teaching*. Princeton, N.J., 1990.

College Board. *College Bound Seniors: 1993 Profile of SAT Achievement Test Takers*. New York, 1993.

Holmes Group. *Tomorrow's Teachers*. East Lansing, Mich., 1986.

Maeroff, Gene I. *Don't Blame the Kids*. New York: McGraw-Hill, 1982.

Maeroff, Gene I. *The Empowerment of Teachers*. New York: Teachers College Press, 1988.

Maeroff, Gene I. *Team Building for School Change*. New York: Teachers College Press, 1993.

Maeroff, Gene I. *Teaching and Learning in English Urban Schools*. Washington, D.C.: Council of the Great City Schools, n.d.

Metropolitan Life Insurance Company. *MetLife Survey of the American Teacher: Violence in America's Public Schools*. New York, 1993.

Murname, R.J.; Singer, J.D.; Willet, J.B.; Kemple, J.J.; and Olsen, R.J. *Who Will Teach: Policies that Matter*. Cambridge, Mass.: Harvard University Press, 1991.

Senge, Peter. *The Fifth Discipline*. New York: Doubleday Currency, 1990.

Recruiting New Teachers. *Teaching's Next Generation*. Belmont, Mass., 1993.

Wise, Arthur E. "A Vision of the Future." *Phi Kappa Phi Journal* 73, no. 4 (1993): 8-10.

INDUCTION, RETENTION, AND COLLEGIALITY

BY DONOVAN R. WALLING

Donovan R. Walling is Editor of Special Publications for Phi Delta Kappa and previously was a teacher and education administrator.

The induction of new teachers, whether into the profession or into a specific school, is unsystematic. In many districts, newly hired teachers receive only a brief orientation to their new school before being cast adrift. They are isolated not only from the once-familiar, supportive environment of academe, but also from their new colleagues, who are too busy dealing with the myriad details of their own classrooms to nurture their fledgling peers. Few schools offer a truly collegial induction for either new teachers or for incoming veterans who have taught elsewhere.

Collegial environments promote a more rapid, successful induction of newcomers than do noncollegial environments. And collegiality can enhance retention by serving as a "safety net" when teachers experience uncertainty and frustration in their work.

New teachers often feel alone and beleaguered, and their response may be simply to withdraw into their classrooms, to become isolated. Perhaps a majority will find their own way or seek the support of another teacher. But many new teachers who have the potential for success will not find that success on their own. If their feelings of isolation are unrelieved and their initial experiences are negative, then they may choose to leave teaching. Dissatisfied teachers who leave the profession — whether after a short time or after a number of years in teaching — seldom directly cite isolation as the reason; but many of the problems that affect retention are related to isolation. The stress and "burnout" from which teachers suffer might be alleviated through collegial support.

Collegiality does more than enhance the induction and retention of teachers. It also is a powerful mechanism for teachers' self-improvement and, in turn, for the improvement of the profession.

Nurturing Collegiality

Collegiality implies mutual support. Teacher colleagues share ideas and plans, work together to solve individual or common problems, and help one another to improve teaching practices. But collegiality also embodies the notion of shared power and authority. True colleagues are, by definition, equals.

This notion of equal power and authority is difficult to achieve in practice. The education profession is fundamentally hierarchical: new teachers are "outranked" by veteran teachers; regular classroom teachers have less authority than specialists; and so on. The hierarchy of teachers often is informal, but it mirrors the more formal lines of authority that give principals more power than teachers or department heads but less power than central office administrators and the superintendent. Consequently, in order to create an environment in which collegiality can be nurtured, it first is necessary to remove traditional barriers that exist between teachers.

This essay is limited to the hierarchy among teachers. While there are good reasons to examine the larger hierarchy and to modify the lines of authority between teachers and administrators, I am concerned here with collegiality among teachers, not among teachers and administrators.

A number of initiatives have been developed to promote interactions that are characterized as collegial but that, in fact, do not equalize teachers' authority. An example is the "peer assistance and review" (PAR) model, which was developed in the Toledo, Ohio, public schools and can be found in similar forms in a number of districts (Zimpher and Grossman 1992). Most such programs use a consultation model to assist teachers and include review by a peer panel that has the power to recommend continuation of a teacher's contract or termination. Both the consultation and review functions are antithetical to collegiality.

Consultation presumes a client-expert relationship. The new teacher (as client) seeks out or is assigned to a veteran teacher who functions as a consultant (expert). The consultant, or mentor, fills the role once occupied by the new teacher's college supervisor. In some instances, there can be a "handing off" of the new teacher from the college supervisor to the on-the-job mentor, particularly if the teacher has been hired in the school or district where he or she was a student teacher. In some cases, the mentor may have been the new teacher's cooperating teacher.

While mentoring relationships can be valuable, they are not collegial. Most mentors fall into a teacher-student role with the new teacher. Consequently, while the mentoring relationship may be productive and individually helpful, it does little to enlarge the scope of collegiality. The new teacher does not engage in the wider professional dialogue as an equal among the other teachers on the staff. Indeed, the reverse may be true: Because the new teacher is assigned to a mentor, he or she may be seen as "inferior" because veteran teachers normally are independent of such helping relationships.

The review dimension of PAR and similar programs is wholly out of step with the "equal authority" aspect of collegiality. This type of "collegiality" might be better characterized as shared decision making. It reduces the authority barrier between teachers and administrators by giving some teachers a share in the traditional power of administrators to evaluate staff and to recommend retention or dismissal of an employee to a yet higher authority (usually the superintendent and the school board). However, the status inequality of the review function precludes collegiality among teacher reviewers and those teachers under review. Moreover, new teachers are unlikely to be chosen as reviewers; and so they remain powerless in this inferior-superior positioning of supposed equals.

These concerns are at the heart of collegiality. If collegiality is to break the isolation that many teachers — especially new teachers — feel, then truly collegial strategies must be developed that foster teacher-to-teacher connectedness, where all participants are on an equal footing. Ideally, these strategies should be employed during preservice teacher education, during the induction of new teachers, and throughout professional practice in order to enhance self-improvement, improvement of the profession generally, and retention of successful teachers.

Collegiality in Preservice Education

Strategies that connect prospective teachers to one another during their professional education not only enhance skill acquisition through peer support, but also teach collegiality as an effective means of self-development. An example of one such strategy is peer coaching.

Neubert and Stover (1994) describe peer coaching as "a collegial relationship between student teachers who provide reciprocal, in-class assistance to one another as they attempt to incorporate new teaching skills, strategies, and approaches into their teaching." Neubert and Stover believe that:

Teachers tend to embrace peer coaching as a collegial activity because it excludes the evaluation component of observation from the professional growth process; provides camaraderie to the teachers from an "equal," especially as they find themselves experiencing the disequilibrium of a learner; reduces the isolation of teaching; builds communities of teacher-learners; and encourages a new sense of professionalism. (p. 9)

Effective use of peer coaching requires college and school personnel to rethink philosophical and structural aspects of teacher education. In order to foster collegiality, the college supervisor and the cooperating teacher must regard student teachers not only as individuals but as cohorts. Schedules must be constructed to allow pairs or groups of student teachers to work together — to observe one another's teaching, to hold conferences with one another, and to meet as a group with supervisors and cooperating teachers. It may mean assigning a pair of student teachers to the same cooperating teacher, a departure from traditional pairing of a single student with a cooperating teacher. And cooperating teachers may need training in facilitating peer coaching.

The reward for this effort is the induction of new teachers, in the words of Neubert and Stover, "into their teaching careers with an expectation that teaching can and should be a collaborative activity." A benefit to the veteran cooperating teachers is the introduction of a collegial model that they can adapt for their own professional development.

Colleagues in the Process

In schools, the peer coaching model can be extended as a staff-development strategy. Most veteran teachers seldom, if ever, observe a contemporary in action. Few have done so in a systematic way to learn new instructional methods or to provide constructive feedback. Thus peer coaching offers a strategy not only for professional skill development but, fundamentally, for the enhancement of mutual trust and understanding.

Krovetz and Cohick (1993) describe how collegiality can lead to school improvement, citing a Santa Cruz, California, program that uses Professional Development Support Teams (PDSTs). Key elements, say the authors, "are choice, support, stimulation, trust, and respect for the judgment of peers." The PDSTs are structured as vehicles for professional development in which teachers train together and then coach one another to apply newly acquired skills. The Santa

Cruz program, which is relatively new, is specifically tailored for experienced teachers:

> Tenured staff members with effective or outstanding evaluations in all areas for at least the last five years are now free to choose to participate in the PDSTs for up to three consecutive years and are exempt from the formal evaluation process for that period. (p. 332)

Experience with this type of limited peer coaching program may eventually lead to a broadening of the eligibility requirements, thereby opening up a range of collegial staff development options for all teachers, newcomers as well as veterans. Likewise, if a district realizes positive benefits from this type of initial program, school leaders may be encouraged to adapt the model to involve teachers who are less effective and less successful, thereby generating improvement where it is critically needed.

Collegiality also can be nurtured through shared professional experiences in various forms of teaming. Two such forms are: 1) interdisciplinary teams and 2) team, or paired, teaching. Neither form is new, but both have been reinvigorated by recent school reform initiatives and so bear revisiting.

Interdisciplinary teams in their modern incarnation gained prominence a number of years ago when the movement began to transform junior high schools into middle schools. During such a transformation, departmental structures often are discarded in favor of interdisciplinary teams. A team might comprise a science teacher, a language arts teacher, a math teacher, and a social studies teacher. Four-teacher teams usually are assigned an equivalent number of students (100 to 120) who rotate among the four subjects. Fully functional teams become truly collegial, collaboratively designing instruction, sharing curricula, and working cooperatively to meet the educational and social needs of their students.

More recently, school reform initiatives have moved some schools to broaden the authority base of their interdisciplinary teams, to create different team configurations, or to adopt teams where none previously existed. Elementary and high schools have instituted their own forms of interdisciplinary teams, often incorporating shared decision making to bridge the collegial gap between faculty and administration.

McCarthy (1991) enumerates nine activities in which teams should engage in order to function professionally:

1. Planning and coordinating the constantly shifting schedules of all students and teachers on the team;

2. Assuming responsibility for the manner in which district-adopted curricular programs shall be implemented;
3. Coordinating instructional materials from different disciplines to facilitate an interdisciplinary approach to skill development and concept mastery;
4. Selecting objectives, content, learning activities, modes of instruction, and media to be used;
5. Developing procedures for the continuing evaluation of each student's progress;
6. Grouping students for different instructional purposes;
7. Recommending budgets for supplies, materials, equipment, and personnel;
8. Hiring new team members and other personnel; and
9. Organizing classroom and space allocation. (pp. 18-19)

Empowering teachers to make these kinds of decisions redefines lines of authority in addition to creating the equality among teachers that defines collegiality. However, even an imperfect realization of this profile may significantly encourage a level of collegiality that was previously unattained, or thought to be unattainable.

Similarly, team teaching – usually limited to pair configurations because of tight budgets or difficult schedules – offers opportunities for teachers to initiate and maintain collegial relationships. Again, the activity is not new to the profession; but it recently has been given new impetus by reform initiatives. At the high school level, one notable impetus is Tech Prep.

The philosophy that undergirds Tech Prep is summed up in the phrase, "applied academics." Green and Weaver (1994) identify the target population for Tech Prep programs as the majority of students "who are now unprepared for either college or work," and thus Tech Prep offers "a curriculum that integrates academic study with workplace applications" (p. 7).

To meet the requirements of Tech Prep, which Congress included in its 1990 amendments to the Perkins Vocational and Applied Technology Act, many high schools are developing applied academic classes. Examples are Chemistry of Foods, combining basic chemistry taught in the context of food preparation (part of vocational home economics), and Physics of Technology, combining basic physics with traditional industrial technology. The team for a Chemistry of Foods class would be a chemistry teacher and a home economics teacher, who jointly plan and deliver instruction.

Team teaching allows teachers to observe one another and to reflect on curricula, instructional methods, and assessment. With encouragement, teams can expand their collaboration to the level of peer coaching. Teams such as those for Tech Prep classes bring together teachers from various disciplines, and so they increase the scope of collegial communication.

In some schools, as Tech Prep has increased collaboration between academic and vocational areas, such collegial ventures have encouraged other types of teams. For example, Science Compositions is a class that pairs a science teacher with an English teacher to teach scientific reporting. A class in photojournalism might team a photography teacher from the art department with a journalism teacher from the English department. The possibilities for team teaching are limited only by a school's ability to staff and schedule teamed classes.

Even in constrained circumstances, creative tandem scheduling can accomplish many aspects of team teaching. In a tandem schedule, two coordinated classes of the teamed subject are scheduled back-to-back. For example, students might attend "part one" of Photojournalism one period, followed by "part two" the next period. "Part one" would concentrate on photography and be taught by an art teacher; "part two" would focus on journalism and be taught by an English teacher. Students would receive credits in both art and English, but the teachers would work as a team to coordinate instruction.

Fostering a Collegial School Culture

The traditional view of teaching — one teacher, one group of students, one classroom — is an archetype of isolation. Collegiality requires an alternative vision that dismantles the walls of the classroom "box"; moreover, it requires that teachers dismantle the mental box that constrains collaboration. When collegiality becomes the norm, it transforms the school culture.

Krovetz and Cohick said of the Santa Cruz project,

> We wanted teachers to view their involvement in PDSTs not as time added to what they were already doing, but as time invested in improving the quality of their work. Good teachers, we hoped, would view this as an opportunity to build relationships and grow professionally. (p. 333)

Their experience thus far with the project has proved them to be correct. Given sufficient opportunity and incentive, it is not surprising that most teachers will embrace collegiality.

However, those are two key ingredients: opportunity and incentive. They cannot be taken for granted. Nor can a collegial culture be created to foster collegiality; collegiality first must be developed in order to reshape the school culture. As Carter points out: "Cultural change does not cause new ways of thinking, it is a consequence of those ways" (1993, p. 183).

Therefore, the groundwork for a collegial culture is established by nurturing collegial events that involve individual collaborations, by developing programs that encourage collegial work, and by replicating collegial successes in new contexts.

Astuto and her colleagues (1994) view the development of collegiality that challenges the assumption of competition as the foundation of school improvement. They contend that:

> Establishing competitive environments in schools is at the heart of many personnel policies. Fascination with merit pay and recognition programs for teachers is based on a belief that directly connecting work and rewards will yield increased teacher effort to improve student achievement. . . . A counterargument is that self-motivation is sustained when individuals maintain a sense of self-efficacy and work in a context in which people (teachers, administrators, students, parents) help each other to develop skills, to take risks, and to challenge standard operating procedures. Competitive environments isolate people; cooperative environments bring people together and protect diversity of experience, preference, and interest. (p. 53)

In order to establish a collegial culture, schools must provide time for dialogue between teachers and "access to ideas both within the individual school community and throughout the broader professional arena, including practitioners in other schools, colleagues in higher education, and educational researchers" (Clark and Astuto 1994, p. 516).

Implementing Principles of Collegiality

It would be incorrect to dichotomize the noncollegial and the collegial in schools. Such a dichotomy ignores reality. Schools *are* largely bureaucratic, hierarchical organizations. While educators may reasonably expect to modify the structure of schools — after all, that is what "restructuring" is all about — the likelihood of discarding bureaucracy and replacing it with a wholly new, wholly collegial structure is at best slim.

66

However, those who are nominally educational leaders can reshape the school culture to incorporate principles of collegiality. By so doing, they can foster staff development and school improvement in non-bureaucratic, nonhierarchical ways. Such reshaping is enlightened by a concern for balancing the bureaucratic, presumably necessary efficiencies of traditional school organization with inclusionary, interactive processes that − albeit challenging from the standpoint of strict efficiency − offer more effective means for enhancing the induction, retention, and professional development of teachers. Three such principles are:

1. The work of teachers is naturally collaborative.
2. Academic disciplines are fundamentally interrelated.
3. Professional development is an interactive endeavor.

Each of these principles merits brief discussion. The first, that the work of teachers is naturally collaborative, seems self-evident. Teaching and learning seldom are solitary endeavors. From our earliest experiences, we learn from others, whether the act is tying a shoe lace or factoring an equation. And teachers learn to teach by observing their own teachers, by interacting with their peers and professors in teacher education, and, it is hoped, by collaborating with their colleagues once they move into their careers.

Making the work of teachers a solitary endeavor to be carried out behind closed classroom doors is, if anything, unnatural. Solitary teaching isolates teachers not only from their colleagues, who might help them over the rough spots of daily classroom practice, but also from the currents of professional thought that are shaped in professional collaborations, both formal and informal.

The second principle, that the academic disciplines are fundamentally interrelated, is equally self-evident; but it often is deliberately disregarded, and interrelationships are forestalled by the bureaucratic structure of the disciplines. The elementary classroom, which ought to be a model of interrelated, interdisciplinary curricula in action, instead is often a mirror of secondary school compartmentalization and segmentation of curricula. Elementary pupils "get" reading for a certain number of minutes each week, writing for a certain number of minutes, science, art, arithmetic, and so on. Only recently, and only in some classrooms, have teachers been encouraged to cluster disciplines, for example, teaching writing in the context of science through lab journals and experiment reports.

Bureaucratic devices, such as time mandates for certain subjects at the elementary level and certification by discipline at the secondary level, help to ensure that students receive sufficient instruction and are taught by qualified instructors. But such devices also constrain learning by treating disciplines as disconnected and unrelated. Thus restructuring schools in this regard will require, first, that certain mandates and standards be deregulated in order to allow for the re-emergence of fundamental interrelationships among disciplines. Then it will be possible to encourage collegial approaches to instruction. A fledgling start in this direction has been made with Tech Prep and similar programs. Much more remains to be done.

The third principle, that professional development is an interactive endeavor, should be a natural outgrowth of the reshaping of school culture along the lines of the first two principles. But, as previously alluded to in Carter's comment, reshaping professional development to be interactive and collegial, in turn, will help to reshape the school culture. For example, formal continuing education has been a prime staff development vehicle in many school districts. Requirements for a certain number of credits over a given time, whether required by the school district or by the state licensing agency for recertification, do not create professional development that is connected either to the work at hand or to collegial endeavors in the workplace. When a teacher takes a continuing education class, the work of that class may be related to the teacher's professional practice; but it seldom derives specifically from the teacher's day-to-day work. Nor, unless the class is specifically developed for a school staff, is the class likely to include the teacher's workday colleagues.

Where collegiality is prized, greater priority must be given to professional development that is connected to day-to-day teaching practice and connects teaching colleagues through interactive, mutually developmental activities. Such nontraditional opportunities for staff development will require nurturance. Again, a fledgling start has been made in such programs as the Santa Cruz Professional Development Support Teams. But, again, most schools need to go much further.

Many aspects of school organization and, indeed, of school culture inevitably will remain bureaucratic and compartmentalized, hierarchical and disconnected. Necessary efficiencies and economies argue against radical change. Yet, within such bureaucratic structures, collegiality can be created and nurtured to enhance the environment of teaching and to develop an ethos wherein collaborative engagements are valued.

Much in the successful induction and retention of teachers depends on first impressions that are reinforced by the day-to-day professional culture. Teachers who are welcomed into a community of colleagues are more likely to fare better — to achieve success in the classroom, to grow in the profession, and to stay in education — than are those who merely are assigned to a classroom.

References

Astuto, Terry A., et al. *Roots of Reform: Challenging the Assumptions that Control Change in Education.* Bloomington, Ind.: Phi Delta Kappa Educational Foundation, 1994.

Carter, Gene R. "Revitalizing America's Public Schools Through Systemic Change." In *The State of the Nation's Public Schools: A Conference Report*, edited by Stanley Elam. Bloomington, Ind.: Phi Delta Kappa, 1993.

Clark, David L., and Astuto, Terry A. "Redirecting Reform: Challenges to Popular Assumptions About Teachers and Students." *Phi Delta Kappan* 75 (March 1994): 512-20.

Green, James E., and Weaver, Roy A. *Tech Prep: A Strategy for School Reform.* Fastback 363. Bloomington, Ind.: Phi Delta Kappa Educational Foundation, 1994.

Krovetz, Martin, and Cohick, Donna. "Professional Collegiality Can Lead to School Change." *Phi Delta Kappan* 75 (December 1993): 331-33.

McCarthy, Robert J. *Initiating Restructuring at the School Site.* Fastback 324. Bloomington, Ind.: Phi Delta Kappa Educational Foundation, 1991.

Neubert, Gloria A., and Stover, Lois T. *Peer Coaching in Teacher Education.* Fastback 371. Bloomington, Ind.: Phi Delta Kappa Educational Foundation, 1994.

Zimpher, Nancy L., and Grossman, John E. "Collegial Support by Teacher Mentors and Peer Consultants." In *Supervision in Transition*, edited by Carl D. Glickman. Alexandria, Va.: Association for Supervision and Curriculum Development, 1992.

TEACHING AS LEARNING

BY TED SANDERS
AND NANCY ANN EBERHART

Ted Sanders is Superintendent of Public Instruction for the State of Ohio. Nancy Ann Eberhart is director of the Division of Curriculum, Instruction, and Professional Development in the Ohio Department of Education.

Teachers stand at the center of learning. Their potential for influencing students is immense. Teaching well requires skills, practice, persistence, and insights that are required of few other professions, because what matters most in education happens inside the classroom.

The same qualities that distinguish excellence in other fields also distinguish outstanding teachers. These qualities are embodied in the word "professionalism." Tenacity, the intention to strive for excellence and not give up, is the hallmark of excellent teachers. Excellent teachers are self-renewing and focus on helping students make connections between intention and action. They learn from their mistakes and reflect on their decisions. Excellent teachers are concerned with developing and refining their skills. Each day they strive to do a better job than they did the day before.

Like students, teachers grow and learn through doing. To teach is to learn twice. As teachers confront themselves and examine their practices, self-awareness is essential to change and growth.

Teaching is a creative activity. Confronting the disparity between intention and action is inherent in the creative process. Aspiring to bridge the gap between the ideal and the real is a career-long endeavor. This process parallels the artistic experience where a contradiction often exists between the artist's conception and the finished work. Each day teachers bring greater skill and understanding to their task. This increased awareness provides the means to move closer to the ideal, where each student is actively engaged in learning.

To see teaching as learning is to accept the idea that teachers go through a series of transformations. Frances Fuller (1969) described these stages as moving from survival to mastery to impact, where teachers are most concerned with the degree to which they influence their students. During these stages, teachers refine their techniques and their understandings of students. They build a repertoire of instructional strategies. This continuous process of "becoming" requires time to reflect and opportunities to practice and polish skills.

Samuel Bacharach, writing about organizational research in *Education Week*, suggests an approach for teacher development that "emphasizes collegial goal-setting, individual initiative, and the development of skills that complement the needs of the organization." Says Bacharach:

> Such a system would focus as much attention on the school system's responsibilities to its teachers as it would on the responsibilities of teachers themselves. A real career development system would take teachers' motivations to improve as a given, and would focus instead on the opportunities and resources a teacher needs in order to make improvement possible. (1986, p. 28)

Acting on what we know about organizational support will mean some shifts in the rhythms and routines of a school. Real professional development will occur as teachers and principals work together to identify and solve their problems. As this collaboration occurs, they will establish collegial relationships that are at the heart of meaningful professional development. High-performing schools share the belief that they constantly must work toward improvement in student and teacher performance. To foster this belief, changes in roles and relationships are necessary (Little 1982, 1986).

According to Judith Warren Little (1989) and Susan Rosenholtz (1989), these changes call for a new set of working relationships:

- Teachers and administrators talking together about schoolwide goals and priorities;
- Teachers engaged together in working on curriculum and solving schoolwide problems;
- Teachers observing each other;
- Teachers feeling a responsibility to help each other learn and exchanging ideas and information about teaching practices;
- Teachers and administrators sharing evaluation as a collaborative process.

The behavior of the principal is critical if collegiality is to be practiced. Expectations for cooperation must be not only demonstrated but reinforced through all actions. As Thomas Sergiovanni (1991) has stated, principals of successful schools know that student learning depends on teacher learning. These principals hold high expectations for teachers as learners, and so they remove barriers and provide resources to assist teachers to become active learners. They support cooperative approaches to instruction and help teachers to work in teams. These principals establish norms and practices that support growth and, as Albert Shanker has said, make staff development an ongoing, daily way of life (Shanker 1990).

Seymour Sarason, in *The Predictable Failure of Educational Reform*, states:

> From their inception our public schools have never assigned importance to the intellectual, professional, and career needs of their personnel. (1990, pp. 144-45)

Thus Sarason suggests that if productive learning conditions do not exist for teachers, "the benefits sought by educational reform stand little chance of being realized."

A Model for Teacher Development

Currently, most teachers probably find themselves at some intermediate point between where their profession was in the past and where it potentially could be in the future. How might the transition be made from the known to the anticipated? How can teachers escape from the isolated, restricted world of their forerunners and embrace all of the possibilities that the future holds for their profession?

The answers to these questions can be supplied, in part, through a cohesive, well-planned program of teacher development. We are not talking here about a program that exposes teachers to unrelated "chunks" of new information at various times over the school year. Rather, what we need is a new model for teacher development. At the core of this model is the idea that teacher development should be an ongoing series of connected events from preservice preparation through internships and licensure to advanced certification.

This model envisions teacher development in terms of three phases:

Phase 1, Preservice Preparation: A professional preparation program gives teacher candidates the theoretical and academic base from which to launch a teaching career.

Phase 2, Extended Clinical Training and Assessment: Teacher candidates experience a prolonged clinical phase of preparation as an internship, during which they receive a beginner or conditional license. As an intern, the novice teacher has opportunities to experiment with different teaching practices and models. The assessment of the intern's performance is the basis for licensure. This phase continues at least through the first or second year of actual teaching and concludes when the intern successfully demonstrates teaching knowledge and skills sufficient for a regular license.

Phase 3, Continuing Education: Continuing education occurs throughout teachers' careers, enabling them to stay up-to-date. After several years of competent service and professional growth, teachers should gain recognition through an advanced certification process.

A dynamic and coherent system of teacher development, as outlined, offers teachers a promising route to the future. On one hand, such a system gives them the means to acquire the leadership skills and communication strategies that will be a prerequisite for effective performance in a classroom. On the other hand, its rigorous requirement for growth and for verification of competence at every career level opens the door to the eventual recognition of teachers as true professionals.

The need for a systematic teacher development model comes at a time when some of the most important professional development initiatives for teachers are arising at the grassroots. Schools and districts are placing a higher priority on expanding their teachers' knowledge base as restructuring plans move off the drawing board and site-based management takes root. Locally generated professional development activities are vital because they reinvigorate teachers and expand their repertoire of skills. They are equally important as an avenue through which teachers can exercise leadership.

The challenge now is to implement a teacher development model that incorporates the grassroots initiatives. This challenge can be met if 1) some sound assumptions about effective teacher development are kept in mind and 2) teachers themselves are allowed to exercise leadership over their own professional development through the grassroots programs.

In addition to organizational support, effective professional development programs need a number of things to make them work. For example, professional development must be integral to the life of the school; it must be ongoing, with time as well as funds allocated for planning, implementation, and evaluation; and all dimensions of growth must be addressed, not just skills and knowledge but also collaboration, reflection, and problem-solving practices. Activities must be designed in such as way as to ensure opportunities for practice, feedback, and coaching.

Effective professional development is global rather than problem-oriented. Loucks-Horsley and Sparks (1989) state that an effective professional development program draws on a variety of activities, including:

- Individually guided activities (attending conferences, reading journals and books, taking a course);
- Observation and feedback on performance (peer coaching, clinical supervision);
- Involvement in developmental improvement processes (shared decision making resulting in projects developed to improve schools);
- Formal training (lectures, demonstrations, and practice with feedback);
- Continuous inquiry into how to make practice more effective (conducting action research in the classroom).

By keeping such points in mind, education leaders will be more attuned to the sensitivities of teachers and other members of the school community. Thus fear and uncertainty about change can be addressed in an atmosphere of trust. Similarly, attention to basic assumptions about sound staff development will help education leaders be realistic about the improvements that teacher development can bring.

One result of grassroots teacher development efforts has been increased opportunities for teacher leadership. Besides enhancing morale, such opportunities strengthen teachers' feelings of security by giving them a measure of control over their professional destiny. The implementation of the suggested teacher development model will not limit opportunities for teachers to exercise leadership over their own professional growth. During their internship and after receiving their regular license, teachers should play a key role in planning, implementing, and evaluating their own professional growth activities.

The contributions that teachers can make at each of these stages are worth noting:

Planning. Because there are so many new demands on teachers and because expectations about professional development programs vary, it often is difficult to design meaningful activities. To ensure that programs are relevant, teachers should take the lead in identifying their own needs. They should determine what means will be used to assess these needs and then decide how the results of the needs assessment will be used to set a direction for subsequent learning. Teachers can play a key role by formulating realistic objectives and establishing a sound basis for evaluation and follow-up.

Implementing. Teachers can exercise leadership by creating workbooks, diagrams, illustrations, or other instruments for use in professional development sessions. Such instruments may be more useful than materials from outside sources, since the teachers who devise them will be more knowledgeable about the purposes of the sessions. For the same reason, local teachers may be the best people to deliver the professional development training. This is not to suggest that teachers cannot or will not learn from outside consultants, but maximum impact for teachers can be achieved if teachers take a central role.

Evaluating. Numerous tasks are associated with evaluation and follow-up and offer channels for teacher leadership. These tasks include:

- Determining what knowledge, behaviors, skills, and attitudes should be measured;
- Determining what instruments should be used to gauge results;
- Deciding how, when, and where to administer the instruments;
- Translating evaluation results into effective follow-up measures.

Teacher leadership in the evaluation of the professional development program reinforces the importance of the new learning. Moreover, if the evaluation leads to positive changes in program content or administration, teachers are likely to view the program as effectively serving their needs and subject to their control. Thus the program will be perceived as enhancing, rather than threatening, teachers' professional standing.

Even if many local opportunities for teacher leadership are available, a pointed question still needs to be asked: Should these opportunities be grasped? While some schools and districts might quickly give an affirmative response to that query, others might hesitate. Principals, central office personnel, and others outside of the classroom may feel that they should be involved. Some may fear that giving teachers so much power over their own professional development will give them a license to increase their power in other areas. Teachers themselves may be reluctant to take an active role in their own professional development, believing that taking on such a responsibility will leave them less time and energy for teaching.

Such considerations should not be discounted. Desire to move toward restructuring — including restructuring professional development — is tied to one's presumed standing within the restructured workplace. Jeanenne LaMarsh, a nationally recognized management consultant, points out that the "old ways made us successful for a long time. It's hard to give them up because they defined us and how we saw and interpreted the world" (1991, p. 37).

Regardless of whether resistance arises to the idea of giving teachers a leadership role in their own professional development, educators should recognize three important ways in which the entire school community will benefit from a move in this direction:

First, it encourages teachers to be introspective about their profession, which, in turn, improves the quality of instruction. When teachers are allowed to direct their own professional growth, they are prompted to look at themselves in new ways. They are permitted — temporarily — to separate themselves from their daily routines and to consider what their work really is all about. They can examine the societal issues that affect their profession. They can analyze the artistic and scientific dimensions of their work. They can search for ways to achieve self-renewal and self-confidence in the face of workday pressures. And they can discover strategies that will enable them to open students' minds to new learning adventures.

Holly Thornton, a teacher in Reynoldsburg City Schools, made many such discoveries as a member of the Ashton Middle School Sixth-Grade Outcomes Pilot Team. The team, which "resulted from an environment with sound administrative and teacher leadership," examined the possibility of implementing an integrated curriculum as outlined by Jim Beane in *Rhetoric to Reality*. Team members looked closely at the changes such a curriculum might bring to teacher responsibilities and the day-to-day flow of life within the middle school. Ultimately, Ms. Thornton and her colleagues identified "ten commandments" about pre-adolescent learning that became a unifying philosophy for their school. Among the commandments were the following:

- Learning should be active and relevant to the students' current and future world.
- Students need to work cooperatively and learn from each other and themselves, not just the teacher, in heterogeneous groups.
- Decisions are made together with students in a collaborative environment based on mutual respect, with student needs and interests at the center.
- Quality and depth of learning are more important than completion and coverage (Thornton 1993).

Similar insights are likely to emerge whenever teachers are allowed to analyze their work and chart a course for the future.

Second, teacher-led professional development enriches the entire school culture. Nine years ago, Jon Saphier and Matthew King wrote a perceptive article in which they outlined 12 "norms" that give shape and direction to a school's culture. They argued that "the degree to which these norms are strong makes a huge difference in the ability of school improvement activities to have a lasting, or even any, effect." Among Saphier and King's norms are four that can be nurtured or promoted by teacher-led professional development programs.

Collegiality: When teachers are allowed to take charge of their own professional development, the isolation in which they normally work is punctured. That is because the very act of planning and administering a professional development program requires combined efforts based on cooperation. Ideas must be discussed and brainstormed. Workshops and conferences must be scheduled, organized, and managed. Knowledge gained must be shared and evaluated. None of these things can occur unless teachers help each other and learn to appreciate the special skills that each of them possesses.

Honest, Open Communication: Within the context of a teacher-led professional development program, teachers are likely to feel more at ease about expressing a concern or voicing a criticism. They will know that their words will be heard by peers who may share or sympathize with their feelings. Correspondingly, the fear of offending an administrator will be reduced. In such an atmosphere, teachers will be better able to disagree over difficult issues and still be supportive of each other.

Involvement in Making Decisions: Teacher-led professional development allows teachers to have a voice in deciding their own professional destiny. It allows them to decide what new skills they need to master and the means they will use to achieve mastery. In a broader sense, it boosts teachers' self-esteem by demonstrating to them that they are trusted enough to be granted considerable control over a program that affects the vitality of the entire school.

High Expectations and Experimentation: When teachers are allowed to be leaders in their own professional development, they can more readily challenge themselves and set their sites on lofty goals without feeling that they are being pressured by administrators. They can experiment with new strategies or delve into new information, knowing that their efforts will be reviewed by colleagues who can appreciate their successes and sympathize with their shortcomings (Saphier and King 1985).

If one accepts Saphier and King's analysis, then to the degree that teacher-led professional development promotes collegiality, honest and open communication, involvement in decision making, high expectations, and experimentation, it fosters a strong, dynamic school culture that stimulates all members of the school community.

Third, teacher leadership of their professional development can be a force that drives improvement in other parts of the school community. It can sensitize educators to the need for comprehensive school change and motivate them to take action. Just as important, it can encourage educators to believe that their efforts to achieve change will bring positive results.

Michael Fullan and his colleagues have constructed a diagram that illustrates how significant improvements in teacher learning can be translated into both classroom improvement and school improvement. The diagram portrays the "teacher as learner" as a large gear that has four smaller gears inside it: the "teacher as researcher," the teacher's "technical repertoire," "reflective practices," and "collaboration" with other teachers. As teacher-led professional development turns each of these smaller gears, the large "teacher as learner" gear also is turned. As it moves, this large gear also moves two other large gears on either side: "classroom improvement" and "school improvement" (Fullan, Bennett, and Rolheiser-Bennett 1990).

Assuming that Fullan and his colleagues are on the mark with their diagram, it is worth asking just why a successful teacher-led professional development program has this kind of "carry-over" effect on an entire school system. The answer may lie partly in the modeling that such a program offers to other members of the school community who might be considering ways to improve their own mode of operation. As they watch the teacher-led professional development program unfold, these people may be alerted to program components or strategies that might be applied to their own situations. And as the program gives evidence of success, they may be motivated to try out the borrowed ideas.

Another point that a teacher-led professional development program would support is one that Fullan and Miles also have identified: "all large-scale change is implemented locally." As such a program evolves, overcoming resistance and bureaucratic snags along the way, it will make the entire school community acutely aware that "change is learning, change is a journey" and that "local implementation by everyday teachers, principals, parents, and students is the only way that change happens" (Fullan and Miles 1992).

In *Teaching as Learning: The Personal Dimensions of Teacher Growth* (1987), Robert Mertz describes recurrent themes from discussions with teachers. Beyond a commitment to making a difference in students' achievement, the themes involve personal and professional responsibility, organizational and collegial support, need for more time, and greater continuity in professional growth and learning activities.

Growth is a process, not an event. Teachers learn as they strive for excellence. They know, as Kenneth Eble points out in *The Craft of Teaching* (1976), that "learning and teaching are constantly interchanging activities. One learns by teaching; one cannot teach except by constantly learning."

Teacher-led professional development will lead to instruction that is more skillful, more inspiring, and more nurturing than it was. Teacher-led professional development should be built into the fabric of everyday school life. It should be a part of the school culture that helps to enrich the lives of everyone in the learning community.

References

Bacharach, Samuel. "Career Development, Not Career Ladders." *Education Week*, 12 March 1986, p. 28.

Eble, Kenneth. *The Craft of Teaching: A Guide to Mastering the Professor's Art*. San Francisco: Jossey-Bass, 1976.

Fullan, Michael G.; Bennett, Barie; and Rolheiser-Bennett, Carol. "Linking Classroom and School Improvement." *Educational Leadership* 47 (May 1990): 15.

Fullan, Michael G., and Miles, Matthew B. "Getting Reform Right: What Works and What Doesn't." *Phi Delta Kappan* 73 (June 1992): 744-52.

Fuller, Frances. "Concerns of Teachers: A Developmental Characterization." *American Educational Research Journal* 6 (March 1969): 207-26.

LaMarsh, Jeanenne. "Lowering Our Resistance to Change." *Circuitree Magazine* 4 (June 1991): 37.

Little, Judith Warren. "Norms of Collegiality and Experimentation: Workplace Conditions of School Success." *American Educational Research Journal* 19 (Fall 1982): 325-40.

Little, Judith Warren. "Seductive Images and Organizational Realities in Professional Development." In *Rethinking School Improvement: Research, Craft, and Concept*, edited by Ann Lieberman. New York: Teachers College Press, 1986.

Little, Judith Warren. "The Persistence of Privacy: Autonomy and Initiative in Teachers' Professional Relations." Paper presented at the annual meeting of the American Educational Research Association, San Francisco, March 1989.

Loucks-Horsley, Susan, and Sparks, Dennis. "Five Models of Staff Development for Teachers." *Journal of Staff Development* 10 (Fall 1989) 40-55.

Mertz, Robert. *Teaching as Learning: The Personal Dimensions of Teacher Growth.* Columbus: Ohio Department of Education, 1987.

Rosenholtz, Susan. *Teachers' Workplace: The Social Organization of Schools.* White Plains, New York: Longman, 1989.

Saphier, Jon, and King, Matthew. "Good Seeds Grow in Strong Cultures." *Educational Leadership* 42 (March 1985): 68-71.

Sarason, Seymour. *The Predictable Failure of Educational Reform.* San Francisco: Jossey-Bass, 1990.

Sergiovanni, Thomas. *The Principalship: A Reflective Practice Perspective.* Boston: Allyn and Bacon, 1991.

Shanker, Albert. "Staff Development and the Restructured School." In *Changing School Culture Through Staff Development*, edited by Bruce Joyce. Alexandria, Va.: Association for Supervision and Curriculum Development, 1990.

Thornton, Holly. "Educational Change and Implementation." *Ohio Middle School Journal* 20 (Fall 1993): 13.

CELEBRATING EDUCATION AS A PROFESSION

BY MARLIN L. TANCK

Marlin L. Tanck is director of teacher development at Marian College in Fond du Lac, Wisconsin.

To improve schooling and to empower teachers as leaders, we must build and celebrate education as a profession. We are not sausage makers.

Some who would have us be sausage makers would have us improve schools by mimicking business and industry. Privatize the schools. Run them like businesses. Give the customers choices among competing retailers. Use total quality management. Use site-based management. Be one-minute managers. Emulate industrial profiles of excellence. Wear Lee Iaccoca masks. Learn to turn back odometers and get government subsidies to compete and excel.

Others who would have us be sausage makers recommend their favorite recipes. Use cooperative learning. Use whole language. Use ability grouping. Use heterogeneous grouping. Use individualized instruction. Use whole-group instruction. Use multiple media. Use aural-oral development. Teach to learning styles. Teach to outcomes. Be student-centered.

There is no evidence that buying into the business-industrial metaphor for schools improves them. Indeed, some of those who use the metaphor also criticize schools for being too much like factories. There is some evidence that some of the recipes do help some students learn. But each is only a part of the larger perspective of what makes great teachers and great schools. And there is much evidence that great teachers have a major impact on student learning and school success.

Great teachers are great professionals. They have a depth of knowledge of their subject matter and of pedagogy. They artfully engage learners in their personal development. They are dedicated to the development and dignity of each learner and to the fidelity of his or her learning. They are loyal to their profession and dedicated to building a learning community. They have a passion for what they teach, for serving each learner well, and for celebrating the joys of learning and life.

We Americans know three leadership ethics for improving public administration: the efficient administration model, faith in Jacksonian democracy, and the civil service professional ethic (Kaufman 1956). We call on each ethic at different times — and sometimes invoke all three at once — to seek solutions to public problems. The confusion of multiple ethics can be cleared by demonstrating that the professional service ethic is best suited to the educational enterprise and to the school reform process.

The efficient administration model calls for strong executive leadership, efficient procedures, and scientific management. Historically it is exemplified by the Hoover Commission study of streamlining the executive branch of the federal government. It also borrows concepts from business management science and applies them to public administration. Educators find themselves emulating the one-minute manager, corporate profiles in excellence, industrial automation and technology, quality management and marketing, and strategic planning. As the public sector latches onto each new wave of management jargon, business and industry move to newer management models, leaving schools discussing last year's model without developing and testing its meaningful application.

The faith in Jacksonian democracy is based on the beliefs that all people have equal rights and that their needs will best be met if they control and manage public institutions. The town meeting and the rule of the majority in referenda represent and implement this ethic. California's Proposition 13, the referendum on school choice, and the Chicago approach to local school management embrace this ethic.

The efficient administration and popular democracy ethics certainly have their roles in public education. It would be folly to ignore efficient management of buildings and grounds, fiscal efficiencies, and appropriate personnel management and leadership principles from the management sciences. It certainly is appropriate for public education to have major policy and budget decisions set by a process of representative democracy. Yet neither management science nor popular democracy, nor the two ethics together, get to the heart of education: the learning and development of individual students. Indeed, majority rule and administrative efficiency may limit the dignity and diversity that nurture individual development.

The civil service professional ethic involves hiring knowledgeable experts, insulating them from the pressures of politics and special interests, and expecting them ethically and competently to serve their clients. Thus the Manhattan Project developed the atomic bomb during World War II before our adversaries did. Thus through the years, county agriculture agents have contributed greatly to the prowess of American agriculture. Thus NASA took the first steps for mankind on the moon and repaired the Hubble telescope. Thus professional educators have served their students through the years.

Through his professional passion and dedication, Jaime Escalante in Los Angeles inspired disadvantaged Hispanics to master calculus. Marva Collins, with professional pride and persistence, taught Chicago inner-city youth to be self-confident and self-directed learners. Through professional dedication and insight, Anne Mansfield Sullivan found the keys to unlocking and developing the hidden potential within a blind, unspeaking Helen Keller. Through his personal attention and support, Peter Davis helped young Louis Armstrong to nurture his love of music when the juvenile Armstrong was incarcerated. Eleanor Roosevelt credited the high expectations and discipline of Mlle. Souvestre for developing her thinking and character (Board 1991).

It is the nature of learning that makes the professional civil service ethic most appropriate to education. Learning is a process characteristic of diverse individual development, not a product like sausage. The idiosyncrasies and complexities of learning require artistic nurturance through the competent application of professional knowledge. The individual dignity and diverse potentials of learners demand that professionals honor individual differences. Recognition of each learner's singular potentials and aspirations is the essence of the professional educator's ethic.

The professional service ethic not only is best related to making a difference in what and how much students learn, but also it is the most likely to help attract and retain capable educators who can make a difference. Hertzberg and his colleagues (1959) long ago clearly established that capable professionals derive satisfaction from their own confidence and from the recognition of their competence. Yet much of the rhetoric of school reform ignores those who are most likely to make a difference and who ardently want to do so. As a veteran English teacher quoted by Maeroff put it,

> The rest of the culture outside of the school doesn't give a
> damn about you or the kids you are trying to teach. The school
> system itself almost regards you in that way. You are in the
> place where the bells are ringing, but the people who are call-

ing the signals for the schools are in places where they can't even hear the bells. (Maeroff 1988, p. 1)

In order to retain the best teachers and to further school improvement, it is essential that we develop professional practice schools in which the professionalism of the teacher is nourished and celebrated.

The Professional Educator

Great professional educators have the same qualities as other professionals:

1. Knowledge-based competence
2. Service orientation
3. Professional collaboration
4. Ethics
5. Accountability

Knowledge-based competence. The professional educator routinely and effectively applies knowledge of subject matter, pedagogy, and learning theory in a personal, professional artistry that maximizes student learning and development. A synergy of knowledge bases is melded in a style that communicates the essence and importance of what is to be learned and actuates student wonder and learning.

The professional educator knows more than the content and structure of subject matter. He or she understands the syntax of the disciplines and can help students understand how knowledge is derived and verified. She or he also knows the field applications and case histories of the disciplines, through which students can experience and develop their own knowledge structures (Shulman 1986, 1987). Inherent in the knowledge of the subject matter is an unspoken passion for knowledge that students find contagious and inspiring. Scholars encourage scholarship.

To develop student understanding and appreciation of the subject matter, the professional educator appropriately uses research-based and experience-based practices for planning, teaching, and monitoring learning. The knowledge of effective pedagogy is based on the literature that describes what occurs in effective classrooms and schools. It is developed in the apprenticeships of teacher education and can be facilitated through inservice professional mentoring. And it is honed with reflective practice.

To teach effectively, the professional educator must nurture a personal style and artistry. Recognizing teachable moments, sensing student engagement, confirming comprehension, and developing meaningful applications of subject matter require astute observation, subtle sensitivity, and informed decision making; simple formulas are ineffective and inappropriate.

Service orientation. The professional educator is dedicated to helping students realize and develop their respective identities and potentials as humans. Professional educators make a personal commitment of time, energy, knowledge, and emotion to maximize student learning; the student's development takes precedence over the educator's personal gain, prestige, politics, or expedience.

There also is compassion and idealism in the service orientation of the professional educator. Great teachers want to be the builders of others' dreams. The ethics of the profession include a premium on individual dignity and democratic rights in a responsible society.

Professional collaboration. The professional educator maintains and renews his or her individual competence through active involvement in a professional community, actively participates in the development of an effective educational organization, and works to establish a vital learning community.

Professional collaboration includes membership and participation in national professional organizations, which publish current professional literature and develop and disseminate rationales, standards, and models for curricula and instruction. Such collaboration also includes links with colleges and universities, which help to develop the professional knowledge base, prepare new members of the profession, and support professional growth. Partnerships among universities and colleges, professional organizations, and local educators are potent arrangements both for better preparing professionals and for maintaining the enthusiasm and competence of practicing educators.

Professional collaboration within the local setting includes at least three types of active involvement: 1) the collegial development and coordination of an effective curriculum, 2) shared responsibility and decision making in a self-renewing school organization, and 3) the nurturance of a learning community. Collaborative curriculum development and coordination provides the vision required for efficient, effective instruction and learning. Involvement in a self-renewing organization includes induction and mentoring of new teachers, collaborative inservice professional development, and participation in an information-based, collegially planned school improvement process. The nurturance of a learning community includes communication and coordination with other community agencies and the meaningful involvement of parents and students in the educational process.

Ethics. The professional educator consistently models and actuates the values inherent in professional competence, service orientation, and collaboration The professional educator honors each student's worth as a person and learner; respects differences in culture, social background, personality, and aptitude; promotes the rights of all students; and provides fair and appropriate developmental opportunities for all.

Efficacy of the Professional Educator

Education falls short as a profession. It falls short because educators do not control licensing and admission to the profession and, collectively, are not responsible for the sanctions of the profession. Also, critics rightfully call attention to instances in which educators have not fully satisfied the standards of professional competence, service, collaboration, ethics, and accountability. But the professionalization of education is the only true hope for the reform of education, and professional aspiration is the only thing likely to attract and keep the brightest and best in the field.

The efficacy of professional effort is clearly reflected in a recent review and analysis of 11,000 statistical studies from 50 years of research about what helps students learn (Wang, Haertel, and Walberg 1993). This review found that the most powerful constructs affecting student learning were student psychological process and instruction. The most powerful categories of influence, in order, were: classroom management, metacognitive processes, cognitive processes, home environment and parental support, student and teacher social interactions, social and behavioral attributes, motivational and affective attributes, peer group, and quantity of instruction.

These most powerful influences on learning involve the essential functions of professional educators, abilities of students that professional educators can help develop, or contextual factors that professional educators recognize and nurture. Classroom management includes the elements of competent practice. Metacognitive processes involve the students' planning and monitoring of their own learning, processes that the professional educator can help students develop. Cognitive processes include other factors that professional educators address. Teachers also are responsible for the positive student-teacher social interactions that support learning and for the full engagement of students and the wise use of instructional time, all of which affect

88

the quantity of instruction. They also take responsibility for helping the students to develop the social/behavioral and motivational attributes that affect their learning. Knowing the effects of home environment, parent support, and peer groups on learning, they work to develop meaningful involvement of parents and to structure positive peer influences.

The least powerful constructs affecting student learning were school organization, state and district governance, and organization. The least influential categories, in order, were: parental involvement policy, classroom implementation support, student demographics, student use of out-of-school time, program demographics, school demographics, state and district policies, school policy and organization, and district demographics.

These policy and organizational variables have received much attention in the school reform debates, but they are least likely to help students learn. "If practitioners and teacher educators want to enhance school learning," wrote the authors of this research analysis:

> they must attend to proximal variables such as: (a) psychological variables, especially metacognition and cognition; (b) classroom instruction and management, and student and teacher social and academic interactions; and (c) the home environment. Findings from cognitive psychology, including the importance of prior knowledge, individual aptitudes, and metacognitive processes, should inform teaching. . . . Findings on the salience of classroom instructional variables should also inform teacher's practice. (Wang, Haertel, and Walberg 1993, p. 278)

Such knowledge-based competence is the very essence of professional education.

The essential characteristics of professional education also are factors likely to keep competent educators on the job. Studies of teacher commitment, morale, and retention indicate that professional autonomy, participation, collaboration, and learning opportunities support teacher morale and commitment. In a major review of research on teacher commitment and differential incentive policies, Firestone and Pennell (1993) reported that autonomy in teaching, meaningful participation in school decisions, and collegial collaboration opportunities enhance teacher commitment. They found that collaborative learning opportunities to acquire, share, and develop pedagogical knowledge can significantly influence teacher commitment. They concluded that such differentiated incentives as merit pay and career ladders may undermine teacher commitment.

Chapman and Green (1986) reported that, following personal traits and initial commitment to teaching, the quality of the first teaching experience and the professional and social integration into teaching are significant factors in teacher retention. Nidich and Nidich (1986) named teacher consensus on goals, principal's support of professional development for teachers, and teacher voice in school decisions as predictors of good teacher morale. A survey by the American Association of School Administrators (Brodinsky 1984) identified professional autonomy, recognition of work well done, involvement in school decisions, a support network, and good inservice education as contributors to high teacher morale.

Thus teacher professionalism addresses the factors most likely to make a difference in how well students learn in schools and promotes the type of working environment most likely to affect the commitment, morale, and retention of the best and brightest staff. This makes the development of professional aspiration and teacher leadership essential to the improvement of education and to the attraction and retention of capable teachers.

Building a Climate for Professional Aspiration

The development of professional aspiration, subsequent professional practice, and highly professional service to students requires the development of schools in which professional education is emphasized and supported.

A priority for such schools is to hold an institutional membership in one or more professional organizations, such as Phi Delta Kappa, the National Society for the Study of Education, or the Association for Supervision and Curriculum Development. In addition to the journals and publications, institutional membership offers other media and staff development kits. Membership in professional organizations appropriate to the teacher's assignment is vital to contribute to the sense of professionalism and to the knowledge bases shared in professional practice.

In addition, the administration should support the development of and recognize the leadership of the profession. The school administration can nurture professional aspiration and teacher leadership by changing from a more traditional, directive, managerial mode of supervision and leadership to a largely non-directive, facilitative mode. This transition can be accomplished through the use of differentiated and developmental supervision models.

Differentiated supervision empowers teachers by actively involving them in a professional growth process (Glatthorn 1984, 1990). Each educator is involved in selecting appropriate professional development goals as the focus of his or her supervision and professional development. Beginners may be required to start with goals centered in basic pedagogy and learning principles. Once those basic professional competencies are demonstrated, they join the rest of the staff in selecting developmental goals appropriate to their needs.

Differentiated supervision also provides three modes of supervision and professional development — cooperative clinical supervision, collegial development, and self-directed development. In the first mode, the supervisor and teacher agree on developmental goals and work together in cycles of classroom observations and conferences. In the collegial development mode, teams of educators with the same goals work together in collegial development teams. In the self-directed mode, each professional plans, monitors, and reports his or her own professional growth. The collegial development mode uses the strengths of professional collaboration. Self-directed development, of course, embraces the individual competence and self-monitoring characteristic of a profession.

Developmental supervision (Glickman 1984, 1990), involves selecting a style of supervision — directive, collaborative, or facilitative — that is appropriate to the stage of professional development of the teacher and using a progression of interactions to develop professionalism. The facilitative style empowers those teachers with high levels of professional knowledge and commitment to plan and monitor their own professional growth.

In schools that support professional education, there is an emphasis on moral leadership based on the ethics and values of the profession. When school routines and decision making honor the service orientation and ethics of the professional educator, there is a higher level of moral leadership. When staff and community members are involved meaningfully in the planning and implementation of instruction, there is a supportive, middle level of moral leadership. However, when school routines and decision making are characterized by control and bartering, there is a lower level of moral leadership. The focus is on organization and control, rather than on professional competence and student development.

The nature of moral leadership is portrayed to the staff and the public by the way in which things typically are done and how resources usually are used. Provision of higher-level moral leadership, which stresses professional ethics and service to students, is strongly stated by allocating adequate time for professional collaboration and by making instruction councils the focus of school organization.

Uninterrupted time for learning and instruction are, of course, the premium for maximum service to students. In order to use that time effectively, the school must provide adequate time for professional development and collaboration. Time spent on professional growth, coordination of instruction, curriculum research, and reflective self-monitoring maximizes student learning and development.

Professional leadership can be supported by including all faculty in a school instruction council. The instruction council provides coordination and vision for a learning community. Instruction councils plan, coordinate, and support effective instruction. They develop curricula consistent with the knowledge bases. They plan professional development and school improvement efforts to support learning and instruction. They coordinate resources in support of effective instruction. They conduct curriculum research and promote action research to help assess learning and instruction.

The council may be divided into smaller groups that focus on ad hoc needs or on specific areas of instruction. Larger secondary schools may function with an instruction council steering committee, composed of department chairs or other staff representatives, that coordinates council efforts between whole-council sessions. All faculty also are members of district ad hoc or subject area instruction councils, each of which is represented on a districtwide instruction council.

If norms of collegiality and shared knowledge characterize school operation, professional collaboration and service to students are supported.

Providing a Professional Data Base

Data for making informed decisions and reporting objectives are essential to the operation and leadership of the profession. A school data profile can describe the context in which learning occurs, some of the processes that influence learning, and the resulting attitudes, achievement, and performance of students. Such information provides a tool for setting goals, a context for individual classroom planning, and a basis for objective reporting to the public. It is vital to professional competence and accountability.

The school profile should contain four major sections on school context, school resources, schoolwide student performance, and some diagnostic data specific to school improvement efforts (Northwest

Regional Educational Laboratory 1989). The school context section describes the school community and documents student demographic trends. It includes data on student gender and ethnicity, on student socioeconomic and cultural variables, on student exceptionalities, and on patterns of the demographic variables in school enrollments in recent years. Awareness of shifting school demographics provided by such a profile is essential to planning for school success in these changing times.

The school resources section of the profile describes the resources that the school has to serve the student population. It includes data on staff and their credentials, provides a summary of regular and special school programs and services, and describes important features of the facility and equipment. It also may list district and community resources available to staff, students, and families. This section provides an important overview of professional competencies and school strengths in programs and resources.

The schoolwide student performance section of the profile reports how students are performing in a variety of areas, including academic achievement, social behaviors, and attitude. Academic achievement data go beyond test scores to provide summaries from performance assessments and portfolios, reports of student awards and recognitions earned, and records of units and courses completed. Social behavior data include attendance, discipline, and participation factors. Attitudinal data include motivation, self-concept in school, sense of efficacy in school, and satisfaction with school. All the student performance data should be disaggregated by key demographic variables to support analysis and planning for success with the variety of students in the school population.

A diagnostic information section of a school profile may be added to support analysis and planning for a specific school improvement effort. For example, if a faculty has decided to work on improving student study skills and high expectations, the diagnostic section would provide baseline study skills and motivation data, document process data related to improving study skills, and chart progress on study skills and motivation over time.

Many data for a school profile are readily available. Others need to be developed. The process of profiling begins with organizing available data and then augmenting the profile as other data are provided. Providing the resources and involving staff to develop a meaningful school profile are basic factors in empowering staff to make decisions and document progress. Without the profile, a school lacks a basic tool in promoting professional practice and developing related confidence, accountability, and satisfaction.

Promoting Professional Practice

A combination of meaningful collaborative involvement and self-directed performance and accountability is what makes a profession strong and keeps competent persons in it. Collaborative involvement may include shared decision making in school improvement projects or instruction councils and collegial professional development with peer coaching. Autonomous performance may include development of professional knowledge, self-directed professional development, and individual classroom accountability.

While there is evidence that site-based management *per se* does not improve student achievement in schools (Cotton 1992), there is evidence that a collaborative focus on effective school practice does enhance student learning (Robinson 1985). One highly productive and meaningful way to provide collaborative involvement and professional leadership by teachers is to organize site-based school improvement projects, such as the Onward to Excellence model of the Northwest Regional Educational Laboratory (Butler 1989) or those that many state departments of education promote. Such projects involve all staff, with guidance by a leadership team, in a schoolwide process of improving results for students. The process starts with analyzing the need to improve student performance by reviewing a school data profile, such as the one described above. The staff then are involved in agreeing on a related school improvement goal, identifying research and experience-based practice likely to support the goal, planning how to better implement such professional practice, carrying out the plan, and monitoring the results. Time and resources must be allocated for the collaboration if it is to make a difference; the investment is rewarded by improved professional practice and better results for students.

A second productive, meaningful way to build teacher professional leadership and collaboration is to make an instruction council the true locus of faculty leadership. The council can take charge of the school data profile. It can provide the coordination and select the leadership team for the school improvement project. It can conduct cycles of curriculum evaluation. It can process, review, and update professional knowledge by using the institutional professional association membership and other professional media. And it can coordinate the professional development effort in support of the school improvement project, improvement of instruction, and updating of professional knowledge. As with the school improvement project approach to collaborative professional leadership, adequate time and resources must be committed to make the instruction council effective; but the investment is worthwhile if the collaboration focuses on competent professional practice and student performance.

Small-group collaboration in professional improvement through collegial development teams or peer coaching also can contribute to professional practice and teacher leadership, as teachers share their expertise and provide mutual support. Much has been written about peer coaching, in which teachers observe each other and provide feedback on the efficacy of professional practice. In collegial development teams (Tanck 1992), teachers work together in small groups, ideally four to six persons, to analyze and achieve a shared professional development goal. Together they process related professional knowledge and report on and review its implementation in their classrooms. Participants in collegial development teams report a strong commitment to the process and agree that their efforts improve instruction and student achievement (Tanck 1991).

While collaborative leadership and collegial professional development are important and powerful means of improving professional practice, self-directed professional development must not be overlooked. The essence of being a professional is taking responsibility for individual competence and for meeting the needs of students. Adult learners want to assess their own growth needs, control their own learning procedures and schedules, and see practical results in their work. Even in collaborative settings, professional development depends on individual participation, understanding, and performance.

There also are practical reasons for promoting self-directed professional development. Persons in singular assignments or pilot projects may have unique professional goals. Schedules sometimes make group participation difficult or impossible. Some persons prefer independent learning or do better in it. Self-directed development and reflection provide a change of pace from collaborative involvement and can provide checks for "group-think" pressures.

Self-directed development can be promoted and formalized by making it an option in the process of supervision and professional development. Rather than participate in clinical supervision or group staff development, staff members may elect to submit a self-directed professional growth plan at the start of a school year, to implement the plan during the year, and to report results at the end of the year

(Tanck 1994). Adequate time must be scheduled for the process. A current professional development media collection, consultant services, and suggestions for self-monitoring are among other resources needed to support self-directed professional development. However, most vital to self-directed growth are an awareness of the changing subject area and pedagogical knowledge bases and an atmosphere of respect and trust (Duke 1993).

Training staff and providing resources for action research can provide an exciting and useful vehicle for self-directed growth and accountability. Teachers learn to identify and define problems or goals they want to address by finding related research or experience-based practice, setting observable goals, defining a plan of action, implementing and monitoring the plan, and organizing data to know if they reached their goals (Livingston and Castle 1989; Sagor 1992). The research process lends structure and accountability to the self-directed development process. Sharing the action research report can build professional pride and add to the case-study knowledge base of the profession.

Celebrating the Profession

How does one recognize and celebrate the competent and dedicated work of professional teachers in order to build their morale and keep them leading? No Golden Apple Awards, please. And, please, no Teacher-of-the-Year programs. Such extrinsic, token rewards can demean and divide the profession. Rather, do what research says will motivate good teachers. Recognize and celebrate their competence and accomplishments.

Routinely recognize achievement. Rotate the location of faculty functions among classrooms so that host teachers can briefly share with colleagues the projects and activities they are doing with students. Change the open house to a school report night, at which student projects and portfolios are displayed in each instructional area. Compile and publish a three-ring binder of the successful instructional activities that teachers have used. Publicize instruction council functions and decisions, and describe classroom projects in the school newsletter. Report in the school and district bulletins the work of curriculum committees, graduate study by staff, professional association involvement of faculty, and instructional innovations under way in classrooms. Start district curriculum evaluation and teacher action research journals. Report the academic and social accomplishments of students in the same ways that co-curricular and athletic accomplishments are reported.

Meaningfully use the experience and talents of staff. Have experienced staff members be mentors for newcomers. Have peers share their expertise in planning and conducting staff development opportunities. Use faculty focus groups to assess trends and issues and brainstorm responses. Establish collaborative action research teams for the most pressing problems or issues of the school. Name faculty resource persons whom parents might consult in specific areas of concern. Establish teacher assistance teams to help colleagues diagnose student problems and plan interventions. Recommend and encourage promotion from within the school and district. Involve staff in the process of hiring new faculty members.

Be personable and congenial. Observe teacher appreciation week for all teachers at the toughest time of the year and see that all get flowers the first day and notes of thanks each day of that week. Write at least one letter of thanks a year to each teacher for extra duty assignments, special efforts, or performance in difficult circumstances. Document unsolicited compliments and expressions of appreciation from parents and students. Periodically collect parent and student feedback and anonymously publish selected favorable comment; use the less favorable anonymous comments with faculty focus groups and inform your public of the process and resulting action plans. Say "Thanks for caring" whenever you see a teacher take a fearful hand, clarify a doubt, build student competence, or recognize the joy of learning.

Finally and most important, keep the professional service ethic prominent, for great teachers are the molders of students' dreams. Professional educators build the dreams of those children who come to us with little hope and few expectations. We also help those who come with more abundant hope and higher expectations to shape their special dreams.

References

Board, J.C., ed. *A Special Relationship: Our Teachers and How We Learned*. Wainscott, N.Y.: Pushcart Press, 1991.

Brodinsky, B. "Teacher Morale: What Builds It, What Kills It." *Instructor* 93 (April 1984): 36-39.

Butler, J.A. *Success for All Students: How Onward to Excellence Uses R&D to Improve Schools*. Portland, Ore.: Northwest Regional Educational Laboratory, 1989.

Chapman, David W., and Green, M.S. "Teacher Retention: A Further Examination." *Journal of Educational Research* 79, no. 5 (1986): 273-79.

Cotton, K. *Topical Synthesis #6: School-Based Management*. School Improvement Research Series. Portland, Ore.: Northwest Regional Educational Laboratory, 1992.

Duke, D.L. "Removing Barriers to Professional Growth." *Phi Delta Kappan* 74 (May 1993): 702-704, 710-12.

Firestone, W.A., and Pennell, J.R. "Teacher Commitment, Working Conditions, and Differential Incentive Policies." *Review of Educational Research* 63, no. 4 (1993): 489-525.

Glatthorn, A.A. *Differentiated Supervision*. Alexandria, Va.: Association for Supervision and Curriculum Development, 1984.

Glatthorn, A.A. *Supervisory Leadership: Introduction to Instructional Supervision*. New York: Scott, Foresman, 1990.

Glickman, C.D. *Developmental Supervision: Alternative Practices for Helping Teachers Improve Instruction*. Alexandria, Va.: Association for Supervision and Curriculum Development, 1981.

Glickman, C.D. *Supervision of Instruction: A Developmental Approach*. 2nd ed. Boston: Allyn and Bacon, 1990.

Hertzberg, F.; Mausner, B.; and Snyderman, B. *The Motivation to Work*. New York: John Wiley & Sons, 1959.

Kaufman, H. "Emerging Conflicts in the Doctrine of Public Administration." *American Political Science Review* 50, no. 4 (1956): 1057-73.

Livingston, C., and Castle, S. *Teachers and Research in Action*. Washington, D.C.: National Education Association, 1989.

Maeroff, G.I. *The Empowerment of Teachers: Overcoming the Crisis of Confidence*. New York: Teachers College Press, 1988.

Nidich, R.J., and Nidich, S.I. "A Study of School Organizational Variables Associated with Teacher Morale." *The Clearing House* 60 (1986): 189-91.

Northwest Regional Educational Laboratory. *Onward to Excellence: 2. The Research and the Profile*. Portland, Ore., 1989.

Robinson, G.E. *Effective Schools Research: A Guide to School Improvement*. ERS Concerns in Education. Arlington, Va.: Educational Research Service, 1985.

Sagor, R. *How to Conduct Collaborative Action Research*. Alexandria, Va.: Association for Supervision and Curriculum Development, 1992.

Shulman, L.S. "Those Who Understand: Knowledge Growth in Teaching." *Educational Researcher* 15, no. 2 (1986): 4-14.

Shulman, L.S. "Knowledge and Teaching: Foundations of the New Reform." *Harvard Educational Review* 57, no. 1 (1987): 1-22.

Tanck, M.L. *Report of Staff Feedback on Differentiated Modes of Supervision of Instruction*. Sheboygan, Wis.: Sheboygan Area School District, 1991.

Tanck, M.L. *The Collegial Development Team: Who? Why? How? When? Where? Who, Me?* Sheboygan, Wis.: Sheboygan Area School District, 1992.

Tanck, M.L. *Self-Directed Professional Development: A Powerful Option in Differentiated Supervision*. Fond du Lac, Wis.: Marian College, 1994.

Wang, M.C.; Haertel, G.D.; and Walberg, H.J. "Toward a Knowledge Base for School Learning." *Review of Educational Research* 63, no. 3 (1993): 249-94.

PART III
EMPOWERING TEACHERS THROUGH PROFESSIONAL DEVELOPMENT

TEACHER EMPOWERMENT IN A TIME OF GREAT CHANGE

BY WILLIAM E. WEBSTER

William E. Webster is a professor of educational administration at California State University at Bakersfield.

School-site management and participatory decision making have been identified as key elements in many of the improvement and re-structuring efforts taking place in schools across the country. Implied in site-based management and decision making are teacher involvement and teacher empowerment. My research indicates that these notions are being implemented in so many different ways that there is no single paradigm to represent teacher involvement, nor is it easy to find an operational definition of teacher empowerment.

The complexity of high schools and their uniqueness were continually reinforced in my recent research visits to schools. Although there were recognizable similarities, such as subjects taught, departments, and number of periods, so varied were the structures, interpersonal relationships, and communities served that they made each high school a distinctive institution.

In this essay I present findings from a four-year research effort that I have been conducting to investigate the varied roles of the high school principal and how these roles are carried out within the school structure.* I also discuss a school reform effort titled Project 2000, of which I am the co-principal investigator, emphasizing how teacher empowerment was implemented in this program and its positive effects.

Limitations on Teacher Empowerment

Before reviewing these findings, I must note some general limitations on teacher empowerment caused by the nature of the job and

---

*This study also is the basis of a new book to be published by the Phi Delta Kappa Educational Foundation.

the organization of the school. Teachers, in most cases, have no control over whom they teach. With the exception of busing, children come from the neighborhoods surrounding the school; thus teachers have no selection of clientele as do doctors and lawyers. Even where there is "choice," the parents, not the teachers, have the choice.

Also, teachers have limited control over whom their colleagues will be, although my findings indicate that this is beginning to change, and teachers in many cases are being involved in the selection process.

Although teacher committees sometimes select textbooks and materials, more often teachers must accept assigned texts, and there is very little room for deviation. As with teacher selection, I present findings that indicate that teachers' roles in choosing textbooks are growing. However, intervention at the state policy level can have a major impact on the nature of texts that teachers are allowed. Recently in California, under the leadership of the state superintendent, the state's elementary reading program was changed from a basal-reader program to a literature-based program. In order to be on the list of acceptable textbooks from which districts made their selections, publishers had to adhere to the literature-based philosophy. And teachers had no choice but to change teaching styles, a decision over which they had little or no control.

Historically, schools have been hierarchical, bureaucratic, top-down organizations that work against teacher empowerment. Through the years, teachers have not made important decisions affecting district policy other than through the collective bargaining process. Rather, they have been restricted to decisions within their own classroom. This means there has not been a system to involve teachers in the process, and one of the purposes for the study was to find out if structures for teacher decision making were emerging.

Another element of school life that impedes teacher empowerment, described in Dan Lortie's influential book, *School Teacher: A Sociological Study*, is teachers' isolation from one another. At the high school level, the master schedule reinforces the isolation by providing little time during the school day for teachers to work together.

Research Findings

In my work with the school reform effort called Project 2000, in my role as an author-lecturer for Phi Delta Kappa, and in a study I conducted on secondary year-round education in California, I had opportunities over several years to meet and talk with dozens of high school administrators in various parts of the country. I became interested in how high schools were managed, and that interest grew into a formal study of the role of the principal and the high school as an institution. I developed an interview protocol to organize the research and then tape recorded interviews with more than 100 high school administrators and scores of teachers in 23 states. I also interviewed principals and teachers in 7 foreign countries; and though the data and conclusions reported here are based almost exclusively on American high schools, I mention two examples relating to teacher empowerment in Brazil.

The principal interview covered a variety of topics. Following are questions related specifically to teacher empowerment:

- Describe your relationship with the teaching staff.
- How do collective bargaining and contract management impinge on that relationship?
- Do you have a system to involve the teaching staff in making significant decisions relating to the operation of the school? If yes, what is the nature of that system?
- How would you describe your management style?
- What are your strategies to motivate teachers to continually improve?
- Do you consider yourself the instructional leader of the school?

I focused questions to teachers on their roles in the decision-making process and their perceptions of teacher empowerment.

Advisory Groups

The school structure involving teachers that was mentioned most often was the advisory committee. Such a committee was organized in a variety of ways and called by such names as school-site council, principal's advisory committee, or principal's council. In most cases, the organization seemed informal, almost ad hoc; generally, no agenda or minutes were kept and issues were addressed in no formal order.

In several schools there were two such groups. One had responsibility to advise on the day-to-day operation of the school, such as tardiness policies and discipline procedures. A second group took responsibility for school improvement planning, such as developing programs of integrated learning or initiating a tech-prep program. In all cases, the principal and teachers made it clear that these groups were strictly advisory; the principal made any final decisions.

A small number of schools had a regular structure with annually elected teacher members, a mission statement, and a yearly plan of activities. These more formal groups operated where major restructuring efforts were under way. Rather than being called simply advisory committees, these groups were called restructuring teams or school improvement teams. Although they were considered advisory, in operation they were seen by teachers and principals to be more than that; and it was apparent that if the principal were to countermand or redirect the team, it would be with the establishment of a clear rationale for the change and through persuasion rather than direction.

In one case, the school had an advisory committee made up of the principal and teachers elected by the faculty, with a chair elected by the committee. In this situation the principal was an equal of the teachers and had only one vote. Only if a decision violated school district policy or the law did the principal have veto power over a group decision.

Another school had a committee of parents and teachers. The group was described as having "legislative powers." The principal served as the executive, and differences were resolved through negotiation and compromise.

One area where teachers were being given greater responsibility was the hiring of new staff. Typically, the principal established an ad hoc group that included an assistant principal, department chairs, and teachers of the discipline involved. The responsibility of this group was twofold: 1) to screen application files prepared by the central office and 2) to conduct interviews of the prospective colleagues. Although principals emphasized the importance of teacher involvement in the hiring process, in almost every case the teachers' role was advisory, with the final decision being made by the principal. In no case did I find that teachers were involved in the evaluation process or in the decision of whether an individual would receive tenure.

The involvement of teachers in textbook selection varied. In districts with one high school, the selection was made by the teachers of the discipline involved; no principal indicated that he had used his veto power in this process. In some large districts, textbook selection also was a site decision involving the respective disciplines; but a far more common practice was the establishment of districtwide committees with representatives from each school, thus giving each school and its teachers a chance to influence the process. The final decision was a districtwide selection.

Influential Groups

During the interviews, several teachers identified the ability of senior faculty to form informal but influential groups. One teacher stated, "There are really two power structures in the school: the formal structure made up of principals, vice principals, and deans, and the informal structure made up of senior respected faculty."

Another teacher confirmed the notion of the influential informal group when she said, "To get something done, you cannot operate alone. You have to get a large enough group of important teachers if you are really going to influence the administration."

Supporting these observations are several examples of informal empowerment by teachers themselves, either by establishing new groups or by influencing the formal organization. In one school the principal had an advisory committee that was not always taken seriously; but in informal discussions it was given more power through the support of senior faculty, most of whom were not members of the advisory group. In one instance, the teachers were concerned that the administration was not giving enough attention to maintaining a safe and orderly campus. This informally expanded advisory committee designed a plan that it presented to the administration, accompanied by a strong suggestion that either the principal adopt the plan or the teachers were prepared to go to the superintendent and the board. The plan was adopted; and by the end of a semester of operation, it was being touted by the administration at public meetings as a sound strategy for managing a large urban high school.

A group of Hispanic teachers in a large urban high school told the principal they were organizing a committee made up exclusively of Hispanic teachers in order to design a program to reduce what they thought was a dangerously high dropout rate among Hispanic students. They emphasized that they wanted the committee to include only Hispanic teachers. The principal, not Hispanic, explained to me that through district affirmative action policies, over the years the Hispanic teachers had created, as he termed it, "a critical mass," which enabled them to empower themselves. Some non-Hispanic teachers filed a grievance with the union protesting the committee's makeup; but it was ignored by the principal, and the union chose not to press the issue. Eventually the committee involved the entire faculty and community and developed a comprehensive improvement effort under the motto, "School of Champions." The principal told me that graffiti, truancy, and overall discipline problems had been reduced to such a degree that he thought the program, then in its second year of operation, was working and that he was hopeful that the dropout rate would fall in the future.

In another district, following the success of an elementary school multi-track, year-round education program, the board, with what many faculty members felt was insufficient involvement by them, decided to implement year-round education districtwide, which included its two large high schools. A storm of group protests led by senior high school faculty followed. However, the plan to implement high school year-round education went ahead — as did faculty opposition. After two years of high school year-round education and with the opening of a new school, high school year-round education was abandoned. Many observers attributed the reversal to the actions taken by senior faculty in the high schools.

Individual Empowerment

Sometimes charismatic teachers operating alone were able to empower themselves. One example occurred where an individual teacher was responsible for almost derailing a major restructuring effort. For most of a year the school had been looking into restructuring to a four-period day, following a program that had been instituted by another high school in a nearby district. A faculty advisory committee had thoroughly analyzed and discussed the plan, including holding a series of open, reasonably well-attended community forums to discuss the planned change with parents and interested community members. In addition, teachers and parents had visited schools where the four-period day was in operation. With the support the faculty and those who attended the community forums, implementation was scheduled for the fall.

After the scheduled change was announced, an unanticipated intervention took place. The director of instrumental music, who also lead a highly honored marching band, concluded that the proposed four-period day would seriously limit his ability to conduct rehearsals and related activities that were necessary for the continued excellence of the marching band. Without informing the principal, he convinced his booster club and band alumni that the change would seriously affect the quality of the music program, particularly the quality of the marching band. Large numbers of individuals from these groups began attending the community forums, often changing orderly discussions into raucous shouting matches. It appeared for a while that the whole restructuring plan would have to be abandoned or at least delayed for a year. However, the principal, working with respected teachers and community members over a two- or three-month period, was able to explain to the satisfaction of the concerned parents that the fears of the band master were groundless. The program got under way as scheduled.

An area where energetic and committed individuals acting on their own can have a significant impact is technology. In school after school that I visited, where there were substantial computer labs, almost invariably the principal would report that an individual teacher was the driving force behind the introduction of the labs to the school. The strategy seemed to work this way: An individual teacher would become enamored of computers, at first bringing his or her own computer to school and buying programs at personal expense. Then, by demonstrating the computer's usefulness to other faculty, this teacher would gain peer support and convince the principal, who often was reluctant to embrace the new technology, to move ahead with developing computer capabilities in the school.

Empowerment Through Resistance to Change

Principals often cited teacher reluctance to change as a source of frustration. Such inertia can be a form of group empowerment. One principal mentioned that he had hoped to link up with Ted Sizer's Coalition of Essential Schools, but faculty resistance to any change had postponed the linkage indefinitely. The most-cited example of resistance to change concerned the development of programs to meet the needs of limited- and non-English-speaking youngsters. In several of the schools that I visited, principals explained that over the past decade or so there had been an influx of many youngsters for whom English was not their native language. The principals also reported that there was substantial faculty resistance to meeting the needs of these students. One principal summed up the problem, stating, "What they really say is, If they come to school speaking English, we'll really help them. But I'm a math or science or English teacher, and it is not my job to teach them to speak English."

Traditional Role of the Principal

The conventional thinking of principals about their leadership roles often affected teacher empowerment. Many remarks by principals similar to the following indicate how they saw the principalship: "I've been given the responsibility to run this school, and I'm also accountable for what happens here. It's all well and good to involve teachers, and I do, and they can influence my decisions. But since I'm responsible and held accountable for what happens here, I must reserve the right to myself to make key decisions and veto faculty decisions when appropriate."

The time-honored way in which principals think about their jobs and their relations with teachers again came to the fore when they were asked to identify strategies they used to motivate teachers. The most frequent response was, "through evaluation and follow-up conference," with no principals noting motivation by empowering teachers.

Answers to a question about the characteristics of the principal's management style covered a wide range. Some principals said they were directive and authoritarian. Others identified participation and collegiality as elements of their management style. In the entire sample, only one principal responded by saying, "I manage through the empowerment of teachers."

Schools in Crisis

Principals who were appointed to take charge and "straighten things out" in crisis situations limited any movement toward teacher empowerment. Taking charge was interpreted by the principals that I interviewed as assuming a directive, non-participatory management style that left little or no room for teacher empowerment. A typical comment was:

> The superintendent asked me to come to the school to straighten it out. Through the years, things had really deteriorated. You would not believe the condition of the school when I got here last year — graffiti, halls a mess, kids wandering around, even teachers missing classes. I had to take action on my own to get the school straightened out before I could take the time to set up structures to involve the teachers in decision making, and I really wondered if some of them were really capable of making decisions with the condition the school was in when I got here. I had a faculty meeting and expressed my opinions on what I had seen and told them we were going to get the school in shape; and if they did not like my methods, they could apply for transfers, and I'd help them get them. I told the vice principal that if he wanted to continue to be vice principal, to get here early and see that the graffiti was gone before the kids got here.

One principal said that the big problem on his arrival was student tardiness to class. He unilaterally introduced a program where teachers were directed to close their doors when the second passing bell had sounded, and all late students were ordered to go to the cafeteria to meet with the principal to get a pass to return to class. He told me that five tardies would lead to a suspension. He said at first there were well over 100 youngsters who showed up in the cafeteria. The day I was there, two youngsters showed up, both of whom had plausible excuses that were accepted by the principal.

In another example where the principal was "putting the school back together," at about five minutes before the dismissal bell the principal asked me to accompany her on a quick tour of the school grounds. The purpose of this tour, she explained, was to check on teachers who were dismissing students early, a practice that had been widespread before she became principal three months earlier. Indeed, there were clusters of students shuffling toward the exits. She quickly shepherded them back to their classrooms, and in each case she directed the teacher in question to meet with her immediately after the youngsters were dismissed at the proper time.

A Model of Teacher Empowerment

One high school used an innovative, unusual arrangement that involved teachers in hiring personnel and organizing the school. The school was given a number of "personnel points" based on enrollment; and the staff could decide how to allocate points to develop administration, clerical support, and teacher ratios. As a result, the faculty and administrator working together decided to do without a vice principal and to create the position of curriculum coordinator in all the major disciplines. The coordinators were assigned to teach one-half of their time and to work on curriculum and to serve as mentors for the other half. Teachers participated in the selection of individuals to fill these roles.

This approach was interesting from two aspects: First, teachers were participants in the process that determined the organization of the school and, second, individuals who were basically teachers gained expanded responsibilities, thereby empowering them to have a greater influence on instructional quality.

Teacher Empowerment in Project 2000

Project 2000, a major reform effort now in its fifth year in Bakersfield, California, just graduated its first group of students and gives evidence of how small class sizes, a degree of teacher independence and decision-making power, and teacher teamwork can better educate students. The project is in the Kern High School District of 25,000 students, with an average high school size of about 2,000. The major goal of the project is to increase the numbers of students going on to post-high school education and at the same time to reduce the dropout rate among project participants. (The district had a dropout rate of 30%; of the 70% who did graduate from high school, only 26% went on to higher education or specialized vocational training.)

Selected by a competitive process, four of the district's 10 high schools assigned 100 students each to participate in the reform effort. At each project high school, an additional 100 were added each September. Students were selected in a random process from those at each school who scored between the 25th and 65th percentile on standardized achievement tests in the eighth grade — in other words, average and slightly below average students. The minority representation at each school in the project would equal or exceed the percentage of minorities at that site. Project teachers had little control over individual project participants.

Project teachers were paid for planning time during the summer prior to the inauguration of the project. During this time they selected texts and other materials and decided on organizational strategies, such as team teaching and curriculum integration. Teachers in the project had a teaching load of 100 students (the district averaged between 140 and 165 students) and taught a four-period day, allowing two periods for group planning and decision making, processes that had started during the summer. When the project moved into the second year, participating teachers were given the opportunity to select new team members to work with the project students in their sophomore year. The reduced load, time to work together during the summer, and school-day planning time were key elements in the project's determination to empower teachers to make key educational decisions for project students.

Evaluation of the project by a team from California State University, Bakersfield furnished evidence that the project is succeeding. Part of the evaluation design called for a matching control group of 400 students who would mirror the project group, reflecting the same achievement test score limits and minority participation criteria. The evaluation results indicated that the project group had taken substantially more college preparatory classes, the dropout rate was 5% for project students and 20% for the control group, and many more of

112

the project students had made application for higher education than had students in the control group.

At the end of the four years, the evaluation team asked the project teachers to complete a survey instrument composed of three parts: multiple-choice responses, statements relating to the project, and a comment section. A member of the research team followed up the questionnaire by conducting focused interviews at each of the project schools.

Following are results from the survey relating to the empowerment of teachers:

- 100% of the Project 2000 teachers enjoyed teaching in the project;
- 88% believed they had adequate time to select and implement instructional strategies based on student needs;
- 95% felt they were encouraged to make decisions concerning development and make revisions in programs of instruction;
- 95% saw a high level of mutual support among project teachers;
- 100% believed project teaching staff were willing to be accountable for the effort's instructional accomplishments.

By contrast, in their responses to statements comparing their roles in Project 2000 to the overall operation of the school, project teachers reported the following:

- 44% felt the entire school staff was actively engaged in and committed to the school's plan for improvement;
- 32% felt that, as a group, teachers were a major influence in setting school policy;
- 53% felt staff and community were actively involved in working together to solve significant problems confronting the school.

It is interesting to note that project teachers, while positive about key aspects of the project, also were able to identify the more traditional operations of the school in which the project was located.

In the comments section of the questionnaire, teachers zeroed in on the major components of the project. One teacher said, "The most significant part of our project is the meeting time each day when we make decisions about curriculum and students."

Working together also was noted by another teacher: "I've had an opportunity to work in a team situation with a dedicated group of educators."

Another comment reinforced this notion: "One of the things I valued most is the colleague interaction and support I have received.

I have enjoyed the freedom to make decisions that we as a team see will best meet student needs."

In the focused interviews, which gave the team of teachers the opportunity to react to the results of the questionnaires, themes similar to those in the comment section emerged: "One of the key things about the project is our getting together as a group. We are able to talk together about students over a long period of time and together design strategies that we as a team think will do the best job."

Another teacher remarked, "The kids know that we make decisions and that we can make the changes that help them. And they really like that. They know we meet as a team, and they really feel they are part of it."

One teacher summed up a general feeling by saying,

> I felt that for the two years in the project, I was the luckiest teacher in the world because we have decided on the curriculum we want, we have small class sizes, and we said to our administrators as a group that we wanted to do this or that and they treated us as professionals and said, "Do that." That has meant a lot to me to have that happen.

Teacher Empowerment in Brazil

While visiting high schools in Brazil, I learned about two components of their education system that, although very different from one another, certainly could be viewed as teacher empowerment. I had the opportunity to visit high schools in five large cities and talk to officials in five states and in the office of the Secretary of Education in Brasilia, the national capital. In Brazil the federal government, states, and municipalities have their own systems of education. The federal schools that I visited were technology schools, of which there was one in each of Brazil's 23 states. The remainder of the schools that I visited were state schools.

In my first visit, I was introduced to the principal, the vice principal, and the *orientador*. This last position has implications for teacher empowerment. I was told that this position existed in all Brazilian schools, and on subsequent visits I talked to the *orientador* at each school. The *orientador* is a teacher elected annually by colleagues at the school site and appears to be a leader on issues and problems related to students and curriculum. They have the power to call meetings and to conduct studies and, in general, serve as the school's quality control officer.

114

Probably the best example of the *orientador* in action emerged in interviews in a large school in a major city on the Amazon River. More than 50% of students taking algebra had failed the first semester. The *orientador* organized meetings of groups of parents and groups of students to determine the kinds of homework assignments that had been given, teaching styles used, and grading procedures. She also met with teachers and interviewed them to determine what they thought caused this unusually high failure rate. When the data had been gathered from the three groups — students, parents, and teachers — she met with the teachers; and together they designed a course of action aimed at improving the algebra program.

I talked to many teachers and found them universally supportive of the *orientador*. They saw the person serving in this role as a colleague and supporter and repeatedly reminded me that the *orientador* was not an administrator but, indeed, a peer.

The second example was the vote of confidence for the principal that occurs every three years in every school in Brazil. Teachers vote on whether the principal should continue as the school leader. This is an advisory vote that the teachers union has been trying to make binding; but I was told that if there is an overwhelming negative response, the principal almost invariably is removed.

Observations

As school districts move haltingly and unevenly toward site-based management, equally uneven efforts to empower teachers are being made. Teacher empowerment takes many forms and is influenced by traditional organizational arrangements, perceptions of administrator and teacher roles and functions, institutional cultures, and state mandates.

The principal plays a key role in teacher empowerment through his or her management style. The principal either is supportive by establishing structures to facilitate teacher empowerment or is obstructive by managing schools in a traditional, authoritarian, top-down manner. The perception of many principals that they are solely accountable for what happens in schools results in feeling that they, therefore, must be the final authority on all important issues, thereby severely limiting the role of teachers in making decisions. The almost total absence of empowerment as a motivation strategy or as part of a principal's management style strongly suggests that many principals do not see empowerment as important in how schools operate.

Although principals often express anger and hostility when they feel they are not being empowered by boards and superintendents to make the necessary decisions to conduct the business of their schools, many of these same individuals have not thought seriously about or developed structures to allow for an organized teacher role in school-site decision making.

Decision-making structures go from none to very complex, with informal groups (exclusively advisory) being typical, usually with department chairs playing a key role. The power of teachers, either individually or acting as groups, can have a major impact on what happens in schools; and without a structure, self-assumed power can be positive or negative.

The role of collective bargaining appears to be more often an impediment than a support to teacher empowerment, though several principals and teachers did note that by working together they had created a structure that violated elements of an existing labor contract.

Recommendations

For teacher empowerment to influence today's reform efforts, there has to be an understanding on the part of the board, central office administrators, principals, teachers, and unions that education is in a period of flux. Traditional roles and relationships are going to change. And change will be accompanied by confusion and, in some cases, conflict. Living with ambiguity and confusion is going to be part of living with the myriad of new paradigms that are emerging in schools across the country.

There will be no single way to empower teachers; but for teacher empowerment to become an enduring institutional fixture, the following conditions should prevail:

- Principals understand and accept that real empowerment might mean some conflict; but it also can increase energy, commitment, and creativity on the part of teachers.
- The board and superintendent work with the principal to develop the understanding that he or she is not solely responsible for everything that happens in a school and that teachers share in responsibility and accountability.
- There is a formal, organized structure and sets of procedures that are not too rigid or bureaucratic but provide for consistent and organized teacher participation in school decision making.

116

- Organized training, both pre- and inservice, for teachers and administrators enables them to participate effectively in the school's restructured processes.
- Necessary funding is allocated, but creativity and ingenuity are exerted to provide for teacher meeting time during the school day.
- Greater understanding on the part of unions and school officials recognizes that collective bargaining agreements need to be flexible enough to allow for various organizational structures to exist at different schools in the same district.

The movement toward site-based management has gained momentum across the country, often supported by state legislative actions. A major challenge to school administrators is going to be to involve teachers as substantive players at the site level in order to ensure that this latest reform effort becomes an enduring part of America's schools and not just another reform movement that disappears, as has happened so often.

EMPOWERING TEACHERS AS LEARNERS AND LEADERS

BY MARY HATWOOD FUTRELL

Mary Hatwood Futrell is director of the Institute for Curriculum, Standards, and Technology at George Washington University in Washington, D.C.

> *I believe we need common standards, but it is obvious that whoever developed these does not understand the culture of the school in which we teach. They do not understand the conditions of teaching nor the diversity and complexity of today's student population.*
>
> — a teacher

> *The assumption is that all that is necessary now is to take the reforms back to the local school districts and, Voila! teachers can implement them effectively and efficiently.*
>
> — a school administrator

> *How can we help teachers implement the proposed reforms if we don't know what they are or what they mean? Or, if we ourselves don't know how to implement them?*
>
> — a teacher educator

Comments like these about education reform increasingly are being voiced both formally and informally. Teachers, school administrators, and teacher educators recognize the need for reform. They recognize society's demands for an education system that will prepare people to live, work, and socialize in a more complex society. At the same time, educators are expressing genuine frustrations about the schools' limited capacity for reform.

According to the *Status of New State Curriculum Frameworks, Standards, Assessments, and Monitoring Systems* chart, 45 states are implementing or planning to implement new curriculum frameworks, 31 are implementing or planning to implement standards linked to performance levels, and 41 are implementing or planning to implement performance-based assessments.[1] However, calls for new standards, new curriculum frameworks, new forms of assessment,

119

and new certification requirements for teachers are raising questions about the ability of those in schools, namely teachers, to implement all of these reforms.

This essay puts forward a discussion, first, of teachers' professional development as a critical component on the continuum of education reform. Second, it focuses on efforts to rethink and to redesign the whole concept of teachers' professional development. It briefly highlights three models that have the potential to revolutionize the way teachers engage in professional development activities. These models – the Christa McCauliffe Institute, the Minority Mathematics and Science Teachers Leadership Corps, and the National Board for Professional Teaching Standards certification process – are good examples of how professional development is being restructured to strengthen teachers' roles as learners and leaders. Third, this essay examines whether administrators and teachers are being provided with the resources needed to transform their schools.

Education Reform

For most of the 20th Century, the education system in the United States has been in some state of reform. According to Linda Darling-Hammond:

> The criticisms of current education reformers . . . are virtually identical to those of the Progressives at the turn of the century, in the 1930s, and again in the 1960s. Many of the reforms we are pursuing today were pursued in each of these eras.[2]

Such reforms as interdisciplinary learning, team teaching, cooperative learning, alternative assessments, and curricula to develop higher-order cognitive skills also were advocated in earlier eras.[3] However, as creative, relevant, and significant as these initiatives were, they did not succeed. They failed for numerous reasons; but at the top of the list is the failure of reformers, policy makers, and communities to address the capacity of schools and the teaching profession to implement the reforms. Today we are about to repeat history.

Current proposals to reform education in the United States consist not of one movement, but of several.[4] There are movements to establish common national standards for schools and for the teaching profession, a more rigorous curriculum, and performance-based assessments. Simultaneously, movements to decentralize schools through such initiatives as site-based management, shared decision making, and school choice are in action. These movements, although different, are not incompatible.

It is not unusual to have several major reforms converging on the schools at the same time. What makes the current reform "movement" different is that for the first time in the history of American education, all levels of education, kindergarten through graduate school, have been linked.[5]

Reform initiatives that currently are being debated were developed for the most part by reformers and policy makers who are external to the education system. An analysis of major education reform reports issued during the last decade indicates that the vast majority of the membership of the task forces, commissions, and committees represented the business community or policy makers. Only 5% represented educators. This partially explains the failure to address such issues as teachers' and teacher educators' professional development, conditions in the schools, equity and the changing demographics of our student population, and the increased needs of a growing number of students. It also explains why, with the exception of the Carnegie Report, *A Nation Prepared: Teachers for the 21st Century*, and the Holmes' Group report, *Tomorrow's Teachers*, none of the reports addressed the critical role of teachers as central to efforts to reform education.[6]

Generally, the rationale for reforming education and restructuring the education system focuses on four basic issues:

- Faith has declined among many segments of the American people regarding the ability of our current public education system to educate all students adequately for a technological society.[7]
- Mobility of the American people over the course of the last two decades has increased; and broad cultural, demographic, and technological forces have softened regional identities and crystallized national interests in the education of students and teachers.[8]
- As corporations have become less constrained by geography, many communities have realized the importance of being able to ensure a quality workforce as a means of attracting and retaining businesses in their areas.[9]
- The global economic and political status of the United States has declined, and a strong sense of community or national identity has diminished.[10]

The Culture of Schools and the Capacity to Change

The culture of schools and the capacity of the current teaching staff to implement reform initiatives are indispensable elements for restructuring and reforming our education system.

In America today, 30% of all school-age children come from language or racial minority groups.[11] Further, an increasing number of America's children come from families living in poverty. Seventy percent of these children are concentrated in urban centers where the schools they attend are more likely to be run down and have inadequately equipped facilities. The instructional programs in these schools tend to focus on rote memorization and discipline, rather than on higher-order thinking skills. The curriculum tends to be narrow and segmented, rather than reflective or interdisciplinary.

Arthur Wise and Jonathan Kozol argue that poor children and minority children are far more likely than children in more affluent school districts to be taught by teachers who are not qualified to teach the core subjects. These children also are more likely to have teachers who completed an alternative certification program and are more likely to have more substitute teachers.[12]

During the early days of the current reform era, reformers deliberately ignored the vast majority of educators. They did so out of concern that the education establishment might try to derail or stall efforts to change the current system. Others believed that educators had little to offer, else why had they not implemented reforms to stop the slide toward mediocrity? Still others believed that educators did not understand or appreciate the magnitude of the challenges facing the nation or the critical role that education plays in helping address these challenges. Therefore, teachers were viewed as being part of the problem and were excluded from the policy-formulation phase of the reform movement.[13]

Now, 11 years later, some reform has taken place; but comprehensive, systemic reform has not occurred. The slow pace of change can be attributed in part to the sheer size of the nation's education system. But it also is the result of the failure of most reformers to understand the complexity of reforming our education system, as well as their failure to identify who must be involved in the monumental shift needed to implement reform — that is, classroom teachers.

Reforms will continue to be implemented sparingly and selectively unless educators are provided with the resources to reform our system of education. This means that both the 3.2 million school staff working in the approximately 90,000 elementary and secondary schools and the faculty in the 1,500 higher education institutions that prepare the nation's teachers must be involved; their expertise must be used.

If education reform is to be successful, it is imperative to provide vastly improved and more readily available professional development. Also, we must restructure teacher education programs to prepare future teachers for the realities of the changing student population and school culture.

A Problem of Fit

Judith Little writes that there are "five streams of reforms focusing on: subject matter teaching; problems of diversity; authentic student assessments; the social organization of schools; and the professionalization of teaching."[14] All must be considered if education is to be reformed. However, Little argues that there is "a problem of 'fit' among the five streams of reforms and prevailing configurations of teachers' professional development."[15] She argues that the dominant model of professional development is not adequate to the ambitious visions embedded in the reform initiatives. In other words, there remains a serious disconnection between education reform and teachers' professional development.

Most professional development programs for teachers are provided by state education agencies or local school districts. Programs to meet the needs of teachers are designed, organized, and delivered by outside experts (usually central office staff or contracted consultants or trainers). These programs deliver skills and knowledge that others believe teachers need, rather than allow teachers to identify their own needs and design programs to address them.

Generally, one or two staff development days are scheduled before the beginning of the school year. On average, an additional three or four staff development days may be scattered throughout the school year. Sometimes these days are designated as "in-school or inservice work days," meaning that teachers usually remain in their school preparing report cards, attending faculty or departmental/grade level meetings, or simply "catching up."

Districtwide staff development programs usually consist of workshops or seminars designed by a committee, the central administrative staff, or state education agencies. Teachers often characterize these as "we can leave the school for lunch" days. Seldom are teachers asked what issues should be addressed during these programs. Rarely is follow-up provided to help teachers implement the strategies or skills they have been given. More often than not, teachers are expected to return to their schools and implement the changes in isolated environments that are neither conducive to nor supportive of change.

If reform initiatives are to receive serious consideration, professional development must become a central concern. These programs must be restructured to guarantee that ongoing, meaningful interaction among educators will take place at all levels of the system. School- or district-mandated workshops delivered by external experts three or four times a year will no longer suffice. They never did suffice, but now they are even less relevant.

Leadership Teams

Educators are responsible for implementing the reform initiatives that have emerged during the last decade. It is their responsibility to help assess the situation in their communities and to determine how to implement the initiatives that have been developed by state and national reformers. It is their responsibility to determine which reform initiatives "fit" with providing a quality education for their students. Contrary to what is sometimes advocated, reform proposals are not "one size fits all."

One way to institutionalize a collaborative model of professional development is to create a leadership team in each school. The leadership team would be responsible for working with and supporting the faculty in addressing reform issues, including the professional enhancement of school faculty. This team should comprise all segments of the school staff, parents, community leaders, policy makers, and representatives of regional college and university faculty. Teachers should constitute a plurality, if not the majority, of the leadership team. Thus teachers would be regarded as full partners, not simply as implementers of initiatives promulgated by others. The leadership team should communicate regularly with the full faculty and respond to the faculty's concerns.

If the leadership team includes non-educators, it is vital that they recognize that teachers do not have the same opportunities to be involved as do other leaders. Because of the nature of the school structure, teachers do not have the flexibility to meet, to reflect, or to set aside time during the school day to review drafts of the change initiatives unless such time is built into the process. Therefore, in order for teachers to be part of this process, arrangements must be made to ensure that they are able to participate fully in efforts to initiate, implement, and institutionalize education reform initiatives in their schools and school districts.

The first step is to make sure teachers have access to information. Eleven years after *A Nation at Risk*, seven years after the National Council of Teachers of Mathematics standards, and three years after the National Education Goals were promulgated, hundreds of thousands of teachers have not seen these reports and are not familiar with their recommendations. Too often, these and other such reports stop at the superintendent's or the principal's desk and are not made available to teachers. The successful implementation of reforms will be determined by whether teachers are given the opportunities, time, and autonomy to decide how reforms should be implemented.

The Role of Professional Development

Professional development is a lifelong process, a continuing program of personal and professional growth. In this essay the term *professional development* includes deliberate learning activities undertaken by individual teachers or groups of teachers to improve policy, curriculum, or their professional knowledge and skills with a view toward more effectively teaching all students.

Teachers who design professional development programs can identify ideas and concerns that warrant immediate or long-range attention. Teachers know the students and the schools on which the reforms will have an impact. They know their own strengths and weaknesses. By embracing and respecting teachers as professionals who are part of the reform effort, instead of individuals on whom reform is imposed, teachers' attitudes and behavior change from cynicism to cooperation — from "this too shall pass" to "how can we really make our schools work better." Empowering teachers to become leaders of reform means ensuring that they share in the responsibility and authority of transforming schools.[16]

Education reform should be approached with an attitude that all participants bring expertise to the table. However, these efforts will be superficial unless resources are allocated to ensure full implementation of the new programs.

New Models of Professional Development

Traditional models of professional development are designed to "do it to teachers" or "to tell teachers what to do." However, an analysis in 1991 by Wallace and Aman of 20 promising "new" professional development programs revealed a growing number of organizations attempting to reconceptualize this component of teachers' professional growth.[17]

Scrapping the traditional "package" approach of staff development, in which programs are designed and delivered by external experts, several organizations are working with teachers to redesign professional development programs to ensure that they are focused on the individual school and keep students and teachers central to any redesign. These organizations include the Christa McCauliffe Institute for Educational Pioneering, Foxfire Teacher Outreach Networks, and the Center for Educational Leadership. Their new programs have rejected the traditional "stand and deliver" model for teachers' professional development. They recognize that while teachers need guidance and help, they bring considerable experience and expertise to the reform discussion.

The repertoire of models designed by these organizations reflect teachers' ideas, values, and needs. They are designed to place teachers and students at the heart of efforts to reform our education system. Networking, conferences and institutes, workshops, courses, research and development, and consultations are among the approaches designed and implemented by teachers working with the various organizational staffs.

Professional Development that Empowers Teachers

Two good examples of professional development programs that put teachers in the roles of both learners and leaders are the Christa McCauliffe Institute fellows and the Minority Mathematics and Science Teachers Leadership Corps.[18]

The 100 Christa McCauliffe Institute fellows were selected because of the innovative ways in which they are integrating technology into their classrooms. The fellows are from 29 states and teach at all grade levels. Each year the CMI fellows attend several two- to three-day seminars that they design in order to share ideas about what is or is not working for them in their classrooms. CMI fellows also design a two-week institute in which they work with university staff and other experts in such fields as the fine arts, mathematics, science, technology, social studies, or language arts to design and field test innovative programs to implement in their home schools. To maintain ongoing collaboration and planning, the teachers have established an electronic network.

These teachers are working together to make schools more effective for all students, especially those who have been placed at risk. They believe the best way to accomplish this goal is through the professional enhancement of teachers as learners and leaders of education reform.

An equally promising program for professional development is the Teacher Leadership Corps (TLC), which consists of 100 elementary and secondary teachers. The TLC teacher leaders are located in five states. All are minority teachers (African-Americans, Hispanic Americans, and Native Americans) who teach mathematics or science. Each of the five states has a cadre of 20 such teachers (6 elementary, 6 middle or junior high, and 8 high school) that works with a core group of five university faculty members in their region. Each cadre of TLC teacher leaders is responsible for working with their school faculty and other community leaders to design and implement programs that will enable their students, especially minority students, to be more successful in the study of mathematics and science.

TLC teacher leaders experience continuous professional development opportunities through seminars, conferences, and workshops. However, the TLC teacher leaders also provide professional development opportunities by sponsoring miniconferences for their peers and interested members of the community. In addition, they conduct inservice programs for the staff in their schools and use their classrooms as models for implementing reform initiatives related to their discipline. TLC teacher leaders also engage in electronic networking to plan future activities.

All of the teachers involved in these two programs are risk takers who are willing to experiment with new ideas and strategies. The programs are designed to encourage teachers to teach other teachers, to be innovators and implementers of the best teaching practices, and to be education reform leaders in their schools and communities.

A Conversation About Professional Development

The reform initiative with perhaps the most far-reaching potential for reconceptualizing and restructuring education is the assessment and certification process advocated by the National Board for Professional Teaching Standards (NBPTS). (See also the essay in this volume by James A. Kelly, president of NBPTS.) The certification process is a conversation about professionalizing teaching that has broad implications for initial teacher preparation, professional development of practicing teachers, and teacher certification.

Teachers seeking to become board certified are participating in a multifaceted assessment process that requires them to demonstrate that they are exemplary teachers. Through portfolios, candidates demonstrate knowledge of their subject matter, understanding of their students, and use of what they consider to be best practices in teaching. Through writing case studies about their students, videotaping their classes, maintaining journals, and documenting professional service activities, these teachers further show what they know and are able to do as teachers. They also are required to analyze their teaching, work collaboratively with other teachers, and demonstrate that they can teach a variety of students.

Numerous teachers participating in the pilot phase of the assessment and certification process have commented that it is the most intensive, reflective professional development program in which they have ever participated. Many have stated that it is the first time they have made an in-depth self-examination of how they teach and how students learn. Thus the NBPTS assessment and certification process has major implications for the professional development of practicing teachers and for the restructuring of the teaching profession.

Preservice teacher education programs also will be affected. As more school districts and states recognize the NBPTS certificate as a sign of teaching excellence, they will expect future teachers to work toward a certificate. To ensure that their graduates are prepared to successfully complete the national assessment and certification process, schools and colleges of education will need to radically rethink how they prepare teachers.

Who Will Train the Trainers?

An important consideration is the role of higher education in school reform. Who provides college and university faculty members with the experiences and expertise that will enable them to help teachers and others effect school reforms? Do higher education faculty members model in their classrooms the methodologies they advise K-12 teachers to use? Are they preparing the next generation of teachers as in the past, or are future teachers being prepared to facilitate the transformation of schools from hierarchical factories into learning communities?

Currently the links between elementary, secondary, and higher education are weak. There is limited interaction between K-12 school personnel and college and university faculty. This observation is underscored in Joni E. Finney's report, *At the Crossroads: Linking Teacher Education to School Reform*:

> It is uncertain to what extent colleges and universities will play a strategic role in preparing teachers to reform schools; it is even less certain whether they will have a role at all in the professional development of teachers and other school leaders. . . . Efforts to link schools, colleges and universities . . . are largely ad hoc.[19]

Professional development schools, an approach strongly advocated by the Holmes Group as a way to enhance teachers' professionalism, are one possibility for strengthening the linkage between K-12 and university faculties. These schools are designed to bring together practicing teachers, student teachers, and university faculty to work in regular schools. A key component of the professional development school is to strengthen relations among members at all levels of the teaching profession through the cultivation of collegial relationships.

Equally important, professional development schools are designed to provide opportunities for teachers and administrators to contribute to the development of professional knowledge and practice and for university faculty to increase the professional relevance of their work. Such schools would provide opportunities to test different instructional arrangements under different working and administrative conditions. Further, K-12 and university faculty could work together to develop, demonstrate, and evaluate programs designed to implement key education reform initiatives. However, while the concept of establishing professional schools holds great promise, few such schools exist.

All of the above models are designed to reconceptualize professional development programs so that teachers can design new learning environments. They signal movement of the discussion about teachers' professional development from the conversational phase to the action phase. These models will be used as the foundation for a new conception of professional development and of teacher preparation programs. They will strengthen efforts to professionalize teaching and to improve teaching and learning. They are designed to ensure that teachers are active participants in education reform.

A Matter of Time

As efforts are made to transform schools, the question must be raised about time constraints. Unlike other institutions (such as

129

churches, hotels, shopping malls, and so on) that can shut down while taking inventory, remodeling, or reconstituting the leadership team, schools must continue to provide learning experiences for students while changes in pedagogy, curriculum, and the organizational structure are being implemented. None of the education reform reports have addressed the issue of time — that is, how and when school personnel, especially teachers, will be given the time necessary to implement changes.

Time constraints, rather than learning, control what is taught in school. The 35- to 45-minute blocks of time allocated for teaching the various subjects allow for little creativity, cooperative learning, or mastery of content. And with bathroom duty, hall duty, cafeteria duty, or bus duty, teachers have no time to reflect on their teaching, read professional journals, or collaborate with their peers. Since 30% of America's teachers are working second jobs to augment their salaries, few teachers have time to volunteer to meet after school to discuss how to improve education.

Thus, largely because of school schedules, teachers continue to be isolated in classrooms, lecturing to 25 or 30 students, while waiting for someone at a higher level to announce the next round of reform initiatives. Schedules effectively deny teachers opportunities to be involved in curriculum planning. Current schedules ensure that decisions about teaching and learning are made by people far removed from the classroom and guarantee that professional development will continue to be unrelated to the improvement of instruction. These time and structural constraints reflect and reinforce the image of teachers as deliverers, not creators, of knowledge; as followers, not leaders.

In other countries the school day has been structured to guarantee that teachers have the time they need.[20] In Asia, for example, time is allocated for teachers to get together with their colleagues each day to exchange information and ideas. Teachers in Japan and Taiwan are allowed up to 40% of the school day to interact with colleagues, plan and assess, tutor students, or participate in activities that are professionally enriching.

Countries such as Great Britain and Australia, like the United States, are struggling to reform their education systems and are addressing many of the same issues, including time for teacher involvement in school reform and professional development.[21]

The message is very clear: If teachers are to enhance our nation's efforts to ensure that all students can excel, they must be part of the decision-making process and must have the resources, including the time, to become fully involved.

Funding Professional Development

Most of the reports advocating reform are silent on the issue of resources. They are silent because, as one task-force commissioner prophesied, the inclusion of any reference to funding would draw attention away from the recommendations and become the central focus of the report. Yet the issue of funding cannot be ignored.

Although 31 states have mandated staff development programs for teachers, only 17 have provided funding to implement these mandates.[22] Reforms will not be implemented, much less institutionalized, unless new resources are earmarked to support these efforts.

Teachers' professional development is a critical component of efforts to reform our education system. It deserves a substantial investment of funds. However, efforts to determine how much money school districts, states, and the federal government spend on professional development activities has produced little of substance.

Telephone interviews with government officials, at least six professional organizations, and three research groups yielded such responses as "No such information exists" or "There is no specific information about professional development or staff development programs for teachers."[23] Many policy makers and community leaders do not link teachers' professional development with efforts to improve teaching and learning. Therefore, funds for professional development usually are scattered throughout the school budget and cannot be identified easily.

The most current information on the topic appeared in an article by Robinson and Protheroe, which stated that in 1992-93, school districts set aside 1.5% of their budgets for curriculum development and staff inservice.[24] This is only a 0.4% increase since 1983. The average per-pupil expenditure in 1992-93 was $5,378, with a range from $3,871 for low-expenditure districts (primarily rural and urban school districts) to $8,829 for high-expenditure districts. Multiplying the per-pupil expenditure figures by the 1.5% allocation reveals that an average of only $80.67 per student was spent on curriculum development and staff inservice. The range of expenditures for curriculum development and staff inservice would be $58.07 to $132.44, which means that high-expenditure districts spent 2.3 times more on those two program areas than did low-expenditure districts.

This underscores the point made by Wise and Kozol about America's unrealistic expectations regarding what schools and teachers are able to do. The playing field is definitely not level for all children. Teachers in resource-poor school districts are less likely to receive professional development assistance than their peers in more affluent districts. If we raise academic standards but do not provide the necessary resources to meet them, the playing fields of education will become even more uneven.

An urgent need exists to educate policy makers and budget managers about the critical role that professional development plays in school change. Teachers cannot and will not implement reform if they are unequipped or ill-equipped to do so. School reform requires that teachers be empowered to become both learners and leaders. Without programs to enhance teachers' professional development, the best plans and the most innovative and ambitious reform initiatives may be to no avail.

The Clinton Administration seems to understand the link between teachers' professionalism and education reform. In new education legislation, teachers' professional development is a central component. The proposal to reauthorize ESEA and other federal programs makes professional development a high priority in reforming education. Federal initiatives will build on existing professional development efforts that are intensive, systemic, long-term, and well-designed. In particular, emphasis will be placed on programs that give teachers more say in school decisions and help teachers develop more instructional strategies while expanding their knowledge base.[25]

ESEA, in particular, will encourage the establishment of school support teams consisting of experienced teachers and others to help schools design and implement schoolwide programs that focus on reforming instruction, with a special emphasis on meeting the learning needs of at-risk children. In other words, school staff, especially teachers, would become leaders, creators, implementers, and evaluators of professional development opportunities in their schools and districts.

However, making teachers' professional development a high priority at the federal level is insufficient. It must be a priority at the state and local levels as well. After all, that is where school reform will really occur.

Summary

Efforts to reconceptualize the professional development process for teachers remain small. However, the models described here demonstrate that reformers and policy makers are beginning to recognize that it is critical for teachers to become empowered, to be advocates and implementers of reform.

The traditional views of teachers' professionalism are inadequate and insufficient for the tasks at hand. Teachers themselves must be learners and leaders. All those involved — teachers, teacher educators, researchers, and school officials — must constantly evaluate new methods for delivering professional development opportunities to all school staff. Also, professional development must be supported with adequate resources. Professional development needs to be an ongoing process. It cannot be a one-shot deal.

Nearly everyone involved in education reform has come to realize that the current level of support is not sufficient to implement comprehensive, systemic reform. Unless teachers are supported and are confident in their ability to implement change, and unless the culture in schools is conducive to change, reform will not be realized. Without broad-based, sustained community support, some change may occur; but the system as a whole will remain what it is today — a system that allows too many students to fall through the cracks and, thus, jeopardizes our nation's future.

Footnotes

1. United States Department of Education, "Improving America's School Act of 1993: The Reauthorization of the Elementary and Secondary Education Act and Amendments to Other Acts," *Education Week*, 20 October 1993, p. 20.
2. Linda Darling-Hammond, "Reframing the School Reform Agenda: Developing Capacity for School Transformation," *Phi Delta Kappan* 71 (June 1993): 755.
3. Ibid.
4. John I. Goodlad, "Studying the Education of Educators: Values-Driven Inquiry," *Phi Delta Kappan* 70 (October 1988): 104-11; Mary Futrell, "National Education Reforms: Is America Moving Toward a National Curriculum?" *Phi Kappa Phi Journal* 72 (Fall 1993): 30-34; Judith E. Little, "Teachers' Professional Development in a Climate of Educational Reform," *Journal of Educational Evaluation and Policy Analysis* 15 (Summer 1993): 129-51.
5. John Goodlad, ibid.
6. Carnegie Forum on Education and the Economy, *A Nation Prepared: Teachers for the 21st Century* (Washington, D.C., 1986); Holmes Group, *Tomorrow's Teachers* (East Lansing, Mich., 1986).
7. National Commission on Excellence in Education, *A Nation at Risk: The Imperative for Educational Reform* (Washington, D.C.: U.S. Department of Education, 1983); Secretary's Commission on Achieving Necessary Skills, *What Work Requires of Schools: A SCANS Report for America 2000* (Washington,

D.C.: U.S. Department of Labor, 1991); Mary Futrell, *Analysis of National Leaders' Perceptions of Major Education Reform Policies Centralizing Effects on Public Education* (Washington, D.C.: George Washington University, 1992).

8. Bennett Harrison and Barry Bluestone, *The Great U-Turn: Corporate Restructuring and the Polarization of America* (New York: Basic Books, 1988); Harold Hodgkinson, *The Same Client: The Demographics of Education and Service Delivery Systems* (Washington, D.C.: Institute for Educational Leadership, Center for Demographic Policy, 1987).

9. National Alliance of Business, *A National Education Examination System: Introduction to Discussion* (Washington, D.C., n.d.); The Business Roundtable, *A Primer for Business on Education* (New York: National Alliance of Business, April 1991).

10. William H. Kolberg and Foster C. Smith, *Rebuilding America's Workforce: Business Strategies to Close the Competitive Gap* (Homewood, Ill.: Business One Irwin, 1992); Marshall S. Smith and Jennifer O'Day, "Systemic School Reform," in *The Politics of Curriculum and Testing*, edited by Susan Fuhrman and Betty Maylan. Philadelphia: Falmer, 1991.

11. Harold Hodgkinson, op cit.; Harold Hodgkinson, *A Demographic Look at Tomorrow* (Washington, D.C.: Institute for Educational Leadership, Center for Demographic Policy, 1992).

12. Jonathan Kozol, *Savage Inequalities: Children in America's Schools* (New York: Crown, 1991); Arthur E. Wise, "Equal Opportunity for All?" *Quality Teaching* 3, no. 1 (Fall 1993): 4.

13. Gene I. Maeroff, *The Empowerment of Teachers: Overcoming the Crisis of Confidence* (New York: Teachers College Press, 1988), p. viii; Mary Futrell, "K-12 Education Reform: A View from the Trenches," *Educational Record* 74 (Summer 1993): 6-14.

14. Little, op cit., pp. 130-32.

15. Little, ibid., p. 132.

16. Maeroff, op. cit., pp. 34, 99.

17. David K. Wallace and Mary Aman, *An Analysis of Leadership and Professional Development Programs for Teachers*. A report prepared for the National Foundation for the Improvement of Education (Washington, D.C., October 1991), pp. 1-11.

18. The Christa McCauliffe Institute for Educational Pioneering is a project of the National Foundation for the Improvement of Education, which is located in Washington, D.C. The Minority Mathematics and Science Teachers Leadership Corps is a project of the Quality Education for Minorities Network, which is located in Washington, D.C., and is funded by the Annenberg/CPB Foundation.

19. Joni E. Finney, *At the Crossroads: Linking Teacher Education to School Reform* (Denver: Education Commission of the States, October 1992), p. 2.

20. National Education Association, *It's About Time* (Washington, D.C., n.d.), p. 4.

21. Ray Bolam, "Recent Developments in England and Wales," and John M. Owen, "Perspectives from Down Under," in *Changing School Culture Through Staff*

Development: The 1990 ASCD Yearbook (Alexandria, Va.: Association for Supervision and Curriculum Development, 1990), pp. 147-81.

22. Van E. Cooley and Jay C. Thompson Jr., "Mandated Staff Development in the Fifty States: A Study of State Activity 1983-1989," pp. 4-7. Paper presented at the Annual Conference of the National Council of States on Inservice Education, Orlando, Fla., November 1990.

23. Interviews with staff from the following organizations were conducted to gather information about funding allocated for teachers' professional development: American Federation of Teachers, American Society for Training and Development, Association for Supervision and Curriculum Development, Council of Chief State School Officers, Education Commission of the States, Educational Research Services Inc., OERI's National Center for Education Statistics, National Council of States on Inservice Education, National Education Association, National Governors' Association, and the National Staff Development Council.

24. Glen E. Robinson and Nancy Protheroe, "Local School Budget Profile Study," *School Business Affairs Magazine* 59 (September 1993): 32-41.

25. United States Department of Education, "Improving America's School Act of 1993: The Reauthorization of the Elementary and Secondary Education Act and Amendments to Other Acts," *Education Week*, 20 October 1993, p. 21.

REDEFINING RESULTS: IMPLICATIONS FOR TEACHER LEADERSHIP AND PROFESSIONALISM

BY MICHAEL J. SCHMOKER AND RICHARD B. WILSON

Michael J. Schmoker is research analyst and coordinator of libraries for the Amphitheater Public Schools in Tucson, Arizona. Richard B. Wilson is superintendent of the Amphitheater Public Schools.

As we consider the best ways to improve the quality of education for our students, it is instructive to reflect carefully on the words "leadership" and "professional." If "teacher leadership" ever gets the chance it deserves to truly improve education, then it must move beyond a limited concern with new roles and release time toward that which the word "leadership" should always imply: knowing where to go and how to get there.

"Professional" is defined in most dictionaries with the word "learned." Thus "teacher leadership" and "professionalism" raise profound questions: What is a professional? What must a professional know? What responsibilities does a professional have to his or her clients? And what is leadership? That is, what are the goals of the teaching professional, and how can professionals lead us toward these goals? We contend that any meaningful understanding of these two concepts must center on tangible, measurable accomplishment, on results. Leadership and professionalism derive meaning from what they help us to achieve.

The linchpin, then, to creating opportunities for professional leadership for teachers may be disarmingly simple: It may require, more than anything, a radically explicit and aggressive commitment to making connections between professional knowledge and activity and educational results. This is important both to teachers and to the students and public they serve. Just as important, our notion of results must be redefined to acknowledge more fully the teacher's role in their establishment and refinement.

137

Historically, educators have resisted an emphasis on results. The emphasis, instead, has been on activity — on instituting innovations and programs without checking them for their educational impact. A recent conversation with a well-known education consultant is an example of this approach. This consultant has a long and impressive list of school districts with whom she has worked regularly and extensively. When we asked her if, in the last several years, any of her clients had realized any improvement as a result of new programs or new approaches to instruction, she indicated that such a concern was premature and that much more training was required before efforts could be expected to "evolve" into actual results.

This tendency to avoid results not only postpones benefits, it inhibits meaningful effort. Results are the stuff of purpose; they are what drive and sustain any improvement effort. Because so much depends on our understanding of this concept, the notion of results must be reconceived and made more friendly; "results" must take on a meaning that teachers will embrace rather than resist. And this new understanding must reflect a new trust in teachers, a faith in the power of their cumulative and collective knowledge and capacities. A less threatening but still rigorous emphasis on results would have far-reaching implications for everything from preservice preparation and student teaching to staff development. It would make teaching a more attractive profession. More than anything, it would promote a substantially new role for teachers as the primary agents of change and improvement in schools.

We should begin by looking at the relationship between knowledge and results. One of the key elements that defines professionalism is a recognized and respected body of knowledge. This is not to say that this knowledge is fixed or permanent, but that it represents the acquired wisdom that enables its possessors to perform with proficiency and acumen.

It can safely be said that we now know more than enough to improve our schools, more than enough to make the school experience far richer for both students and teachers. But what we do with this knowledge is what defines an occupation not only as a career or an activity but as a profession. In general, the real work of teaching is not sufficiently concerned with professional knowledge.

Not long ago, President Clinton made political hay with the expression, "Without a vision, the people will perish." We've gone from a disparagement of "vision" to popular acceptance of the idea that collective achievement requires those in an organization to share a clear and compelling sense of where the organization is headed. Organizations, schools among them, have spent record amounts of time creating mission and vision statements.

The irony is that for all our vision and mission and purpose statements, the average school is not, in fact, vision-driven. That is, having crafted these visions, we cannot point, in concrete terms, to much that constitutes their fulfillment. We have overlooked the fact that vision is as vision does: The better part of vision − like the better part of leadership − is the extent to which it influences what we do and what it enables us to accomplish.

Leadership must be less tolerant of disparity between aspiration and achievement. A more vital professionalism would address this disparity. We are referring here to our collective inattention to what we know about how to help students learn better, by which we tacitly deny both students and teachers the benefits of existing knowledge. Peter Senge may not be far from the mark when he enthuses, "What we have learned in the last fifteen years about more effectively teaching children is one of the most impressive achievements in our 200-year history" (1992). And yet, evidence abounds that we have yet to implement even the most promising discoveries in education. As Bruce Joyce and his colleagues argue:

> Of the twenty or more most powerful teaching strategies that cross subject areas and have a historical track record in terms of student effects, we speculate that fewer than 10 percent of us − kindergarten through university level − regularly employ more than one of these strategies. (Joyce et al. 1993, p. 38)

By comparison, promising discoveries in other fields are implemented with an urgency that is lacking in education. One of us was a kidney donor. At one point it looked as though there wasn't an adequate genetic "match" between donor and recipient to warrant the risk, and so surgery was canceled. That changed six months later, when hundreds of doctors returned from a conference in Chicago where they learned about recent discoveries that could greatly enhance the chances for a successful operation even in the case of a poor genetic match. Within months, people with no hope were off dialysis and thriving. Vision, combined with knowledge, led to a valued result. But the knowledge itself was only as good as the willingness of professionals to use it. A failure to appreciate and apply such new information toward clear and beneficial results strains the notion of education professionalism.

The real mark of professionalism, of leadership, is its proactive determination to make a difference. Education might take a page from William James. Like John Dewey, James is best known as a pragmatist. James' legacy is to urge new criteria for evaluating ideas, even for legitimizing their exploration. He held that abstract ideas were only as good as their "cash value." "The whole function of philosophy," wrote James, "ought to be to find out what definite difference it will make to you and me." Breakthroughs in education research, however painstakingly realized, will not make a difference in children's lives until they are acted on. Like vision and mission statements, they have no "cash value" unless they bring us closer to a valued goal.

Results and the Importance of Goals

Enamored as we are with vision, there are strong indications that the typical school has an aversion to achievement goals. Schools and districts seldom get down to the difficult but meaningful work of establishing goals and then finding ways to meet them — especially academic achievement goals. Susan Rosenholtz says that "the lack of agreed-upon goals for teaching makes schools organizational exceptions" (1989, p. 18). In the corporate sphere, goals and results increasingly are seen as essential to making vision a reality. In *The Wisdom of Teams*, Jon Katzenbach and Douglas Smith emphasize the distinction between an organization's "purpose" and its "goals." For them, it is crucial that employees, "Transform broad directives into specific and measurable performance goals. . . . Purpose and specific performance goals have a symbiotic relationship; each depends on the other to stay relevant and vital . . . goals help teams maintain their focus on getting results" (1993, pp. 53-55).

A healthy organization needs goals that recognize not only long-term but also short-term results, which give employees something to celebrate and by which they can gauge their effectiveness. Short-term accomplishments help stimulate high performance. We are reminded of Mihalyi Csikszentmihalyi's simple discovery that frequent and continual feedback is the key to sustained effort — that effort toward long-term goals can only be sustained by short-term feedback. Feedback, in the form of what Katzenbach and Smith call "small wins," must be seen as one form of results. In that vein, Robert Schaffer advocates that some projects be geared for getting "better results right now," emphasizing people's need to see "the successful accomplishment of a tangible goal. . . . Immediate successes are essential if people are to increase their confidence and expand their vision of what is possible." He adds, "By 'results,' I mean a measurable success," the pursuit of which "releases so much force and energy in reaching important short-term goals" (1988, p. 60). "Important" should not be taken for granted; schools may set goals, but they are almost invariably procedural. Schools fail, Rosenholtz points out, to set "goals for teaching."

The implications of this principle and of Rosenholtz's findings are monumental. If schools are, in fact, goal-shy, then there is far less mystery to why traditional leadership has not helped us to realize major school improvements. Awash in vision, mission, and purpose statements, schools are unique in their avoidance of that prerequisite to improvement: a commitment to clear, concrete improvement, to "goals for teaching." Viable goals take us beyond the general — and too tolerant — spirit of most vision and mission statements that require little in measurable terms. In the absence of such goals, with only the most flaccid conception of leadership, we flounder.

A more explicit commitment to goals and their achievement would have far-ranging benefits. In her studies, Rosenholtz identified what she called "moving schools," those that exhibited measurable growth and improvement. They are characterized by two things: 1) common awareness of the school's academic achievement goals and, more important, 2) a continual awareness by teachers of where they are relative to the achievement of those goals. Such awareness implies frequent measurement of results. Short-term results represent incremental progress. For Rosenholtz, this is essential to sustained effort. A number of schools vividly demonstrate the power of this principle, whether their efforts are called outcome-based education, total quality, action research, accelerated, essential, or effective schools (Schmoker and Wilson 1993; Joyce et al. 1993).

An examination of the conventions and routines teachers live by — conventions and routines that constrain teachers in their pursuit of a more confident professionalism and the leadership opportunities that go with it — has implications for morale and professional self-efficacy. According to Katzenbach and Smith, we underestimate how "the opportunity to meet clearly stated customer and financial needs enriches jobs and leads to personal growth" (1993, p. 13). Teaching would be better situated to see and meet its customer's needs if we did more to "clearly state" those needs we deem most important, by teacher team, by faculty, or by district.

Similarly, Csikszentmihalyi's studies reveal that people work hardest and most happily when (echoing Rosenholtz's findings) they have a clear and compelling goal to work toward and receive regular feedback. This is especially true when these goals are altruistic and concerned with the welfare of "the wider community," flowing from a "strongly directed purpose that is not self-seeking . . . not concerned primarily with advancing their own interests" (1990, p. 92). But altruism is not enough. Once we identify a goal we care about, regular feedback, combined with the sense that we are continuously learning and growing, nourishes our sense of optimism and control (p. 65). Even setbacks will not deter us under these conditions; they are less important than a precise sense of where to go and what to try next, which defines leadership.

We are goal-oriented beings, an orientation that is fostered by the interplay between purpose, goals, new knowledge, and feedback. Almost twenty years ago, sociologist Dan Lortie found a relative indifference among teachers toward professional knowledge, even to the knowledge that they had acquired through experience. He found teachers to be "hesitant and uneasy" about their own knowledge and abilities, and that subsequently "teachers find it difficult to rate their performance; and there are indications that doubts about one's effectiveness can spoil the pleasures of teaching" (Lortie 1975, p. 212). Chris Zajac, the well-reputed teacher who was the subject of Tracy Kidder's micro-study in *Among Schoolchildren*, is the picture of the hardworking but demoralized teacher, who laments her inability to gauge her own effectiveness (Kidder 1989). This might help to explain Robert Evans finding that "disenchantment is rampant" among about 70% of the teaching force (Evans 1989).

Dona Kagan's recent interviews confirm Lortie's 1975 study. If the relationship between what we know, what we learn, and our sense of what we are achieving is important, then Kagan's recent interviews with teachers paint a less-than-inspiring picture of the state of teaching. She found that teachers "did not see classroom teaching as a predictable applied science" and that they regarded "research as relatively useless" (1993, p. 28). This helps to explain Joyce's speculation that only a small number of the most powerful innovations are operative in the classroom. Again, Lortie found that teachers rejected the "knowledge-building" ethos that assumes some "underlying order" to their work and encourages and informs a "scientific approach" to the teaching enterprise (1975, p. 212). No profession can sustain such a divorce from its knowledge base without damage both to its professional image and its ability to lead.

142

The potential for education improvement and teacher leadership toward that improvement is severely limited by a breakdown of the links between professional activity, professional knowledge, and an appropriate concern with goals and results. This breakdown undermines the entire education improvement effort, affecting everything from teacher effectiveness to more spiritual, but crucial, elements such as hope, optimism, and morale.

The place to begin improvement efforts is with an emphasis on measurable evidence of student learning. This is not to circumvent but rather to embrace what is essential to getting better results: a greater attention to the processes that promote better results, such as better preservice and inservice training, a more rigorous and intelligent teacher induction process, and a more respectful regard for professional knowledge.

Results: A New Paradigm

There is an attractive logic to rejecting a strong emphasis on results. "Results" carries with it the specter of top-down mandates, of annual and unfair public comparisons, and of an onerous accountability that denigrates professionalism. Peter Senge has disparaged overemphasis on results, likening it to a basketball team that fixates on the scoreboard, rather than on skills and strategies. Such thinking is understandable in a climate of annual comparisons of standardized test scores, an occasional analysis of which would suffice. In reality, most schools suffer from an inattention to more meaningful results. Our mania for standardized test scores notwithstanding, schools exhibit a systematic disregard for the effects of new processes and innovations.

This stems from a failure to understand and appreciate the variety of results. Results should mean simply evidence of learning and improvement and should be stated in terms that are intelligible to students, teachers, parents and the community. The types of results to be examined might be chosen by teachers and students in concert with the wider community, which includes business people, parents, and educators in higher education. Some types of results, to be sure, would be more useful to some parties than to others; but generally the results should inform teachers, parents, and the public about what schools do well and what they are learning to do better.

For example, if teachers experiment with prewriting strategies that help students to write with more passion about topics that touch them, the results might include both the quality of the writing and whether the students enjoyed writing about the topics they chose. These results, regularly discussed, would drive an examination of every aspect of the writing process, from how we teach students to write arresting introductions to how we help them to brainstorm for supporting details in a persuasive essay. Teachers around the country are seeing both the energizing effect and the public relations value of sharing student growth and achievement with the wider public. These are meaningful results.

We might do more to monitor, even to advertise, our achievements in some areas. A school in North Carolina adopted a hands-on science program to replace the previous text-driven science curriculum. What was the result? In one year, the number of students who said they enjoyed science rose from 37% to 87% (O'Neil 1992). If that is not useful information for parents, teachers, the administration, and the wider community, then nothing is. Evidence such as this helps to counteract criticism that "despite calls for curricular reforms that emphasize 'doing' science, lectures and textbooks continue to dominate science instruction" (Rothman 1992a) or that most students find the traditional biology curriculum as "boring or irrelevant" ("Biology Education," 1990). Results such as these will play well on every stage, from faculty meetings to the front pages of district newsletters. They reveal the potential difference that teachers, given adequate support, can make.

For all the potential that such information holds to spur improvement and boost morale, the traditional lack of enthusiasm for generating and using such data and information is not hard to understand. Richard Stiggins, who has done extensive work on assessment, says,

> To the extent that you are clear and specific about the outcomes you take on as your instructional responsibility, you open yourself up . . . your supervisor may be able to use your own focused, high quality classroom assessment to muster evidence that you did not succeed in doing what you were hired to do − produce achievement results. (1994, p. 64)

Similarly, Fullan tells us, "Monitoring results . . . is frequently misused. . . . In the early attempts at change, people are usually wary of gathering information." However, he adds that once the right kind of improvement effort "is under way, teachers and others close to implementation are those most insistent on gathering and examining the results of their efforts. Good change processes develop trust, relevance and the desire to get better results" (1991). Monitoring results

144

is essential; but the conditions have to be right. This helps to explain the popularity of the Total Quality movement, with its simultaneous emphasis on closely monitoring progress while taking equal pains to "dispel fear" by gathering data on a constructive, nonpunitive, and collective basis.

Under such conditions, where trust runs both ways, teachers will become more comfortable with data and with gathering and analyzing their own results, as well as published results, on the most demonstrably effective methods to teach children to write, estimate, calculate, comprehend, analyze, present, research, and solve problems in every area. What results are we getting using these methods — by individual assignment, by unit, by grading period, by semester, or by school year? Only by regularly monitoring results will we note improvement and be able to promote a regard for professional knowledge. Only so manifest a goal-orientation will ensure that effort is focused and self-refining.

Benefits of Being Results-Oriented

Such goal-oriented analysis not only informs improvement efforts, it also gives us something meaningful to share with a public hungry for evidence that schools are doing their best to equip our children for the future.

"Results" in this model would enable teachers to take back the education agenda. No one is, or ever will be, in a better position than teachers to make judgments about what is best for students. But teachers must be ready to change or adjust goals as students' needs change. This underlines the importance of inviting the community to help establish the standards by which results are judged. If we are smart, we will find ways to demonstrate consistency among goals, results, and the desires of the community.

The establishment of goals in this manner will require an unprecedented willingness to negotiate consensus and to commit to common rather than purely individual goals and methods. For many teachers, the majority of whom work in virtual (in some ways, comfortable) isolation, this process may seem like an invasion of professional privacy. But we must consider the manifold benefits.

An emphasis on measurable improvement will overcome the pervasive cynicism about professional knowledge and generate greater attention to relevant research in ways nothing else could; improvement would be inevitable. It would address disputes that currently drive a wedge between practitioners. Many teachers understand relatively little about matters that affect the quality of instruction because they disregard the value of "research" and thus reject those teaching practices that are manifestly essential to improvement. For example, NAEP surveys demonstrate that "reforms are rare" in the teaching of writing. Despite all we have learned about how to promote good writing, students still write relatively short pieces on an infrequent basis, and there is "little evidence of the types of practices school-based writing assessment is expected to capture, such as the use of prewriting strategies" (Rothman 1992*b*).

Such cynicism could be addressed by providing more precise, vivid references to student success, whether through data or samples of student work — or both. It is hard to believe that educators, in the face of continual exposure to such evidence, would continue to deny students the benefits of the best we know. We have given up too easily in the fight to bring the best information into the classroom. Research will continue to be a dirty word only as long as we fail to invite teachers to generate and study results themselves and to gather and examine the evidence that makes change worthwhile. We can make a far better case for professional knowledge merely by demonstrating — and helping teachers collectively to realize — the measurable superiority of certain methods over others. We must address what seems like thoughtless "resistance" not by resenting but by appreciating the "show-me" spirit that is the mark of rationality and professionalism.

Consider the effects of such measures on the public perception of teaching. The very fact that education's claim to be a profession is debated is telling. There is, despite evidence that teaching is perhaps better than it has ever been, a lingering suspicion that "those who can, do; those who can't, teach." There is a suspicion that the ranks of teachers are full of "deadwood," that teaching is primarily a custodial rather than a professional occupation. Frank Eccles, in an essay for *Education Week* (1993), averred that the presence of "obviously ineffective teachers undermines public respect for teaching as a true profession." Our failure to better equip (or in the worst cases, remove) such teachers leaves education especially vulnerable to criticism.

We should remind ourselves of the unique relationship that schools have with the public on whom they depend for support — especially fiscal support. An excellent example of the failure to see this can be seen in the lament of a recent *Educational Leadership* article. "Why," the writer asks,

146

aren't teachers given credit for finding credible solutions? Why don't educational commentators presume that teachers are already doing good things? . . . All teachers ask is that others respect our contributions. (Negin 1993)

Unfortunately, those contributions seldom are made available. We have made it extremely difficult for commentators, or anyone else, to "presume that we are already doing good things" or are finding "credible solutions." There is little mention of any compelling evidence of credible solutions in the public press. The only real evidence of achievement that the public has access to is test scores. If that is all they have, then all that we deplore, from school and district comparisons to inconsistent financial support, is inevitable.

Against this backdrop, the absence of better, more legitimate evidence of quality and improvement takes on real meaning. With better evidence, educators could take back the education agenda and begin to assert themselves as professionals who know, more than anyone, what constitutes quality education and the extent to which students are receiving it.

Without such evidence in the form of meaningful results, schools must rely on less informative means by which to impress their public, some of which may do more harm than good. Schools and districts receive a variety of awards and accolades, but few are awarded on the basis of student achievement. Many appear to be politically motivated or are awarded on the basis of impressive-sounding programs; measurable student achievement is not even referred to in most cases. Teachers at such award-winning schools sometimes are embarrassed by these accolades.

A related situation was cited by American Federation of Teachers president Albert Shanker, who took then-Secretary of Education Lamar Alexander to task for giving a prestigious award to the Baltimore school system that had decided to let a private company manage it. Alexander grandly praised this effort before even it began, before the results − any results − were in. This is analogous, said Shanker, to giving a Nobel prize in medicine to a doctor before his or her treatment was field-tested. It must seem strange to those in other fields to see this cavalcade of self-congratulation sans any evidence of learning or improvement.

Better evidence of improvement and what is really being learned in schools could go a long way toward impressing a skeptical public, whose opportunities to see how well our schools actually teach math, writing, speech, or music is severely limited. It is time to start

147

telling them. We are fully convinced that a conscientious attempt to monitor the effects of the best research would result in improvement that would make for an abundance of good news to share. In virtually every case, such efforts even raise standardized test scores.

More important, a new emphasis on results and the incorporation of professional knowledge into teaching would increase opportunities for teacher leadership. As teachers have told us, and as Vivian Troen and Katherine Boles point out, "Teacher leadership and risk-taking are not valued in the schools." Even worse:

> When teacher leaders emerge, they encounter resistance not just from the principal, but from other teachers who have been heard to say, "Just who does she think she is?" (Troen and Boles 1993, p. 27)

"Myriad difficulties and obstacles confront the institutionalization of teacher leadership," say Troen and Boles. But there is an absence of evidence in their article that, for all the difficulties and expense, their effort would lead or has led to making schools richer or more productive for students. Our failure to see this as the root of so many of our problems undermines the case for teacher leadership.

But what if the best teachers in our schools and districts were made lead-teachers, or were given release time to teach and facilitate the adoption of high-impact staff development and follow-up? And suppose, with this new guidance, that teachers and students began to achieve clear, measurable goals? To what extent would this mitigate, if not eliminate, the resentment felt toward teacher leaders? In this way teachers could see that these new structures — and roles — are indeed a good investment, that they "make a difference" in terms they value and understand. Such circumstances would be far more hospitable to these new roles, because teachers would be growing professionally, feeling more competent, and expanding their vision of what they can achieve. An altogether more effective case thus might be made for financial support to fund such leadership roles.

Experience should indicate how grossly we underestimate the effect of our failure to demonstrate the educational value of difficult and expensive new arrangements, even when to do so is well within our means. This applies to school overrides and levies that could provide extra funding for local schools to create new arrangements. How often, after the community has voted to increase school bond or operating budgets, is the public given evidence that their higher taxes have resulted in higher levels of learning? The recent case of the

Kansas City schools is instructive: After an infusion of $1.2 billion into new, state-of-the-art facilities, test scores (in the short term) remained unchanged. Whether we are asking the public to fund better facilities or new arrangements, we would win more consistent support by demonstrating that these make a difference in ways other than test scores — and, indeed, perhaps also in test scores, but over a longer period.

Teacher preparation programs could play a more vital role in making teaching more results-oriented. They must begin to furnish our schools with a new breed of teacher who arrives at the classroom door with an informed idealism, knowing how to use and refine the best instructional methods and having a capacity to think deliberately and pro-actively about results. Student teaching must be designed to be more meaningful and purposeful. In a nonjudgmental, self-assessing atmosphere, student teaching can provide a rich opportunity to refine the prospective teacher's ability to effectively implement methods and measure the real impact of those methods.

An emphasis on results not only would promote unprecedented levels of professional capability, confidence, and prestige; it would do much to attract those looking for a profession that is intellectually alive and socially purposeful. It would broaden public and fiscal support for the essential arrangements that favor teacher leadership. And it would lead to and sustain the effort to reach an ever-increasing number of children with an increasingly higher-quality education, which is the richest reward of all.

References

"Biology Education." *ERS Bulletin* (December 1990): p. 4.

Csikszentmihalyi, Mihalyi. *Flow: The Psychology of Optimal Experience*. New York: Harper Perennial, 1990.

Eccles, Frank. "Should Incompetent Teachers be Protected?" *Education Week*, 3 November 1993, p. 40.

Evans, Robert. "The Faculty in Mid-Career: Implications for School Improvement." *Educational Leadership* 46 (May 1989): 10-15.

Fullan, Michael. *The New Meaning of Educational Change*. New York: Teachers College Press, 1991.

James, William. *Writings: 1902-1910*. Edited by Bruce Kuclick. New York: Viking, 1987.

Joyce, Bruce; Wolf, James; and Calhoun, Emily. *The Self-Renewing School*. Alexandria, Va.: Association for Supervision and Curriculum Development, 1993.

Kagan, Dona. "Snapshots from High School: Teachers' vs. Professors' Views." *Educational Leadership* (March 1993): 28.

Katzenbach, Jon R., and Smith, Douglas K. *The Wisdom of Teams: Creating the High Performance Organization*. Boston: Harvard Business School Press, 1993.

Kidder, Tracy. *Among Schoolchildren*. Boston: Houghton Mifflin, 1989.

Lortie, Dan. *Schoolteacher: A Sociological Study*. Chicago: University of Chicago Press, 1975.

Negin, Gary A. "In Vino, Veritas." *Educational Leadership* 50 (March 1993): 32-33.

O'Neil, John. "School Pushed to Broaden Access, Overhaul Practice." *ASCD Curriculum Update* (September 1992): 4.

Rosenholtz, Susan. *Teacher's Workplace*. New York: Teacher's College Press, 1989.

Rothman, Robert. "Science Reform Goals Elusive, NAEP Data Find." *Education Week*, 1 April 1992, p. 15. a

Rothman, Robert. "In a Pilot Study, Student Writing in Class Gauged." *Education Week*, 22 April 1992, p. 24. b

Senge, Peter. Speech at the annual convention of the American Association of School Administrators in San Diego, 21 February 1992.

Schaffer, Robert H. *The Breakthrough Strategy: Using Short-Term Successes to Build the High Performance Organization*. New York: Harper Business, 1988.

Schmoker, Mike, and Wilson, Richard B. "Transforming Schools Through Total Quality Education." *Phi Delta Kappan* 74 (January 1993): 389-95.

Stiggins, Richard. *Student-Centered Classroom Assessment*. New York: Merrill, 1994.

Troen, Vivian, and Boles, Katherine. "Teacher Leadership: How to Make It More than a Catch Phrase." *Education Week*, 3 November 1993, p. 27.

PART IV

TEACHERS AND THE IMPROVEMENT OF SCHOOLS

CAN TEACHERS BE EDUCATED TO SAVE STUDENTS IN A VIOLENT SOCIETY?

BY MARTIN HABERMAN

Martin Haberman is Distinguished Professor, School of Education, University of Wisconsin-Milwaukee. Vicky Dill is in Exemplary Education at the Texas Education Agency.

The short answer is, "Yes." The longer answer is, "But whether we have the will and the insight to make the necessary changes is problematic." There needs to be an overhaul on two levels: the nature of schooling offered children and youth in poverty and the ways in which their teachers are selected and prepared.

Schools "serving" poor children need to be derailed and redirected. Their present course is taking them closer and closer to the model of the penal institution in a hostile community. Schooling for children in poverty needs to provide the holistic, humane, nurturing, liberating education now offered many advantaged youngsters. But no school can be better than its teachers. Simultaneously, teacher education must be developed anew so that it produces culturally competent teachers who can be effective with children making perfectly normal responses to living in poverty and violence. To achieve this goal, teacher education must change who is selected to teach, what they are taught, how they are taught, and who teaches them. Traditional forms of teacher education need to be held publicly accountable for preparing teachers whose effectiveness with poor children can be tied directly to their training programs and their trainers. Without giving these children the teachers they need and are willing to learn from, the endless advocacies for restructuring schools are so much piffle.

This essay connects the effects of violence on children with teacher practices that exacerbate or alleviate its impact. Positive teacher practices are then connected with the nature of teacher selection and training. Principles derived from teacher education programs already demonstrating some success are proposed as criteria for advancing teacher education still further.

153

Life Looks Different

For children in most of the nation, life is changing rapidly. The cozier school atmospheres that many parents remember are a thing of the past. The reflective glint of metal detectors rings schoolhouse doors; video cameras, convex mirrors, security guards, and drug-sniffing dogs compose an increasingly common image. See-through bookbags have replaced the home-made or nylon type; purses must be small enough not to conceal even one of those pale pink, mother-of-pearl, girl-sized guns. Companies sell bullet-proof vests for school youth able to afford them. Resources for education dwindle as security budgets rise. That the New York Public Schools fund the ninth-largest police force in the nation means fewer resources for teachers, libraries, books, field trips, computers, and gymnasiums. Fourteen million dollars is budgeted for security alone in Dade County, Florida (Reed and Shaw 1993).

The data for samples of inner-city schools is horrendous. For example, only 17% of middle school children report feeling safe in school (Lewis 1993). But the data for the nation as a whole is even worse. Homicide is now the third leading cause of child death; and while the rate for adult homicide has increased 11% in a 10-year period, the rate for child homicide has increased 93% (Children's Defense Fund 1993).

Increasingly, the nation's children daily negotiate a bewildering array of hurdles. Poverty, abuse or neglect, isolation, ill-equipped schools, substandard physical and mental health care, poor parental and community models, and unemployment nibble at their spirits, however ebullient they may have been as toddlers. Gangs spread fear into neighborhoods and schools, causing students to arm themselves. So armed, they end up retaliating in violent ways or, all too frequently, accidentally harming themselves or others. Fear feeds further violence, and a vicious cycle becomes a steady stream of carnage in neighborhoods around schools. Voices loudly call for deterrence, while researchers show and experts remind the public that 100,000 more cops will barely stem the tide.

Few areas of American life remain untouched by violence, and its ubiquitous presence across the nation has affected every child. The crack cocaine industry, spreading from the cities to suburbs and rural areas alike, brings some poor children sudden wealth. They gain access to weapons and a life divided between school time, home time, and "homeboy" time; and they are surrounded by an ethos of "do or die" (Bing 1991). What may appear as a nonchalant gun-toting ethos, even habit, among youth more likely is the result of terror, the need to protect, and a perceived lack of options. Why would children six or seven years old carry a weapon? For most, fear and the desire not to appear weak or vulnerable overcome any hesitation they may have. Even within gangs, loyalty seems a thing of the past. "Sets" or subgroups of gangs fight one another regularly, drafting the youngest children in the neighborhood to be part of the drug trade and, subsequently, the carnage. Being called a bad name, having someone stare at you a certain way, and not retaliating is cowardly. Being a "buster" or someone who won't kill is the ultimate sign of weakness for gang members and aspiring gang members, called "wannabees."

Suburban and rural children are not removed from this culture and the implied virtues of macho revenge. "Show and tell" may mean bringing a weapon to school to intimidate threatening bullies or just to be admired. Nearly every show on television, every toy up and down the retail toy shelves, and nearly every pop, rap, or reggae song alludes to the violence of life in this nation; and guns paraded as protection provide a background drone, a type of subconscious indoctrination to the inevitability of violence in the life of every child.

The embattled American family, frequently composed of a young, poor, single mother with several young children, swims upstream to maintain a living and supervise the children properly. Perceived viable options to gang life dwindle as the child grows older. How does the cycle of poverty lead to violence? How does this affect American families and children?

While poverty may be the best predictor of criminal activity and gang membership, obtaining money is not the main reason that gang members themselves say they joined a gang. Poverty, as the literature makes clear, is a correlate and not a cause of violence (Reiss and Roth 1993). It is what poverty entails − struggling and broken families, scattered and disconnected services, living with and seeing daily environmental aggression, despair, and neglect − that causes violence.

Almost universally, gang members report the need for a family and supportive peer group as the primary reason they were drawn into a gang. Boredom in school and with life also is frequently cited as a reason to join gangs (Vackar 1994). Boredom in school and the need to passively endure it amidst a repressive and relatively meaningless smorgasbord of disconnected classes intensifies the sense of being "on edge," of being a grenade that just one more bullying student or one more sharp teacher comment is about to unpin. Further, evidence is mounting that test-driven curricula and a paucity of viable supports for students who fail tests have combined in the "no pass/no play" era to eliminate even sports as an option from the lives of students in risk-laden environments. Indeed, experts who studied the effect of "no pass/no play" rules determined that such a rule decreases the likelihood that at-risk youth will graduate from high school (Texas Education Agency 1992).

At Home with Poverty

When a child in poverty gets up in the morning, that child's day may not much resemble the day experienced by another child who goes to the same school but who is more broadly advantaged. Poor children may awaken after a night of frequent interruptions from gunplay outside, intoxicated family members or neighbors, apartment rodents or pests, neglected siblings, or general neighborhood noise. The poor night of sleep may or may not be followed by a nutritious breakfast at home, although, to their credit, most schools provide disadvantaged children an early meal.

Trauma in violent neighborhoods affects every child. Witnessing violence, researchers are learning, has a dramatic effect on a child's psyche; the younger and the more inarticulate, the more dramatic the effect (Craig 1992). Violent crimes are witnessed 10% to 20% of the time by young children (Will 1993) and are devastating to young preverbal children who may suppress their feelings and become emotionally numb. Unable to process what they have witnessed, they frequently become suicidal or homicidal later in life (Gelman 1993). The callousness observed by many youth who murder randomly may result from the combination of a violent environment and the lack of a caring adult with whom to process the violence (Centers for Disease and Injury Control 1992). It is estimated that among African-American children, about 10% are zero-parented (Downey 1993). The normal reaction to a life lived in unpredictable, uncontrolled, and violent circumstances is a complex of characteristics known as "post traumatic stress disorder" (PTSD).

Isolation is particularly pernicious for poor adolescents living in violent neighborhoods. If safe after-school gymnasiums, tutoring programs, sports, or other activities are not available in poor neighborhoods, youth must choose between dangerous streets and home time, often spent in front of violent television programs. Providing safe activities is complicated by both expense and the fact that adolescents who enjoy "hunting and stalking" videogames may find many after-school activities too tame.

Given the environment and the choices, it is irrational to think that a youth would choose other than to join a gang and imitate those who are seen as prestigious adults in his or her neighborhood – the "OGs" or original gangsters (Bing 1991). By providing parenting, structure, and a family, the "hood" is the logical step in a seemingly inexorable adolescent passage.

As in other situations of social chaos, seldom does the psyche have a chance to rest. Schedules may vary wildly in the home of a poor child. The idea that one gets up every day and does this, then this, then that, may or may not exist. Maintaining an orderly atmosphere requires that a capable adult supervise and reiterate the order often enough for the child to internalize the order and the logic of the sequence. Adults in the homes of poor children may have erratic work schedules; may, in fact, work at night; may be despondent because of their own overwhelming problems; and may be frayed from lack of resources. Under certain conditions, poverty may cause the parents to behave as victims, foisting roles on young children that are appropriate only for adults. Older siblings may need to awaken, dress, feed, pack lunches for, or otherwise supervise younger siblings while receiving little support or nurturing themselves. Having no external locus of control and having no learned internal rationales for order, older siblings or embattled parents set the tone for what happens in the family – for good or ill.

The inability to think through a problem, challenge, or situation with an adult handicaps children as they seek to overcome barriers of poverty or alienation. They may act out their feelings instead of articulating them, sensing that acting out is to be "cool" while articulation is "nerdy." When bad things happen to an underparented, neglected, or abused child, he or she may think of it as bad luck and not be able to analyze what caused events to coalesce so unfortunately. "Victim" parents may attribute much of their misfortune to bad luck, thus communicating a sense of disempowerment or lack of control to their children. For poor children, the voice of authority often communicates a threat that they adopt and use as they have heard it used with them, instead of hearing the voice of authority as a source of help, support, or resources. As they pour into the school building, it is apparent: There is no magic door. The emotional or affective complex that children bring to school influences what they are able to do, or think they are able to do, or want to do at school.

157

The Total Impact

Five other forces influence youngsters growing up in poverty. First, lacking trust in many of the adults around them naturally leads young children to be suspicious of adults' motives and actions. Appearing to be shy or withdrawing from adults becomes a perfectly normal response. Not expecting or seeking safety from adults or the solution to one's problems from adults might be another logical, reasonable response.

The second force affecting development is the violence typical of urban life today. If those around us are potentially dangerous and life-threatening, then it is normal to avoid interacting with them whenever possible.

The perception of "no hope" is the third force that characterizes urban life for older children and adults in poverty, but hopelessness often is mistaken as a lack of initiative. If one sees no viable options or explains events only in terms of luck, it seems useless to expend effort.

The fourth force affecting development relates to the impact of living under mindless bureaucracies. It becomes natural, normal — even desirable — to give the bureaucracy what it wants, rather than try and respond to it in sensible, honest ways. It is only by responding to the bureaucracy on its own terms that any benefit can be derived. This teaches children who grow up under such conditions to initiate and to reveal as little as possible.

The fifth major influence relates to the culture of authoritarianism. The giving and taking of orders becomes the normal way of life. One's power becomes one's self-definition.

Deep frustration is a major characteristic of both adults and children who grow up and live in poverty and violence. And the result of this abiding frustration is some form of aggression. For many it is expressed as violence toward others. For others it takes the form of passive resistance. For some it is turned inward and expressed in the multiple ways that poor people demonstrate a reckless abandon for their own bodies, including suicide.

In sum, the expectations with which poor children frequently begin school are remarkably positive given their life experiences. Not being certain of or trusting adults, surrounded by family and friends being "done to," living in violence, and having learned to relate to others only by giving or taking orders, most still come eagerly to school. It is up to schools and teachers to construct more than a continuation of mindless bureaucracy and to be something other than overly directive, threatening adults.

At School with Poverty

In accepting the 1990 New York City Teacher of the Year Award, John Taylor Gatto stated that no school reform will work that does not provide children time to grow up or simply forces them to deal with abstractions. Without blaming the victims, he described the behavior of his students as lacking curiosity ("evanescent attention"), indifference to the adult world, having a poor sense of the future, ahistorical, cruel and lacking in compassion, uneasy with intimacy and candor, materialistic, dependent and passive, and frequently masked by surface bravado.

For any who would justify directive forms of teaching, it is important to recognize that John Gatto's description of his students is only the starting point. These characteristics will be reinforced by an authoritarian pedagogy, but they do not represent students' true or ultimate natures. Children and youth can become more and different, but they must be taught carefully. Two conditions must pertain before there can be a serious alternative to authoritarian teaching: 1) The whole school faculty and school community, and not the individual teacher, must be the unit of change; and 2) there must be patience and persistence of application, since students can be expected to resist changes to an unknown system when they can predict and control the present one. Children and youth who have learned to successfully negotiate urban schools by interacting with authoritarian adults will not readily abandon all their know-how to take on some new and uncertain system that they may not be able to control. This makes the task teachers face one of helping students first to unlearn what they think is working.

For any analysis of pedagogic reform to have meaning in urban schools, it is necessary to understand something of the dynamics of teacher-student interactions. The authoritarian and directive nature of the pedagogy offered to poor children and youth is somewhat misleading about who is really in charge. Teachers seem to be in charge (and may believe they are in charge) in that they direct how and at what tasks students will work, as well as the time allotments, materials, and means of evaluation to be used. It is assumed by many that having control over such decisions makes teachers "decision makers" who somehow shape the behavior of their students.

But below this façade of control is a more powerful level on which students actually control, manage, and shape the behavior of their teachers. Students reward teachers by complying. They punish them by resisting. In this way, students shape teachers into believing that some things "work" while other things do not. Most teachers incorrectly assume that when there is compliance, there is learning. By this dynamic, children and youth lead teachers to give directions and conduct activities with which they will comply, thereby systematically limiting and shaping their teachers' behaviors to what they feel like being directed to do. Most teachers are unaware of how they are thus controlled by students. They believe they are in control and are responding to "students' needs" when, in fact, they are more like hostages responding to students' overt or tacit threats of noncompliance or disruption. It cannot be emphasized enough that in the real world, urban teachers are defined as incompetent not because their "deprived," "disadvantaged," "abused," "low income" students are not learning but because they cannot elicit compliance. Once teacher competence was made synonymous with controlling and managing students, it was inevitable that students would sense who was really in charge.

The stake that students have in maintaining teaching based on power and control is of the strongest possible kind: It is the schools that are held accountable for making them learn. In their own unspoken but crafty way, students are not eager to trade a system in which they can operationally make their teachers appear effective or ineffective for a new system in which they themselves would become accountable and responsible for their learning. It would be risky and unwise for students to swap a "try and make me" system they can control for one in which they would ask themselves, "Let's see how well and how much I really can do."

Schools reinforce the self-caricatures of children in poverty as helpless, victimized, inarticulate, and threatening beings in a number of additional ways. Poor children are less likely to be in academically enriched environments and more likely to be repetitively drilled in basic skills. Large-group instruction or computer-generated electronic worksheets do not improve interaction skills in poor youth; rather, youth feel relegated to roles where little value is placed on what they can think and do, while great value is placed on how compliant they can be.

Schools that sort and label instead of support and teach place poor students in ghettos called remedial classes or alternative schools. And while it is manifestly true that violent youth cannot be permitted to harm other youth who are trying to study or stay safe, it also is true that in-school suspensions, alternative schools, juvenile detention camps, and other "justice" solutions tend to sort out students who already feel out of the mainstream of American life and opportunity. In ill-equipped schools where classes are large, behavior is "managed" and no community is created. Students may not have any idea that gentle societies, built on consensus and upheld through supportive authorities, are even a possibility.

How Do Some Schools Make the Problem Worse?

Coercion undermines reasonable authority. In schools where decent behavior is achieved primarily by coercion, students naturally assume that coercing others is the best way, perhaps the only way, to behave. Gang and delinquent behaviors both reflect and reinforce the supposed value of coercion. Individuals who refuse to coerce others (who refuse to intimidate, rob, or "pop" another) are considered undesirable and unworthy. Principals, therefore, have extraordinary responsibility in modeling another, more democratic, way of operating. At the elementary level, where principals are often the only male models in a child's life, it is especially important for principals to "swim upstream," creating ways to obtain their goals without carrying a big stick. At a recent seminar for urban principals, one of the authors asked the group to explain the principle that rational authority is self-eliminating. Not a single participant was able to explain the concept; when told its meaning, they unanimously rejected it as a dangerous way to run a school for poor children.

School bureaucracies are not a fertile source for developing a feeling of community. Why has it been so difficult for site-based decision making to take hold, especially in large, urban environments? There are several reasons. First, bureaucracies tend to function by rules (that is, "operating procedures") that limit participants' behavior and serve to maintain the organization without having to respond to individual needs. Rules are constantly added to deal with special cases so that over time there is a proliferation of restrictions, the reasons for which are long forgotten.

This tendency to think more highly of rules, guidelines, and procedures than of helping individuals achieve the stated goals of the organization dehumanizes schools and places the needs of the bureaucracy over those of the clients. Impersonal bureaucracies make it difficult for teachers to model democratic behavior, because commonsense decisions are precluded by cumbersome guidelines. Teachers may need to go through a four-step permission process simply to walk their kindergarten class around the block. Teachers may wish to visit a child's home to become better acquainted, hear the

161

parents talk about their child, and exchange insights. However, the school already may have delineated and delegated this responsibility to a visiting teacher who has the proper certification, identification, and insurance and gets paid to make home visits.

Teachers may wish to build a curriculum out of a child's world and materials, discussing, for example, international candy and corn trade with Mexico instead of the bonbon imports from France that might be in the textbook. But standardized tests require (frequently by law) greater articulation of curriculum with the test. Teachers find it difficult to individualize a child's education because the bureaucracy has few ways to reward success but many ways to punish teachers who are unwilling to follow school rules at the expense of children.

Second, site-based management runs into difficulty when *de facto* power structures prevent teachers from reaching new and more professional levels of authority and responsibility. Consider, for example, the highly experienced school secretary. She's a "local" who knows everything about the principal's job: where to find vital documents and supplies, who to ask for school adoptions, how to contact central office administrators and school board members, how to key in tests and data for the state department, and how to do payroll. This makes her an indispensable player in the principal's microcosm. She may be easily threatened by changes that lessen her control. Hence, altering the school environment in any way that might better serve students but might deprive her of real power and control is a risk only the bravest of principals would undertake. They will move on, but she will stay.

Such school politics frequently impinge on the establishment of a more democratic vision; the janitor who may be the only one who can communicate with an over-age and delinquent kid may be transferred because he is spending too much time talking to kids and not enough time removing graffiti. The cafeteria worker who may be the only person in the school who says something positive to each child every day is reprimanded for not moving the serving line along fast enough. The successful lesson of the novice teacher causes noise and excitement that is mistaken for lack of control. These and innumerable other incidents occur regularly and disempower those who wish to help youngsters learn that there are alternatives to impersonal, power relationships.

Perhaps the most serious threat to a democratic vision in schools is the widespread use of corporal punishment, institutionalized brutality that replaces skills in negotiation, peer mediation, and problem-solving. In response to a state law that each instance of corporal punishment must be reported in writing, there are, in Texas alone, approximately 275,000 cases reported annually of "shaping up the reluctant." Teaching is the only profession in America legally sanctioned to beat its clients.

Finally, advocacies that once seemed effective may become institutionalized and watered down, defeating the "movers and shakers" who initiated a very different form of change in the first place. As individualized as they are touted to be, pull-out programs for special education students, the language diverse, and others, soon lead to isolation; instruction deteriorates as pull-out classes, tracking, or retention result in concentrations of students who are segregated from advantaged or gifted students. Protection stigmatizes those it is designed to serve. Likewise, inclusion may be overwhelmingly successful with most students. But some students may lose individual contact with important personal friends and teacher/models in their lives by joining large groups of heterogeneously grouped youth. Damion, for example, is a 15-year-old emotionally disturbed youth in eighth grade. He flourished in a pull-out program where an ex-banker-turned-teacher spent concentrated time with him, discussing his family — or lack of it — his grandmother, his guns, and his fears. This year, as an "included" student, Damion has only about seven to ten minutes a day with this teacher. Bureaucracies dehumanize by depersonalizing individuals, including those whose special needs have led to special labels or special rules.

Real Authority Springs from Nurturing Relationships

Certainly leadership is desirable. In a democratic school, leadership is achieved through providing support and model behavior, not through intimidation and coercion. Leadership means helping people demand what is in their own best interest. In the same way that a principal becomes a leader through providing support, the teachers become leaders in their classrooms, schools, and communities through their support of children and learning. Gaining the appellation of "leader" in the classroom is not achieved by power teaching — moving up and down the rows in lecture style, informing the uninterested and testing the intimidated. For children in poverty, school is often an exercise in interminable boredom relieved only by moments of stark terror; this is the legacy of direct instruction and power teaching and should not be confused with educating a free people.

Cooperative learning groups provide a microcosm of democracy by giving each individual the level of responsibility with which he or she can deal successfully and by holding the whole cooperative group accountable for creating a product, becoming informed, or experiencing a process together. Cooperative learning is a way to mine students' strengths, instead of covering an irrelevant curriculum with mindless worksheets.

Levin and others in the accelerated learning schools advise building on students' strengths (Levin 1992). Building on students' strengths assumes a rather deep and personal knowledge of students, their interests, foibles, and strengths. Gathering students into the decision-making process and discussing the nature of learning together takes time; what is learned may not always be measurable by standard outcomes or results-based monitoring. What is communicated and learned, however, is life itself − the ongoing process of articulating a vision, deciding how to move toward the goal, moving ahead, evaluating, and redefining the vision yet again. It should not come as news that effective schooling is not preparation for living but living itself.

For this reason, it might be said that the teacher/leader/nurturer who successfully teaches children in poverty and violence wields not a bat but a mirror, helping the students to see themselves and the consequences of their own actions, where they are going, and what help they need. While predictability and order are important in the classrooms of children living with violence, these characteristics do not result from a system of lecturing, direction-giving, and testing, then more lecturing, direction-giving, filling in the blanks, and testing. Children frequently victimized by chaos, pervasive change, and poverty do indeed need structure; but structure can be created by better means than passively taking direction from mindless autocrats.

Building Wide Bridges

Why is it so critical that students raised in violence have nonauthoritarian teachers and principals? Mothers and especially grandmothers notice that, about the age of two, children in poverty lose the sparkle from their eyes. As the process of growth occurs, individuals seek to turn from victim into perpetrator. In a way that is normal and expected for them, the vicious cycle continues. Experts note that children in repressive, authoritarian structures tend to become manipulative; that is the only behavior they know (Gelman 1993). However, teachers who see children on a daily basis can establish trust and not only suggest but demonstrate another vision of how to get along.

Dondy was the second child of a mixed marriage; Dad was in prison at last communication, and Mom was homeless; food and clothes were scarce. The other kids whispered that she smelled funny, and no one ever picked her for group. Her fourth teacher in one year, Ms. Johnson, provided Dondy with the first and only glimpse she had ever had of a nonthreatening, supportive place to go. Ms. Johnson's gentle approach was unerringly nonpunitive, a style of teaching that requires teachers have an almost endless fund of patience and a firm grasp of their goals. Flexibility and choices are hallmarks of a student-teacher relationship that will "make space" for an angry, highly stressed child, a room full of highly stressed children, or a distraught newcomer who may lash out unprovoked at others. Time and consistent support pay incredible dividends. A teacher may reprimand gently, may move a child away from the group until the anger passes, may discuss the consequences of the child's behavior, and may carefully communicate to the other children ways to help and not humiliate an angry or misbehaving peer. Putting the name of the child up on the board, adding extra humiliation by underlining it or putting a check beside it, delegating pink slips for detention and suspension − the inexorable escalation of humiliations − only exacerbates an already hell-bent cycle. Ineffective teachers prove this is a failed system in schools across America every day.

Being valued by the teacher, on the other hand, helps Dondy know that her classroom is a caring and positive landscape, a flood wall against which the pressures of an unpredictable world pound. Almost any child living in neighborhoods where environmental violence is ubiquitous can be labeled with some arbitrary term and removed from the classroom; the way to keep children in poverty from becoming youth in prison is for teachers to keep them in the class and to move them toward wholeness. This is a schoolwide task. Effective teachers move individuals toward self-understanding and responsibility. They move peers and friends toward flexibility and inclusion of others, however different they may be or however severe their problems.

Power Teaching Versus Gentle Teaching

Locked into a reward and punishment model, beginning teachers assume that their punishments will have sufficient power to make children learn. As they gain experience, they soon feel helpless because their punishments cannot be sufficiently controlling. At this point, many become quitters and failures; a smaller number develop new forms of teaching that seek to engage children rather than over-power them.

There can be no debate about this point. Teachers who begin with the intention of dominating poor children and youth are doomed to failure. Teachers who seek to empower students may or may not become effective. Examples of gentle strategies include the following teaching behaviors. Gentle teachers:

- Generate and use students' interests. Even in assessment-driven systems, they never go through the meaningless motion of "covering" material apart from students' involvement and learning.
- Never use shame or humiliation.
- Never scream, scold, or harangue.
- Never get caught in escalating punishments to force compliance.
- Listen, hear, respect, remember, and use students' ideas.
- Model cooperation with all other adults in the building.
- Demonstrate empathy for students' expressions of feelings.
- Identify student pain, sickness, and abuse, and follow up with people who can help them.
- Redefine the concept of hero. In a variety of media, they show how people who work things out are great.
- Teach students peer mediation.
- Do not expect students to learn from failing. Repeated student failure leads only to more frustration and giving up. Teachers model "learning from our mistakes."
- Devise activities at which students can succeed. Success engenders further effort.
- Focus wholeheartedly on students' efforts and not on inborn gifts.
- Are a source of constant encouragement by finding good parts in all students' work.
- Defuse, sidestep, and redirect all challenges to their authority. They never confront anyone, particularly in public.
- Use cooperative learning frequently.
- Create a family in the classroom and an extended family or "nation" in the school.
- Use particular subject matters as the way to have "fights" — science "fights" about rival explanations, math "fights" about different solutions, social studies "fights" about what really happened in history or politics.

166

- Never publicly ask students for private information.
- Do not try to control by calling on children who are not paying attention and embarrassing them.
- Demonstrate respect for parents in the presence of their children.

Effective teachers see their jobs as helping to create safe havens where, for a good part of every day, the madness of violence will not intrude and their children will experience freedom from fear. Effective teachers engage in gentle teaching aimed at making learning intrinsic and students accountable. Only those who have the self-confidence and strength to function in peaceful ways in volatile and potentially violent situations need apply. Many frail, elderly, female, middle school teachers succeed every day while macho, male, ex-football heroes are driven out. Teacher strength is an inner quality demonstrated by an ability to share authority with children and youth whom most people are unwilling to trust.

Stopping the Chaos

Teachers who build curriculum around the lives of their students, despite bureaucratic pressures, help these students feel a sense of inherent accomplishment, an innate empowerment they may otherwise not feel. Sometimes defined as "learned helplessness" (Craig 1992, p.70), these children's perceptions of life are that it happens to them; they cannot control or stop the events swirling around them. But by helping students use their immediate world as a sourcebook for observation, writing, story-telling, counting, demographics, science, or any interdisciplinary problem, teachers affirm for students the value of a world often communicated to them as inherently worthless.

Communicating an intrinsic dignity to children should be woven into the fabric of school life, a systemic staple. Much has been written about tracking youngsters into homogeneous groups of "losers" and "failers," doomed to move like class-C factory models from transitional kindergarten to over-age elementary kids, to vocational or competency-based high school kids (if they make it that far), to probation, early pregnancy, jail, and welfare. The process of systematically sorting kids, killing them with dehydrated basics and drills, then wondering why they are nonthinking, rebellious, bored, angry, and hostile, must stop if schools are to stop contributing to the violence in the society.

Retention in grade — the honoring of failure as a form of maintaining "high standards" — is a destructive force to be exposed and eliminated. What it does is simply separate advantaged youngsters who can manage in school from those who are disadvantaged and for whom school is an ill fit. Schools made to fit kids are a more optimistic option than kids cut up to fit schools.

Selecting Gentle Teachers

The following attributes typically are used to select people into training programs. Nevertheless, they are predispositions that enable teachers to be successful in performing conciliatory, cooperative, respectful, egalitarian forms of instruction in place of power or authoritarian forms of teaching. What seems to work for star teachers of children abused by violence and poverty?

- They tend to be nonjudgmental. As they interact with children and adults in schools, their first thought is not to decide the goodness or badness of things but to understand events and communications.
- They are not moralistic. They do not believe that preaching is teaching.
- They are not easily shocked — even by horrific events. They tend to ask themselves, "What can I do about this?" And if they think they can help, they do; otherwise they get on with their work and their lives.
- They not only listen, they hear. They not only hear, they seek to understand. They regard listening to children, parents, or anyone involved in the school community as a potential source of useful information.
- They recognize that they have feelings of hate, prejudice, and bias and strive to overcome them.
- They have a clear sense of their own ethnic and cultural identities.
- They are culturally competent and include diverse cultural perspectives in their classroom programs.
- They do not see themselves as saviors who have come to save their schools. While they believe in their ability to affect children, they do not expect their school organizations will change much.
- They do not see themselves as being alone. They network.

168

- They see themselves as "winning" with many of their students, even though they know their influence on their students is much less than that of the total society, neighborhood, or gang.
- They visit parents in their homes or in neighborhood places away from school.
- They enjoy their interactions with children and youth so much that they are willing to put up with the irrational demands of overly bureaucratic school systems.
- They believe that their primary impact on their students has been that they have made them more humane and less frustrated and have raised their self-esteem.
- They derive satisfaction and meet all kinds of needs by teaching poor children and youth. The one exception to this is power. They meet no power needs whatever by functioning as teachers.
- Most of all, they define their work as eliciting effort. Their interaction with the youngsters centers on using effort as the explanation of success for themselves and their students.

What Kind of Teacher Education Will Prepare Such Teachers?

The first step that must be taken to make teacher education function in the real world is to discontinue certain practices. Before we can institute more relevant and viable alternatives, we have to stop doing things that make the situation worse. For example, the practice of using grade point average as the primary criterion for selecting candidates into traditional programs of teacher education must be stopped. GPA predicts who will do well in the university, not who will seek a job teaching children in poor neighborhoods and certainly not who will be an effective teacher in such schools.

The selection practices used in traditional programs of teacher education have not changed in any important ways in 25 years. There is still little or no attempt by schools of education to use selection criteria that have any predictive validity to subsequent teaching practice (Haberman 1994b). This is malpractice and a monstrous hoax; it misleads thousands of undergraduates in preservice teacher education programs into believing that their high university grades qualify them in any way to become teachers of children and youth in poverty. It leads them to believe they fail as teachers because the children are abnormal, rather than because they do not know how to teach these children.

169

In many states the majority of certified graduates never seek jobs because the only openings are in schools in poor, inner-city areas; and these graduates do not want to teach children in the major urban areas. For example, in Wisconsin, 70% of certified graduates never seek such jobs (Haberman 1989). Of the minority who do take teaching jobs in urban areas, more than 10% quit each year; thus half of the small minority who even try to teach poor children are gone in 3 to 5 years. While we hear much complaining from teachers about transient poor children who move from school to school, the more serious problem is the impact on children of having half a dozen or more teachers per year, most of whom are merely passing through.

A second example of a practice that must be stopped before programs of teacher education can become relevant to poor children is that of assuming that completing doctoral-level study prepares people to function as teacher educators. There is no Ph.D. program in any school of education that requires evidence that its candidates were ever successful, effective teachers of children. Indeed, the stated primary purpose of doctoral study is to prepare researchers and scholars, not school practitioners at all! Since the essential expertise required of future teachers is relevant, usable know-how in teaching, the majority of the teacher education faculty should be experienced, currently practicing teachers who have been identified as effective.

A third example relates to the limited knowledge base currently used in teacher education. Before more meaningful knowledge bases can be introduced, counter-productive content must be eliminated. For example, psychology and its offspring, educational psychology, has become the dominant discipline in the knowledge base of teacher education (Haberman 1982). Beginning with the nature of the learner and learning, educational psychology now commonly includes studies in preschool through adolescent development, abnormal development, testing, research, counseling, and school learning. This hegemony of educational psychology over the entire teacher education curriculum is not apparent by simply looking at whether the requirements in a program are labeled educational psychology, since different colleges organize themselves into different departmental structures. The issue is best understood by examining the theoretical constructs and ways of knowing that dominate teacher education courses and experiences. For example, concepts such as motivation, reward and punishment, readiness, retardation, giftedness, self-esteem, self-concept, and the lexicon of terms related to norm-referenced testing (for example, "bottom half") are now an integral part of the syllabi of all courses in teacher education, regardless of whether the particular course is labeled educational psychology. Typically, future teachers are not presented with alternative theoretical constructs to concepts such as motivation, ability, or self-concept as ways of explaining children's behavior. Future teachers are not routinely presented with alternative explanations of human behavior in which the unit of analysis is not the individual. Rarely, if ever, are they presented with ways of explaining human behavior in which individual personality constructs are not assumed to be the primary causes of children's behavior.

Foundation studies of education (for example, history, philosophy, economics, and sociology of education), which focus on societal and ideational influences as ways of explaining human behavior, have always occupied a minor and, recently, a shrinking role in the knowledge base of teacher education (Borman 1990). It is now common for future teachers to take one foundations course in their preparation (many programs require none) and to evaluate "theory" as largely irrelevant to their needs as beginning teachers (Feiman-Nemser and Buchmann 1983). There can be little question that preservice students accept the emphasis in their preparation programs that explains human behavior in terms of the individual personalities involved. The constant and strong criticism made by graduates is not that they were given limited or insufficient paradigms, theoretic constructs, and ways of understanding children and their behavior, but that the knowledge base they were offered was not sufficiently extended into practice. ("Student teaching was not long enough.") What this means is that graduates do not question the efficacy or relevance of the reward-punishment paradigm as a discipline strategy, nor question whether ability measures and constant testing are causes of school learning or whether there are more powerful ways of explaining children's school behavior and learning.

A fourth example of the need for desist strategies relates to how programs of teacher education are evaluated or, to be more precise, not evaluated. The numbers of graduates, their grades, the number and titles of the education courses they have completed, and the length of their programs may be used by the various states to grant licenses; but they are meaningless criteria for predicting teaching success, and they are dangerous since they lead many into believing that schools of education are, in any way, accountable for their graduates' know-how or competence. Every program of teacher education should be judged by how well its graduates perform in real schools with real students. Every beginning teacher's performance should be connected back to the program in which he or she was prepared. Before such genuine accountability can be implemented, the counting of endless irrelevancies that lead to licensure must be stopped. Current requirements in schools of education have nothing to do with making traditional training programs or their graduates accountable for the education of children and youth.

Thus far we have argued that traditional forms of teacher training contribute to violence in schools by selecting the wrong teacher candidates, using individuals with inappropriate expertise as their trainers, and teaching them techniques that intensify an unnecessary power struggle between teachers and students. The traditional system of teacher education might be described as the ignorant teaching the fearful to escalate the violence. Since there is no accountability that connects beginning teachers' effectiveness with their training, the contention may be made that traditional programs of teacher education are without redeeming social significance.

Principles of Preparing Gentle Teachers

We know it is possible for new forms of teacher education to have a positive impact on school violence. Some urban universities and a great many alternative certification programs are demonstrating that this is not only feasible but eminently doable. These successes will not transform American society from a violent one into a saner one, but they will save hundreds of thousands of children and youth from lives of desperation and injury and will provide them with meaningful life opportunities. Following are some of the principles upon which to build teacher education programs for schools serving children and youth in poverty:

1. *Select the "best and brightest."* The profile of the "best and brightest" teachers for culturally diverse children in urban poverty is as follows:

- Did not decide to teach until after graduation from college.
- Tried (and succeeded) at several jobs or careers.
- Is between 30 and 50 years of age.
- Attended an urban high school.
- Has raised several children, is a parent, or has had close, in-depth, meaningful relations with children and youth.
- Currently lives in the city and plans to continue to do so.

- Is seeking and preparing for a teaching position in only an urban school system. (Does not believe "teaching is teaching" or "kids are kids.")
- Has had personal and continuing experiences with violence and of living "normally" in a violent community and city.
- Has majored in just about anything at the university.
- May or may not have an above-average grade point average in university studies.
- Expects to visit the homes of the children he or she teaches.
- Has some awareness of or personal experience with a range of health and human services available in the urban area.
- Expects that the school bureaucracy will be irrational and intrusive.
- Is likely not to be of Euro-American background, but a person of color.
- Is likely to be sensitive to, aware of, and working on his or her own racism, sexism, classism, or other prejudices (Haberman 1994a).

The implication of this sketch is that the typical pool of undergraduates in traditional programs of teacher education cannot possibly produce the body of effective new teachers for children in poverty. While late-adolescent, middle-class, white, monolingual females have every right to seek admission to teacher education programs, they need to be reconceptualized as an ancillary pool of "exceptions." The basic pool for effective teachers for children in poverty will continue to be drawn from the multicultural adults whose profile is cited above.

2. *Star classroom teachers are the best teacher educators.* You cannot teach what you do not know. Since the essential expertise required of future teachers is relevant, usable know-how in teaching, the majority of the teacher education faculty in any program should be experienced, currently practicing classroom teachers who have been identified as effective. Such teacher educators are practitioners whose scholarship derives primarily from an experiential knowledge base of what works in classrooms in the real world; they are expert at evaluating ideas from whatever source (state mandates, expert opinion, administrative policy, research, or theory) in terms of their effects on children and youth in classrooms. These teacher educators are capable of coaching candidates' actual teaching practice and of modeling best practices for them. They also can prepare candidates for the nonteaching schoolwide and community responsibilities of teachers in the real world.

Supporting this cadre of star classroom teachers are specialists drawn from other spheres: university faculty who have developed specific expertise related to the causes of violence and strategies that help poor youngsters learn particular subject matters, health and human service professionals who serve the children and their families, parents, and other community representatives.

3. *The locus of the preparation for teachers of children facing violence and poverty is not an ideal professional development center or teaching hospital, but the typical schools that such children attend.* There are several reasons for this. Learning to deal with the mindless bureaucracy or working under less-than-reasonable principals is a necessary part of a teacher's preparation. So, too, are large classes, insufficient materials, some uncaring parents, colleagues who are burnouts, lack of health and human services, and other conditions faced by students and teachers in such schools. Preparing teachers to instruct under ideal conditions prepares them for the best of all nonexistent worlds. They learn to regard violence, abuse, and even poverty as intrusions that they should not have to face, because such things should not happen. Fantasy is an irrational, dangerous basis for preparing teachers and must be stopped.

4. *The basic process of learning to teach involves actually teaching.* This does not mean that neophytes are simply thrown into a classroom but that they have star teachers who serve as their on-site coaches. Coursework and workshops are of some use after beginners have gained some successful experiences. The neophyte needs to gain a background of teaching experience in order for subsequent courses or workshops to have any meaning. The practice of offering programs comprised of many preservice courses on the assumption that such courses will, in advance, teach neophytes to perform the role of effective teachers in schools serving poor children has been thoroughly contradicted and discredited by the number of failed teachers and the larger number who never even seek positions where teachers are needed.

5. *The content of relevant education for teachers of children in poverty is problem-centered, not totally derived from theory and research.* This means that the present system in traditional teacher education of extrapolating the faculty's favorite data or theory "down" to practice must be entirely reversed. The content of the preparation program for the neophyte must make them face real teaching problems in real schools and learn what star teachers do to respond to such problems. Whenever possible, these teacher behaviors may then

be supported by whatever theory or research is available. But many effective teacher behaviors are craft knowledge that simply work; they need not await total support by theory or research to be continued and improved.

The real knowledge base for teachers in training is the responses of star classroom teachers to questions that university faculty cannot answer in clear, specific terms:

- How do I handle discipline when my classroom rules do not match the building's rules?
- How do I not send "too many" kids to the office?
- How do I deal with violence I did not anticipate?
- What is my responsibility if I have a child who is being abused at home?
- How do I make learning relevant to students who see no future for themselves?
- What can I do if gang loyalties are preventing learning in my class?
- How do I deal with students who cannot read texts or cannot read at all?
- What can I do with students who transfer in and out several times a month?
- How do I make students believe effort is more important than ability?
- How do I work with insufficient supplies or equipment in a particular subject area?
- What can I do about endless classroom interruptions?
- What can I do to get homework − or any assignment − completed?
- What if only outdated texts, maps, and encyclopedias are available to me?
- How can I improve relations between the ethnic groups in my class?
- How can I get parents involved and on my side?
- How can I learn from parents?
- How do I learn more about the neighborhood and utilize more community resources?
- How do I maintain an inclusive class, open to youngsters with all types of handicapping conditions, and meet everyone's needs?
- How do I control the school's paperwork demands?
- How do I cut down on out-of-class duties and demands on my time?

- What should I do about participating in school reform efforts or site-based management?
- How do I counter the negative effects of standardized tests?
- How do I stop burned-out teachers from complaining to the principal about my class projects?
- How do I get permission for my class to take more field trips?
- How do I give my students hope that their efforts will lead to something valuable in their lives?
- How do I maintain a high level of emotional and physical energy?

6. Teacher licensure should not be universal except for those trained in poor schools. Graduates of traditional teacher education programs should have licenses that restrict their practice to schools with less than one-third of their students living in poverty. The effective teaching of poor children and youth is a higher order of teaching and should be recognized by a super license. There is no need for this to be a national recognition. Present state licensing structures permit such recognition.

Current Status

In 1969 B.O. Smith concluded that a major overhaul of teacher education was needed before teachers would be adequately prepared to work with children of any social origin.

> Racial, class and ethnic bias can be found in every aspect of current teacher preparation programs. The selection processes militate against the poor and minorities. The program content reflects current prejudices; the methods of instruction coincide with learning styles of the dominant group. Subtle inequalities are reinforced in institutions of higher learning. Unless there is scrupulous appraisal, unless every aspect of teacher training is carefully reviewed, the changes initiated in teacher preparation as a result of the current crisis will be, like so many changes which have gone before, merely differences which make no difference. (Smith 1969, pp. 2-3)

Twenty-four years later, Zeichner searched the literature and concluded:

> There is a lot of evidence that the situation hasn't changed much in the 24 years since Smith delivered this condemnation of teacher education. . . . If teacher education programs were successful in educating teachers for diversity, we might not have

today such a massive reluctance by beginning teachers to work in urban schools and in other schools serving poor and ethnic- and linguistic-minority students. Just educating teachers who are willing to teach in these schools, however, only begins to address the problem of preparing teachers who will successfully educate the students who attend these schools. Educating teachers for diversity must include attention to the quality of instruction that will be offered by these teachers. More of the same kind of teaching, which has largely failed to provide a minimally adequate education to poor and ethnic- and linguistic-minority students, does not improve the situation. (1993, pp. 4-6)

We can do better. There are literally thousands of star teachers now functioning in the mindless, debilitating bureaucracies of the 120 largest school systems serving 12,000,000 poor children and youth. Recognizing their outstanding accomplishments and tapping their expertise as teacher educators and coaches will enable us to prepare others who also can guide students in poverty through a violent society.

References

Bing, L. *Do or Die*. New York: Harper Perennial, 1991.

Borman, K.M. "Foundations of Education in Teacher Education." In *Handbook of Research on Teacher Education*, edited by W.R. Houston. New York: Macmillan, 1990.

Centers for Disease and Injury Control. *Position Papers from the Third National Injury Control Conference*. Atlanta: U.S. Department of Health and Human Services, 1992.

Children's Defense Fund. *State of America's Children Yearbook, 1994*. Washington, D.C.: Children's Defense Fund, 1993.

Craig, S. "The Educational Needs of Children Living with Violence." *Phi Delta Kappan* 74 (September 1992): 67-71.

Downey, T. "Toward a New Future for America's Children." *Urban Institute Update* (April 1993): 2.

Feiman-Nemser, S., and Buchmann, M. "Pitfalls of Experience in Teacher Education: A Curricular Case Study." In *Preservice and Inservice Education of Science Teachers*, edited by P. Tamir, A. Hofstein, and M. Ben Peretz. Philadelphia: Balaban International Science Services, 1983.

Gelman, D. "An Emotional Moonscape." *Newsweek*, 17 May 1993, p. 52.

Haberman, M. "The Legacy of Teacher Education: 1800-2000." The Hunt Lecture: American Association of Colleges for Teacher Education, 1982.

Haberman, M. "More Minority Teachers." *Phi Delta Kappan* 70 (June 1989): 771-76.

Haberman, M. "Redefining 'Best and Brightest'." *These Times* (January 1994): 26. a

Haberman, M. "Selecting and Preparing Culturally Competent Teachers for Violent Schools." In *Second Handbook of Research on Teacher Education*, edited by J. Sikula. New York: Macmillan, 1994. b

Levin, H.M. *Accelerating the Education of ALL Students*. Restructuring Brief. Santa Rosa, Calif.: Redwood Region Consortium for Professional Development, 1992.

Lewis, A.C. *Changing the Odds: Middle School Reform in Progress, 1991-1993*. New York: Clark Foundation, 1993.

Reed, S., and Shaw, B. "Reading, Writing, and Murder." *People*, 14 June 1993, p. 44.

Reiss, A.J., Jr., and Roth, J.A., eds. *Understanding and Preventing Violence*. Washington, D.C.: National Academy Press, 1993.

Smith, B.O. *Teachers for the Real World*. Washington, D.C.: American Association of Colleges for Teacher Education, 1969.

Texas Education Agency. *An Interim Report on a Study of the Impact of Educational Reform on At-Risk Students in Texas*. Austin, March 1992.

Vackar, K. "Gangs in Public Schools." Speech delivered at Schreiner College, Kerrville, Texas, 11 February 1994.

Will, G. " 'Medicine' for 742 Children." *Newsweek*, 22 March 1993, p. 78.

Zeichner, K. *Educating Teachers for Diversity*. East Lansing, Mich.: National Center for Research for Teacher Learning, 1993.

TEACHER DEVELOPMENT AND SCHOOL IMPROVEMENT: AN ACCOUNT OF THE IMPROVING THE QUALITY OF EDUCATION FOR ALL (IQEA) PROJECT

BY DAVID HOPKINS AND MEL WEST

David Hopkins and Mel West are at the University of Cambridge Institute of Education in the United Kingdom.

In the rhetoric surrounding the professional development of teachers, we frequently hear that "there is little school development without teacher development." Much of our education research, policy, and practice are based on that premise. Although we have no wish to argue against the established convention that to improve schools we need to improve teachers, we are finding in our current work that sustained teacher development is difficult to achieve without reference to a whole-school context. This points to the corollary: "There is little teacher development without school development." Indeed, in order to cope with the demands of a radical national reform agenda, such as we currently are experiencing in Britain, school leaders increasingly are searching for practical ways of bringing teacher and school development together.

Within the IQEA project, this connection is being deliberately made, with reflective classroom practice being linked explicitly to whole-school development. Many of the schools involved are focusing innovative efforts simultaneously on teacher and school development in the context of a clear, well-articulated improvement strategy. Such strategies tend to relate to teaching and classroom organization in a broad sense, rather than to "curriculum" in the conventional sense. Thus, to take one example, many of our schools are using some form of classroom or "paired" observation to help staff work together and to learn from each other. Indeed, peer observation is proving to be a powerful means for establishing ownership, of acquiring new teaching strategies, and eventually of transforming the culture of the school. In such circumstances, once the process has been established, we are finding that leadership comes not from the head or administration, but from the teachers themselves. In this way, by linking teacher development to school development, leaders are being created at all levels in the school.

This is the theme we wish to pursue in this essay. We will tackle it in three ways. First, we describe the principles and approach underlying our school improvement network, Improving the Quality of Education for All. Second, we make an argument for creating conditions within the school that nurture both teacher and school development. Finally, we give some examples from schools with which we work of ways that teachers are taking an active leadership role in promoting their own and their school's development.

Improving the Quality of Education for All

During the past three years or so we have been working closely with some 30 schools in East Anglia, North London, and Yorkshire on a school improvement and development project known as Improving the Quality of Education for All. IQEA involves schools in working collaboratively with a group from the Institute of Education at Cambridge University and representatives from their local education authority (LEA) or a local support agency. The aim of the project is to strengthen the school's ability to provide quality education for all its pupils by building on existing good practice. In so doing, we also are producing and evaluating a model of school development and a program of support. IQEA works from an assumption that schools are most likely to strengthen their ability to enhance outcomes for all pupils when they adopt ways of working that are consistent with their own aspirations, as well as with the current reform agenda. At a time of great change in the education system, the schools with which we are working are using the impetus of external reform for internal purpose.

To describe our work in the project, we often use the metaphor of the journey in an attempt to capture the non-prescriptive and investigative nature of our collaboration. However, there is another, perhaps more important, aspect to our approach to school improvement as a journey. The image was captured recently by the head of a large secondary school when he said at one of our meetings that "we journey as pilgrims, not as nomads." He was reminding us that our collaborative approach to school improvement is based on a set of values that characterize and discipline all our work. So although we all had rejected the blueprint or top-down approach to change, we were not lurching from fad to fad on a whim. Rather, we were journeying in a direction that was, though not always well-posted, informed by goals or by a vision that reflect a set of core values.

At the outset of IQEA we attempted to outline our own vision of school improvement by articulating principles that provided a philosophical and practical starting point. Because it is our assumption that schools are most likely to provide quality education and enhanced outcomes for pupils when they adopt ways of working that are consistent with these principles, they were offered as the basis for collaboration with the IQEA project schools. In short, we were inviting the schools to identify and to work on their own projects and priorities, but to do so in a way that embodied a set of core values about school improvement. Originally, we stated 10 such principles; but as we have continued to work with the schools, we have reorganized these principles into the following five statements. They represent our expectations of the way project schools would pursue improvement, serving as an *aide-memoir* to the schools and to ourselves.

The five principles of IQEA are:

- The vision of the school (the school-in-the-future) should be one to which *all* members of the school community have an opportunity to contribute.
- The school will see in external pressures for change important opportunities to secure its internal priorities.
- The school will seek to create and maintain conditions in which *all* members of the school community can learn successfully.
- The school will seek to adopt and develop structures that encourage collaboration and lead to the empowerment of individuals and groups.
- The school will seek to promote the view that the monitoring and evaluation of quality is a responsibility in which *all* staff members share.

We feel that the operation of these principles creates synergism — together they are greater than the sum of their parts. They characterize an overall approach, rather than prescribing a course of action. The intention is that they should inform the thinking and actions of teachers during school improvement efforts and provide a touchstone for the strategies that teachers devise and the behaviors they adopt.

We underpin our school improvement work with a contract between the partners in the project — the school and its teachers, in some cases the LEA or sponsoring agency, and ourselves. The contract defines the parameters of the project and the obligations those involved owe to each other. It is intended to clarify expectations and ensure the conditions necessary for success. In particular, the contract emphasizes that *all* staff be consulted, that in-school coordinators be appointed, that a "critical mass" of teachers be actively involved in development work, and that sufficient time be made available for appropriate classroom and staff development activities. For our part, we coordinate the support arrangements, provide training for the school coordinators and representatives, make regular school visits and contribute to staff training, provide staff development materials, and monitor the implementation of each school's project. The detail of the contract expresses what we take to be the minimum conditions necessary for a successful partnership with the school:

- The decision to participate in the project is made as a result of consultation among *all* staff in the school.
- Each school designates a minimum of four staff members as project coordinators (one of whom is the head teacher), who attend training and support meetings. (The group of coordinators is known as the *project cadre*.)
- The school will allocate substantial staff development time to activities related to the project.
- At least 40% of teachers (representing a cross-section of staff) will take part in specified staff development activities in their own classrooms. Each participating teacher will routinely be released from teaching in order to participate in these classroom-based aspects of the project.
- Each school will participate in the evaluation of the project and share its findings with other participants in the project.

From the beginning of the project, we were determined to affect all levels of the school. A major purpose of the contract is to ensure that this happens. One of the things that we learned from the research and our previous work is that change will not be successful unless it affects — and is owned — at all levels of the organization. Specifically, our focus is on integrating three levels: the school, the teachers, and working groups. The school level refers to the establishment of policies and overall management, particularly in terms of mobilizing resources and strategies for staff development to support school

182

improvement efforts. At the individual teacher level, the focus is on developing classroom practice. And at the level of working groups, the concern is with collaborative work on the details of and support for improvement activities.

In effective schools these three levels of activity are mutually supportive. Consequently, a specific aim of the IQEA project is to devise and establish positive conditions at each level and to coordinate support across levels. It is in this connection that we require the establishment of a team of coordinators in each school. The coordinators' task includes the integration of activities across the various levels. We refer to these coordinators, in association with advisory colleagues from the local authority, as the *cadre*. They are responsible for the day-to-day running of the project in their own school and for creating links between ideas and actions. In many schools, members of the cadre establish an extended cadre that serves to expand the project in a more formal way within the school.

So far we have summarized our broad approach to school improvement. There remains the issue of how best to support schools through this complex process. Our current thinking and practice can be summarized by describing what we do within and outside the school.

Our within-school work concerns the nature of our intervention. It should be obvious that we explicitly have chosen an interventionist role. This role varies from time to time and place to place. On some occasions it may involve us in questioning our school-based colleagues in order to encourage them to "think aloud" about their work. Often they tell us that simply having an outsider who poses questions in a supportive way and then helps to set deadlines is helpful. Having established a long-term agreement to collaborate with colleagues in a school, and then having invested time in creating a working relationship with those colleagues, it is appropriate that we should be prepared to offer a critique of their proposals and actions. In this way, we seek to balance our support with a measure of persistence that is intended to push their thinking forward.

At times it is important to adopt a proactive role in project schools. We do this in order to provide specific support to school coordinators at particular times. For example, we often contribute to school-based staff development programs, working in partnership with school colleagues. Sometimes this involves team teaching in order to provide demonstrations, practice, and feedback related to particular staff development techniques. We also may assist in the planning and processing of significant meetings. For example, one of us recently helped the head teacher and some of his senior colleagues to devise a plan for a key staff meeting. This assistance involved modeling how the meeting might be managed and then providing feedback as the head teacher and deputy head practiced how they would carry out their tasks during the meeting.

Outside the school, our role focuses mainly on the training sessions we hold for the various cohorts of schools involved in the project. There is a strong emphasis on reflection and inquiry within these sessions. Reflection is the essential building block of professional competence and confidence. The training is based on the conditions we regard as necessary for successful school improvement, which are described later in this paper. The manual that we produced to support our staff development work summarizes these conditions, which we feel underpin school improvement, and includes related training exercises and support materials. We consistently try to model good staff development practice, to share our knowledge of the change process, and to provide time for high-quality planning and consultancy.

We also believe that it is appropriate that a teacher's involvement in school improvement be acknowledged. An advantage of school-university collaboration is the opportunity for teachers to accredit their school-based professional development activities through a series of academic awards.

Establishing a method of working with schools that was both flexible and focused was an issue that arose at the outset. The method adopted in the project was to support each school in relation to the selected objective, while feeding into all schools information about and perspectives on improvement strategies. Within this structure, consisting of many individual school projects, we developed our own action framework. This framework encompasses a series of assumptions on which the project is based. In describing these assumptions, we relate them to outcomes for students and staff, school culture and organization, selected developmental priorities, conditions necessary to support change, and the school improvement strategy.

The first assumption is that school improvement will result in enhanced *outcomes* for students and staff. We define outcomes broadly, and there obviously will be variations in outcomes according to the focus of the improvement effort. For students, the outcomes could be critical thinking, learning capacity, self-esteem, and so on, as well as improved examination and test results. For staff, they could be increased collegiality, opportunities for professional learning, and increased responsibility.

The second assumption is less obvious. *School culture* is a vital yet neglected dimension in the improvement process. It is, of course, a difficult concept to define, though we see it as an amalgam of the values, norms, and beliefs that characterize the way in which a group of people behave within an organizational setting. The types of school cultures most supportive of school improvement efforts, and those that we are working toward in the project, are collaborative, have high expectations for both students and staff, exhibit a consensus on values (or an ability to deal effectively with differences), and support a secure, orderly environment.

The third assumption is that the school *organization* is a key factor in the school improvement process. Few school improvement efforts adequately address organizational factors, which are often the main inhibitors of change. A school's organizational structure inevitably is a reflection of its values. Consequently, there is a strong, but not clearly understood, relationship between a school's organization and its culture.

The fourth assumption is that school improvement works best when there is a clear and practical focus for the development effort. The school's *priorities* usually are some aspect of curriculum, assessment, or classroom process that the school has identified from among the many changes that confront it. In this sense, the priority choice represents the school's interpretation of the current reform agenda. Although the balance of activities varies from school to school, we find that more successful schools set priorities for development that:

- are few in number — trying to do too much is counterproductive,
- are central to the mission of the school,
- relate to the current reform agenda,
- link to teaching and learning, and
- lead to specific outcomes for students and staff.

The fifth assumption is that the *conditions* necessary for school improvement are worked on at the same time as the curriculum or other priorities. Such conditions are the internal features of the school that enable administrators, teachers, and students to get work done. Without an equal focus on conditions, even priorities that meet the above criteria can quickly become marginalized. We also have found that when circumstances exist that are less supportive of change, it is necessary in the initial stages to concentrate much more on creating those favorable internal conditions that facilitate development and to limit work on the priorities until those conditions are in place.

The sixth assumption is that a school improvement *strategy* needs to be developed in order to link the priorities to the conditions. Reflecting our concern that schools constantly seek links that draw together external pressure for change and internal need for development, we take strategy to have both internal and external dimensions. Therefore, an effective strategy is both a device for integrating the school's goals, policies, and actions and a method of harmonizing the school's internal capacities with the opportunities and needs to be found in the external environment.

In encouraging the IQEA schools to identify specific strategies to address their self-generated priorities, we hoped to help those schools to develop an understanding of the potency of the priority-strategy-conditions model in bringing about cultural change. Since cultural change will be necessary if the agenda for reform is to be carried forward in harmony with school improvement activities, knowing how to bring about cultural change will become an increasingly important topic for managers. We hoped, therefore, that the IQEA schools would be explicit about strategy: communicating and publishing strategy decisions and evaluating and re-evaluating these decisions as part of an overall learning experience, an experience that we see as an important stepping-stone for the "moving" school.

Creating the Conditions for School Improvement and Teacher Development

As we note above, in our work with the IQEA project we have begun to associate a number of conditions within a school with the school's capacity for sustained development.

Taken together, these conditions result in the creation of opportunities for teachers to feel more powerful and confident about their work. This is particularly important because difficulties often arise for both individual teachers and the school when development work begins. For example, teachers may be faced with acquiring new teaching skills or mastering a new curriculum. The school, as a consequence, may be forced into new ways of working that are incompatible with existing organizational structures. This phase of "destabilization" or "internal turbulence" is as predictable as it is uncomfortable. Yet many research studies have found that without a period of destabilization, successful, long-lasting change is unlikely to occur.

At present, our best estimate of the conditions that underpin successful improvement, and therefore represent the key management arrangements, can be broadly stated as follows:

- a commitment to staff development;
- practical efforts to involve staff, students, and the community in school policies and decisions;
- "transformational" leadership approaches;
- effective coordination strategies;
- proper attention to the potential benefits of inquiry and reflection; and
- a commitment to collaborative planning activity.

Staff Development Policies. Staff development is inextricably linked to school development. In the quest for school improvement, powerful strategies are required to integrate these two areas in a way that is mutually supportive. In turn, powerful strategies that link staff development to school improvement need to fulfill two essential criteria: First, they need to relate to and enhance ongoing practice in the school and, second, they should link to and strengthen other internal features of the school's organization. Unless the staff development program leads to overall school improvement, it tends to become merely a series of marginal activities.

Further, it seems reasonable to assume that improving the conditions that support teachers' learning will have an impact on the learning conditions for pupils. To this end, it is important for a school to have a considered policy for teacher development. This must go well beyond the traditional pattern of teachers attending external courses or, more recently, one-shot school-based events. Strategies for staff development should be concerned with the development of the staff as a team, as well as with the development of individual thought and practice.

In our work with IQEA schools, we have accordingly been keen to promote a systematic and integrated approach to staff development, establishing that the professional learning of teachers is central to our notion of school improvement and that the classroom is as important a center for teacher development as any other.

Involvement. In the research literature on effective schools there is strong evidence that success is associated with a sense of identity and involvement that extends beyond the teaching staff. It involves pupils, parents, and other members of the school's community. Though it may be difficult for a particular school to establish such community links, it seems reasonable to expect that strategies for the active involvement of two key groups — pupils and parents — should be straightforward. Within the IQEA schools, we have tended,

187

therefore, to focus on ways in which these two groups can be brought more directly into the school's planning and decision-making processes.

The starting point for such involvement is the adoption of clear policies that encourage participation by the various stakeholder groups. There also need to be procedures and methods for bringing such participation into the school; the onus should not be on the groups themselves. Rather, methods for gaining access to the school's deliberations need to be published and supported by appropriate staff attitudes toward potential partners.

Leadership Practices. Studies of school effectiveness also show that leadership is a key element in determining school success. Perhaps such studies have overemphasized "leadership" at the expense of "management," but our own experience suggests that both are important characteristics of the effective school. However, *leadership* is a term of cultural significance for teachers. Most recently, studies of leadership in schools have tended to move away from the identification of this function exclusively with the head teacher and have begun to address how leadership can be made available throughout the management structure and at all levels in the school community. This shift in emphasis has been accompanied by a shift in thinking about leadership itself, with an increasing call for "transformational" approaches that distribute and empower, rather than "transactional" approaches that sustain traditional (and broadly bureaucratic) concepts of hierarchy and control.

Within the IQEA project we have set out to promote discussion about leadership style within participating schools and to help staff from different levels in the school to share perceptions of how leadership operates. Such discussions have identified a number of key aspects of the leadership role. The first underlines the responsibility of school leaders in establishing a clear vision or set of purposes for the school. The methods through which the vision is developed seems to be as important as vision itself in generating staff commitment.

The second relates to the way individual knowledge, skills, and experience are harnessed and the extent to which the school is able to transcend traditional notions of hierarchy or role in bringing together the "best team for the job." Leadership that arises from relevant knowledge or experience seems to be more successful than leadership that stems from authority.

188

A third aspect is the way leadership is used in group or team meetings. Leader behavior obviously is an important determinant of group effectiveness; but a strong commitment to the quality of relationships within the group can sometimes lead to over-cohesiveness, with a corresponding decline in the quality of critical thinking that individuals bring to the group.

Fourth, we have been keen to explore with participating schools the opportunities for "spreading" the leadership function throughout the staff group. This means accepting leadership as a function to which many staff contribute, rather than a set of responsibilities vested in a small number of individuals or jobs.

Coordination Strategy. Schools sometimes are referred to as "loosely coupled systems." This loose coupling occurs because schools consist of units, processes, actions, and individuals that tend to operate in isolation from one another. Loose coupling also is encouraged by the goal ambiguity that characterizes schooling. Despite the rhetoric of curriculum aims and objectives, schools consist of groups of people who may have very different values and beliefs about the purposes of schooling.

Therefore, we have identified the school's capacity to coordinate the action of teachers according to agreed policies or goals as an important factor in promoting change. In our work with the IQEA project schools, we have pursued a number of strategies that, we have found, improve the quality of coordination. At the core of such strategies are communication systems and procedures and ways in which groups can be created and sustained to coordinate improved effort across a range of levels or departments. Of particular importance are specific strategies for ensuring that all staff are kept informed about development priorities and activities, as this is information vital to informed self-direction. We also have found that awareness among staff of one another's responsibilities cannot always be presumed. Indeed, overlaps, both planned and unplanned, need particularly sensitive handling.

A further factor is the informal organization. All schools comprise a number of informal or self-selected groupings, which rarely coincide with formal work units. The attitudes and behavior adopted by these groups often have a profound effect on the individual's willingness to undertake formal tasks. As a consequence, it is important not to overlook the impact of informal organization on formal structures, and a coordination strategy needs to take account of informal contacts that influence (and often can contribute directly to) the quality of effort.

Establishing a cooperative way of working is not a simple matter, not least because it is necessary to do so in ways that do not reduce the discretion of individual teachers. Teaching is a complex, often unpredictable business that requires a degree of improvisation. Teachers must have sufficient autonomy to make instant decisions that take account of the individuality of their pupils and the particular qualities of every encounter. What is needed, therefore, is a well-coordinated, cooperative style of working that gives individual teachers the confidence to improvise the most appropriate responses to the situations they meet. In other words, we are seeking to create a more tightly coupled system without losing the benefits of loose coupling.

Using Inquiry and Reflection. As we have pointed out, national reforms in the education system of England and Wales have produced unprecedented pressures for change at the school level. Changes in curriculum context, processes, and assessment have been enshrined in legislation, requiring adoption at a pace that many schools feel is beyond their capacity. In addition to creating a potentially de-skilling context in which individual teachers must work, the logistics of implementing these changes has proved a severe test for even the most confident of management teams — so much so that it may seem strange to be arguing that schools should actively adopt a focus on school improvement activities at a time when many teachers are finding all their time and energies consumed in trying to assimilate the range of "unavoidable" changes currently required.

However, we have observed that those schools that recognize inquiry and reflection as important processes in school improvement find it easier to sustain an improvement effort around established priorities; and they are better placed to monitor the extent to which policies actually deliver the intended outcomes for pupils, even in these times of enormous change.

Ironically, however, we have found that information gathered by outsiders — whether inspectors or consultants — often is seen as having more significance than information that is routinely available to those within the school community. Further, we have observed that where schools understand the potential of internally generated information about progress or difficulties, they are better placed to exploit opportunities and to overcome problems.

Therefore, a major area of focus in our work with IQEA project schools has been to review the current uses of school-based data and to consider opportunities for improved future uses. Of course, in adopting this focus we are aware that it is sensible to try to work with questions that need to be answered and to use methods that are feasible and neither intrude on nor disrupt the school's patterns of activity. Within these limits, we have urged participating schools to adopt a systematic approach to information collection, analysis, and interpretation, particularly where information about the impact, rather than the implementation, of improvement programs is wanted. We also have encouraged schools to involve all staff in this information-management process. The data routinely available to staff and the sense they make of it are a potentially important aid to decision making. Where a school begins to acknowledge inquiry and reflection as forces for improvement, it is vital to ensure that there are appropriate safeguards so that confidential or sensitive information is handled properly.

Collaborative Planning. The quality of school-level planning has been identified as a major factor in many studies of school effectiveness. Such studies also have identified the nature and quality of school goals as important and collaborative planning and clear goals as key process dimensions. Our own experiences also lead us to see links between the way planning is carried forward and the school's capacity to engage in development work. However, we have noted that there is rather more to successful planning than simply producing a development plan. Indeed, often the quality of the written plan is misleading in respect to its influence. It is the link between planning and action that, in the end, justifies the effort we put into planning activities. This practical focus on the impact of planning, rather than the technical merits of different planning systems or approaches, has led us to stress a number of points when working with IQEA project schools on this condition.

The school's improvement plans need to be linked clearly to the school's vision for the future. Indeed, the notion of priorities for planning arise from the vision; and where there is a lack of congruence between the school's long-term goals and a particular initiative, it is hard to build commitment among staff. One way of tying together school and individual goals is through widespread involvement in the planning process. In some ways, involvement in planning activity is more important than producing plans. It is through collective planning that goals emerge, differences can be resolved, and a basis for action is created. The written plan is really a byproduct of this activity and will almost always need to be revised, often several times. However, the benefits of the planning activity often outlast the currency of the plan.

As we have worked with the project schools on capacity building in these areas, we have begun to observe a number of factors influencing how particular conditions can best contribute to a "moving school" ethos. As a consequence, we have begun to develop a series of propositions about the relationship between the way a school approaches a particular condition and the impact of that condition on the school's capacity for improvement. These propositions inevitably need further refinement and testing; but we believe that they hold the key to the establishment of a school culture that can meaningfully empower all teachers within the school community. These propositions are:

Creating the Conditions for School Improvement

Proposition One

Schools will not improve unless teachers, individually and collectively, develop. Teachers often can develop their practice on an individual basis; but if the whole school is to develop, then there need to be many *staff development* opportunities for teachers to learn together.

Proposition Two

Successful schools seem to have ways of working that encourage feelings of *involvement* from a number of stakeholder groups, especially students.

Proposition Three

Schools that are successful at development establish a clear vision for themselves and regard *leadership* as a function to which many staff contribute, rather than a set of responsibilities vested in a single individual.

Proposition Four

The *coordination* of activities is an important way of keeping people involved, particularly when changes of policy are being introduced. Communication within the school is an important aspect of coordination, as are the informal interactions that arise between teachers.

Proposition Five

We have observed that those schools that recognize *inquiry and reflection* as important processes in school improvement find it easier to gain clarity and establish shared meanings around identified development priorities and are better placed to monitor the extent to which policies actually deliver the intended outcomes for pupils.

Proposition Six

Our experience alongside that of colleagues in IQEA schools suggests that through the *process of planning for development*, the school is able to link its educational aspirations to identifiable priorities, sequence those priorities over time, and maintain a focus on classroom practice.

These six conditions and the related propositions have been the focus of our work with the IQEA project schools. Though we have worked on each condition initially with the school cadre group in a staff development setting, we have taken the major focus of our work to be the way a particular school addresses a particular condition in procuring its own improvement initiatives. This means, in practice, that both sequence and emphasis varies from school to school, according to their own priorities. It also means that conditions need to be addressed in combination, as it is not often that increasing the school's capacity in relation to a single condition will serve meaningful development. But, above all, it means that staff members from the school must take responsibility for leading the improvement effort within the school; the pattern of involvement and support from the IQEA team responds to the demands made by those leading the initiative with the school.

Working on the Conditions: Teachers as School and Staff Development Leaders

Implicit in the descriptions of the conditions that we feel are necessary for successful school improvement is the leadership role that teachers play in school and staff development. In order to illustrate this point, we briefly describe the experiences of some schools that are attempting to implement changes that originated in centralized policies, but that also are in line with their own vision and aspirations.

One primary school had carried out considerable development activity with respect to classroom practice. Their initiative involved the creation of learning centers in which groups of children are able to work on a range of self-directed learning tasks.

During a staff meeting, teachers discussed their anxiety about the quality of engagement that pupils sustained while they carried out tasks in the learning centers. In order to help the staff develop a clearer understanding of what these pupils were doing, the head teacher budgeted time for them to observe children at work in colleagues' classrooms. Time also was allocated for pairs of teachers to discuss their observations in order to draw implications and to plan any necessary modifications to the tasks and activities.

This story is also a particularly good example of how, when head teachers can support colleagues by allocating the most valuable resource that teachers need — time — teachers can begin to play a major role in one another's development. Organizing the school day in a way that allows colleagues to spend time together endorses their activities and creates important new opportunities for professional learning. In this instance, the teachers reported that they had learned as much about themselves and each other as they had about their pupils.

Throughout IQEA we have been struck by the importance of encouraging collaboration in schools. We see the isolation of teachers as a major barrier to improvement. At times it seems as though schools deliberately inhibit meaningful collaboration. It is an indictment of our education system that many teachers do not have the opportunity to observe other colleagues at work in the classroom.

A priority for one of the secondary schools with which we have been working was curriculum access. The term that is currently fashionable with respect to this issue is *differentiation*, meaning the ways in which teachers take account of the individual differences of their pupils in the classroom. To address this issue, task groups were established that involved a majority of the staff. Each group worked in a different curriculum area, though they used a similar action-planning format for their work. Each group appointed a coordinator, known as the "conduit." The choice of this name was to emphasize the role of these people in passing information around the system. All of this activity was coordinated by a cadre of three teachers, one of whom was the deputy head.

This initiative led to a schoolwide debate about the meaning of the term *differentiation*, and the discussions gradually began to identify the complexity of the issues involved in teaching for diversity. Issues about differentiation by task and differentiation by outcome led to heated debates. Indeed, some staff became increasingly uncomfortable about the use of the word *differentiation*, arguing that it might imply forms of teaching that could promote discrimination.

The importance of this story is to show how task groups following a common process can be used to heighten awareness about a vital issue, even in a large secondary school. However, such a strategy does have to be supported and managed if it is to bear fruit. Another dimension to this account is the way in which such a debate necessitates a search for meaning. As we have already suggested, the evolution of new policies and practices within a school requires all staff to establish a sense of personal meaning with respect to the areas to be developed. In this context, curriculum change is not seen as simply the rational implementation of a pre-specified set of ideas. Rather, it is a much more complex process whereby those involved seek to reconstruct their existing understandings and ways of working.

Two staff members of a medium-size secondary school were invited to lead an initiative looking at "pace of learning." This priority was identified as a result of an inspection of the school. Since neither teacher was a senior staff member, they initially chose to work with small groups of staff, rather than try for total staff involvement from the outset. Working with colleagues in pairs, they carried out classroom observation in order to collect data about existing practice and to develop curriculum materials and teaching strategies designed to enhance the pace of learning. Gradually, they involved more teachers in their activities; and as a result, the development work began to have an impact across the school. Time was allocated so that staff could work in one another's classrooms to support the development activities. Toward the end of the year, some of the staff who were involved in this classroom research presented some of their experiences during a staff development day for the whole staff.

This is a good example of the "think big, start small" approach to change. At various stages during the first year of this project, the two school coordinators experienced periods of doubt as to whether their work would have impact on the school as a whole. Their main concern was that, without the involvement of some senior staff, their activities would become marginalized. In fact, the success of the initiative began to draw in senior colleagues, which, in turn, brought about a significant change in the conditions in the school. Indeed, it represented a clear signal that the initiative was seen as important, validating the role played by the two leaders of the development.

Over time the coordinators and senior staff reflected on the changes in teaching styles that had occurred as a result of this work, and they recognized a number of key strategies. In our terms, the school had been successful in recognizing the need to review and adapt certain conditions to support staff in their development tasks. The provision of time to work on development as a group was a significant factor. In addition, the skills of the two coordinators in maintaining momentum and disseminating the work was important. Their decision to find ways of involving students also was recognized as a major strength in their activities. But, most important, the response of senior management was an important factor. The potential for leadership is widely distributed, but the school's management arrangements need to be able to tap this potential if it is to be harnessed.

A final example comes from a special school that was created out of the merger of two schools that were to be closed. In these circumstances, morale often is understandably low, and teachers feel helpless about the situation. The head teacher-designate of the new school was determined to draw a line under such feelings and to launch the school with a renewed sense of purpose. It was felt that this could be achieved by rejecting the familiar hierarchical structure and, instead, organizing the school around four horizontal groups or "syndicates." These syndicates assumed broad responsibility for staffing, student, curriculum, and resource issues. All staff members were elected to a syndicate.

Though syndicates are coordinated by senior members of the staff, the expected level of involvement of all staff in planning and making decisions is high. In effect, all plan and decide for each other according to the particular responsibilities of each syndicate. Even the most junior staff have a structured access to the school's highest decision-making groups, and there is no "senior management team" to reverse or modify recommendations from these groups.

After two years of operating in this way the school feels that it has established a highly collaborative culture that encourages all staff to contribute their particular knowledge and experience to the processes of organizational planning and problem solving. Though by no means perfect, the system is genuinely empowering, tapping into the creativity and the capacity for critical thinking of all staff and representing a significant move toward a transitional leadership model in which all teachers are leaders.

In each of these examples, the schools were seeking effective strategies to increase their capacity to handle change. Being prepared to invest resources and, in particular, time to support teacher development is an important lesson. It may be helpful to locate this discussion of strategies and conditions within our Framework for School Improvement, discussed earlier. The teacher development strategy chosen by the school not only links the priority to the conditions, but also has an impact on school culture and student outcomes. In the schools with which we are working, we have seen many strategies and combinations of strategies used to bring about improvement. Although it is helpful both conceptually and strategically to think of the elements of this framework as distinct, in reality they coalesce. From our work on the IQEA project, we have identified the following themes, which underpin the work of the most successful schools. Taken together, they result in the creation of opportunities for teachers to feel more powerful and confident about their work.

Teachers learning about taking responsibility for their own development. In successful schools, teachers meet together regularly to discuss aspects of their work, share ideas, plan, and help one another to solve problems. They also spend time in one another's classrooms, observing one another's practice and providing feedback on new approaches. In addition, teams of teachers might be formed to plan, implement, and evaluate experimental classroom approaches.

Living with ambiguity. The evolution of new school policies involves the consideration of alternative points of view and the clarification of the policy in use. In this way, policies come to be defined over time through social processes. Therefore, during periods of intensive development, staff members have to live with the uncertainties created by ambiguity. Successful schools seem to recognize the importance of providing support to colleagues during such periods.

Student involvement. An important factor in supporting policy creation can be the reactions of students. When they are unaware of the reasons for change, they may unintentionally act as a barrier to progress. Some of our successful IQEA schools have found ways of overcoming this problem by involving students in the change. For example, the school that is introducing resource-based learning has enrolled some students as resource center assistants.

Tying resources to development activities. As we already have argued, it is helpful if time is allocated to individuals and groups who undertake development tasks. Our experience is that even small amounts of time are seen as being enormously precious and can encourage high levels of commitment. The availability of specific development funds is seen to be equally valuable in engendering enthusiasm and facilitating innovative work.

Vision. Perhaps the most significant role for the head teacher or other senior colleagues is to nurture an overall vision for the school. In one large secondary school, for example, the head teacher occa-

197

sionally holds meetings of the entire staff during which he muses about his views on important educational ideas. Staff members report that this helps them to see their own work within a broader picture of the school's mission. Similarly, in a small primary school, teachers refer to the head teacher's habit of "thinking aloud" about policy matters as she mixes informally with the staff. Again, this seems to help individuals as they think about overall school policy.

Celebrating success. Equally important, staff members celebrate their success. For example, they may positively reinforce one another's work through informal discussion in the staff room; by collecting and displaying press cuttings about the school in the entrance hall; and, in some instances, by accrediting their classroom practice through academic awards. In these ways, they are maintaining enthusiasm and generating ownership of and clarity about the school's aims and vision.

We write from the context of an education system that is undergoing great change. Schools that are surviving with élan seem to be those that are marrying the internally generated goals and priorities with forces and opportunities that present themselves in the external environment. The combination of internal and external circumstances often produces extraordinary results. In these and many other instances where staff commitment has been very high, the outcomes secured were unusually impressive. Teachers in these successful schools are aware that different teachers take on leadership roles. Indeed, many colleagues seem prepared to take the lead at one stage or another. Leadership roles frequently arise through staff working groups, which are appointed with specific goals, a timeline, and considerable authority. In most of these schools, virtually every staff member takes part in a working group sooner or later.

We have argued that the best way for schools to survive and enhance quality in an era of change is through deliberate school improvement efforts. School improvement as a strategy for change focuses not only on the implementation of centralized policies or chosen innovations, but also on the creation of conditions within schools that can sustain the teaching and learning processes and enable teachers to take a leadership role in change. When this occurs, we not only begin to meet the real challenge of educational reform, but we also create classrooms and schools where both our children and their teachers learn.

Resources

More details of our approach to teacher and school development can be found in the following publications:

Ainscow, M., and Hopkins, D. "Aboard the Moving School." *Educational Leadership* 50 (November 1992): 79-81.

Ainscow, M.; Hopkins, D.; Southworth, G.; and West, M. *Creating the Conditions for School Improvement*. London: David Fulton Publishers, 1994.

Hargreaves, D.H., and Hopkins, D. *The Empowered School*. London: Cassell, 1991.

Hopkins, D. *A Teacher's Guide to Classroom Research*, 2nd ed. Buckingham: Open University Press, 1993.

Hopkins, D., and Ainscow, M. "Making Sense of School Improvement." *Cambridge Journal of Education* 23, no. 3 (1993): 287-304.

Hopkins, D.; Ainscow, M.; and West, M. *School Improvement in an Era of Change*. London: Cassell, 1994.

West, M., and Ainscow, M. *Managing School Development*. London: David Fulton Publishers, 1991.

TEACHER LEADERSHIP IN PROFESSIONAL DEVELOPMENT

BY PETER J. BURKE

Peter J. Burke is director of the Bureau for Teacher Education, Licensing, and Placement in the Wisconsin Department of Public Instruction.

> *"Oh Lord, when I die, I pray that it be during a teacher inservice so that the transition is gradual."*

Professional development is the term given to describe an organized approach to lifelong learning for a school staff member. Professional development often is compared to or differentiated from several other activities that have growth and change as a premise. These other activities, such as inservice education, staff development, personal development, or continuing education, all relate to a common theme of providing help to those engaged in the educative process to become better at what they are doing. This essay offers a structure for professional development that encompasses several of the other concepts, but I will use the term *professional development* as the umbrella for all of the other modes of learning involving school people, especially teachers. In addition, the leadership role of the teacher in designing and managing the development program will be emphasized.

One contrast is noteworthy: the relation of professional development to the common concept of inservice education. Inservice education is a structured learning experience scheduled by school authorities for school employees and implemented on school time. The purpose of inservice education most often is to convey a change in basic school operating procedures. This form may be only one component of professional development. Inservice education can play an integral part in the design and implementation of a long-range professional development plan, but it does not substitute for an overall plan.

The following definition will be useful to this discussion:

Professional development is an ongoing, systematic growth process for professional school employees. It is designed to improve professional performance for the benefit of students. Professional development helps all involved achieve organizational goals through the application of acquired knowledge, skills, and attitudes.

This definition focuses on the student. Students of every category − exceptional educational needs, gifted, at-risk, mainstream, economically disadvantaged, socially isolated, culturally different − are equal beneficiaries. All students are under the aegis of the schools, and professional development must be designed with all students in mind.

Organizational goals also are an important part of professional development. The goals of the district and schools should be linked to the improvement of the school system as an organization. Thus organizational development is a concurrent action with professional development. The goals of the organization are developed from state and local policy, federal requirements, immediate and long-term local needs, special interest groups, and other sources. The process of professional development is one of identifying the tensions that exist, prioritizing the needs, designing learning experiences to meet the needs, implementing and evaluating the programs, and recycling the efforts. It is essential that teachers become familiar with this structure if they are to be leaders in their own professional development.

This definition of professional development also stresses the concept of a process − an ongoing and systematic process. Professional development is not an event. Inservice education may be an event and, as such, may be one small component of the professional development process. However, the process of professional development must transcend the knowledge level of providing information and include changing or improving the attitudes, skills, and practices of the target audience.

Change is an essential ingredient of improvement. Environmental and societal conditions have created the need for education to change, and the changes that are made by our education institutions should improve teaching and learning. The purpose of education is to give every student an opportunity to become a productive, self-confident, and moral citizen. Since the characteristics of what it means to be productive, self-confident, and moral are continually changing in our society, it is essential that schools change so that all students graduating from the system gain the foundation necessary for success in the world beyond the school.

One crucial challenge that faces education today is the rapidly changing characteristics of the students who are entering the system. It is essential that educators and others involved in the schooling process not only be cognizant of the shifting demographics but have periodic opportunities to learn how to deal with the impact of these shifts. "Preparation" for the profession cannot end with entry into a teaching position. Lifelong or career-long learning to keep pace with the myriad of changes is essential.

This essay considers how to create a structure that will sustain change to guarantee student success through school improvement. At the district level, this structure begins with school board policy. Policy gives definition to the change that is to occur, but policy does not initiate the change. That comes about through planning.

In this essay, I outline a planning process that considers beliefs, mission, desired results, and policy. This outline is based on the concepts of professional and organizational development as a vehicle for achieving school improvement and sustainable change. Organizational development is a function of the planning process used to create change, with a constant reference to human resource development — in this case, professional development — as a catalyst for action.

Key ingredients in organizational development and change are the principles of adult learning. A basic assumption is that career-long learning is essential to program improvement. Also, it is essential for people to learn how to work together, how to build teams, and how to work effectively in a team to ensure that change will occur and be sustained.

These background concepts form the foundation for the development of a model for change. This model includes a planning process, a process for change, and professional development strategy. Just as policy defines change, professional development serves as the instrument whereby staff learning and practice institutionalize the change.

The Planning Process

In the literature on planning for change, concepts such as quality circles or total quality management and site-based management offer an organizational framework that is the first step in improvement. The planning process I will describe is a "thought before action" structure that has paid dividends in many settings. The four steps in this process include: 1) agreeing on beliefs, 2) defining a mission,

3) specifying desired outcomes, and 4) developing policies or action plans.

Policy must be based on the systemic beliefs of the organization. A commonly held mission will flow from these beliefs, and the mission should lead to specific outcomes that are target goals of the organization. These desired results, when codified, become the policy that gives direction to action for the organization.

Teachers and other school staff must identify and define their beliefs about the school and about their own work. Beliefs about the ability of all students to be successful, the need for an orderly learning environment, or other values are part of this process. The beliefs need specification so that the mission of the organization can be made clear.

The mission statement is an articulation of the desired results of any endeavor. In the case of the professional development plan, the mission should state what the teachers hope to accomplish in terms of the learning and growth that should occur. The mission for professional development should incorporate the needs of the students.

Once the beliefs and mission have been discussed, agreed on, and codified, the planning process should move into a specification of the desired outcomes. These outcomes, while driven by the mission, may vary widely. Also called targets or objectives, desired outcomes form the focus for the policy or action plan. Thus resulting policy statements become a way of directing future action. They form the road map, if you will. Specific events or actions will be discussed in the section on the change process.

These four elements — beliefs, mission, desired outcomes, and policies or action plans — are an important preliminary to the change process. All who are involved in the change process must act on the basis of the same assumptions and goals if order and structure are to prevail. To initiate a change process without a common set of understandings is to invite chaos and failure.

The Change Process

The change process has five phases. They are: 1) readiness, 2) planning, 3) implementation, 4) evaluation, and 5) re-visioning. These phases answer these questions:

Why do we need to change the organization?
For whom will the change be designed?
What will the policy statement or action plan be?

Who will be responsible for which components?
Where will the development take place?
When will it occur?
How will it be provided?
How will program success be measured?

Readiness. Before planning a comprehensive school improvement or program development initiative, change leaders must determine the target group's readiness for change. The readiness phase is the time to answer the question, "Why?" Part of the readiness phase of organizational change is a determination of needs for the development and alignment of these needs with the mission and goals determined in the planning process.

Needs may be assessed through a survey of the staff or may be discerned as a result of observation of performance. Policy changes may be the impetus that creates the need for professional development. Whatever the source, the needs for professional development must be established at the readiness phase to give direction to the change process.

Those involved must consider the question, "For whom?" Planners must understand the attitudes of the staff, their motivation to participate in the program, and the potential impact of the program on the school. They must communicate their vision of what the organizational change will do for the students. The staff commitment to improvement and their dedication to improved student learning are two essential considerations for readiness. The staff must be willing to change and able to envision the results of the efforts that they will put forth. These results should be defined in terms of learning gains for the students.

Contextual factors in the district also must be considered, such as financial constraints, district and building goals, staffing or curriculum trends, conflicts that might exist, external variables, policy concerns, and the basic needs or career stages of individuals involved in the process.

A final component of readiness is to study the governance aspects of the policy. People who are to be assigned to unfamiliar responsibilities need to be identified. In some cases, these people will need added preparation for their tasks. This preparation is the beginning of the professional development component.

Planning. This second planning phase is the time to determine the who, what, where, when, and how of the program. The readiness phase identified who will be involved in organizing the change and who will be responsible for the logistics. This planning phase is a time to give definition to those responsibilities. The extent of the change program is set in this planning phase.

The need for the change also was identified in the readiness phase. Planning now answers how best to meet those needs. Alternatives and "best practices" must be selected. Flexibility should be built in so that feedback from formative evaluation can be used to change direction, if warranted. While program constraints need to be analyzed, not all potential constraints can be identified in advance.

Once a direction is set, both short- and long-range goals need to be determined. The elements of effective professional development that will be discussed later — acquisition, practice, feedback, follow-up, and maintenance — may be used as planning steps in this phase, too. The knowledge, skill, or attitude to be gained should be identified; and the content of the program should be set.

A plan for guided or individual practice of new skills also should be determined at this time. Individuals responsible for the practice should be assigned, timelines for the practice should be set, and goals for successful implementation should be determined. Time and resources need consideration. And the individuals who will evaluate the activity and the criteria to be used also must be specified. These plans should be written down before starting the implementation phase.

Implementation The logistics of the implementation should have been spelled out in the planning phase. Responsibilities for consultants, space, materials, and other resources should be clear; and coordination of the activities already should have been confirmed.

The timeline prepared in the planning phase should be a constant reminder of the activities that are to take place, but there should be flexibility built into the timeline. Specific points should be established as benchmarks for successful completion of the stages of the project.

Monitoring through formative evaluation should be an ongoing part of the implementation phase. Responsibilities for review should be outlined in the plan and should provide accountability in terms of the impact on students. In other words, students should exhibit the desired knowledge, attitude, or behavior change.

Part of the allocation of resources at the implementation phase will be the dispensation of incentives for participation. The rewards for success should be visible and communicated as part of the plan.

Part of a school improvement program might be the acquisition of a new skill for improved practice. This is professional development. Acquisition of the information is followed by practice, which may be independent or guided. Evaluative feedback should occur as part of the implementation phase, and adjustments should be made based on the feedback.

Careful planning is crucial to the success of the implementation, and flexibility is essential so that planned diagnostics can be used to improve the process during the implementation phase. Keeping records of the adjustments to the process also is an important component of the implementation phase, because such records can make future plans more effective.

Evaluation. Program evaluation has three basic purposes. The first is to render judgments on the worth of a program. The second is to assist decision makers responsible for designing policy for the organization. And the third is to serve a political function, for instance, for public relations or program accountability. Two basic types of evaluation are used in any quality change process: formative and summative.

Formative evaluation, which is done during the planning and implementation phases, is used to give corrective directions to the program as it is implemented. Alternate needs, changes in resources, or other unintended outcomes could be reasons for program changes during implementation.

Summative evaluation measures the worth of a project sometime after the end of the implementation cycle and should be planned for the purpose of accountability and to measure the success of the venture.

Both formative and summative evaluation should take advantage of several data sources. For example, participant reaction data can provide value statements about the activities. Anecdotal records can be analyzed to determine program value. Observers can record evaluation data for later analysis. And the impact on the students can be quantified.

The evaluation should be closely aligned to the goals. Results of the evaluation will be important if a second cycle of the project is to be planned. For this reason, the evaluation design should be explicit in the planning phase.

Likewise, responsibility for analyzing the data should be assigned early in the process, and methods of interpretation should be specified. Analysis and appraisal should be completed with the final report in mind. Program evaluation should be more than a checklist administered at the end of a program cycle.

Re-Visioning. One reason for evaluation is to help policy makers judge the worth of the program created through policy and to move forward to newer and stronger programs based on the experience. The results of program evaluation are essential to measure value and to restructure or "re-vision" the organization to future purposes. This might mean a return to the original beliefs and mission that were agreed on at the beginning of the development cycle. Or it might mean a renewal of purpose based on a revised mission statement. It also might mean a redeployment of agency resources, both human and fiscal, to make the completion of desired results more effective or efficient.

The re-visioning phase of the cycle gives energy to starting the process again. People in organizations learn from their experiences, and the result of this learning should be program advancement and improvement. The result of re-visioning could be new or amended policy that would move the program back on track if it has been de-railed for any reason, or it could strengthen an already valuable and effective program. Continued improvement should be the result of re-visioning.

Professional Development Strategy

In this section I describe a strategy for professional development. This delivery model has five elements: acquisition, practice, feed-back, follow-up, and maintenance. Teachers who take the lead in the design of professional development programs must be conver-sant with these elements. These elements will ensure that the acquired new skill or knowledge is actualized in the classroom.

Several sample topics are current today, for example, the full in-clusion of special needs students, instructional modifications for chil-dren at risk, preparing students for the technological world, working with gifted students, or understanding the world of work. These are just a few examples. As society continues to change, more topics will be added to this list.

Following is an explanation of each of the elements, beginning with a definition of each term and followed by a discussion of the ele-ment in the context of professional development.

Acquisition is the act of gaining a characteristic, trait, or ability. The acquisition of knowledge often is the basic goal of inservice edu-cation. Professional development has an expanded concern for ac-quisition. Acquisition for professional development includes acquired knowledge that is embedded in an intellectual understanding and ownership of the new information, new skill, or changed attitude. In addition to new information, acquisition also may deal with review, change of focus, or revitalization of a current skill.

Each professional development program focuses on a topic, theme, or series of subjects. Acquisition of an attitude, skill, or knowledge leads to improved performance. At this stage of the professional development process, the trait to be exhibited must be isolated, identified, transferred to the participants, and understood by the members of the learning group.

Practice is actual performance or application. In practice, the new technique or behavior is modeled for the participants; then the participants try out the new skills through guided and independent experiences. The key to practice is the individual experience, including trial-and-error practice and careful mentoring by a colleague.

Once participants in a professional development exercise have acquired a new technique, it is essential that some practice be a planned part of the program. Without hands-on experience, the anticipated benefits of the change will never be operational for the students.

Feedback is the return to the input of a part of the output of a process or system. If the practice in the new technique is a guided practice, the colleague working with the participant should provide information on the success or failure of the attempt. This information is the feedback on which corrective measures can be based. Feedback is a type of formative evaluation that helps participants to study the results of practice and to decide what works, what does not work, and what needs to be changed.

Certain benchmarks should be set for the practice so that performance can be measured against these benchmarks. Feedback may come from an individual colleague or from a support group of peers who may be working on the same skill. Feedback also may be self-directed. Through reflection, an individual can view one's own practice and determine to improve based on this self-evaluation.

Follow-up means to strengthen by additional assistance or support. Based on evaluation and reflection, follow-up might include restructuring practice to improve skill application. It also might include new or expanded skill acquisition so that the improvement can be made.

Follow-up often can provide for long-range goal setting that may give further direction to the overall professional development plan.

Maintenance means to preserve from failure or decline. The operational effect of feedback should be to maintain and enhance the new skill or knowledge. This is a stage of continued practice, either independent or with the help of colleagues or support groups. The continual involvement of others in the reinforcement process also provides a form of quality control.

One aspect of maintenance that helps strengthen a skill is to teach others that skill. Mentoring or peer tutoring can help both the new learner and the trainer.

Conclusion

As stated previously, professional development should be embedded in the larger context of organizational development. Teachers must direct and participate in all stages of the planning process and the change process.

The policy or action plan is the road map for the program. The change process, with its stages of readiness, planning, implementation, evaluation, and re-visioning, maps the specific steps along the path of the action plan. The elements of the professional development strategy are useful stepping stones.

Teacher leaders who travel the path of designing professional development programs need to begin by considering their own needs. Concepts of adult learning, theories of teacher career stages, and knowledge of team building and interaction are all valuable tools. These skills form the rubric for making decisions at each step of the process. The larger aim is to create and sustain change for the purpose of improvement in school districts.

EXPANDING OPPORTUNITIES
FOR TEACHER LEADERSHIP

BY RALPH FESSLER
AND ANTOINETTE UNGARETTI

Ralph Fessler is a professor and director of the Division of Education at Johns Hopkins University. Antoinette Ungaretti is an assistant professor and chair of the Department of Teacher Development and Leadership in the Division of Education at Johns Hopkins University.

Meaningful school reform will not occur until teachers are recognized as full partners in leading, defining, and implementing school improvement efforts. Too often, school change processes and reforms are designed by education policy makers and administrators who view teachers as pawns in the system who must be moved to predetermined positions and roles to achieve externally defined goals. While the disequilibrium created by this top-down view of leadership and change may have some short-term effects, over the long haul sustained change cannot be accomplished without tapping the rich reservoir of leadership residing at the grassroots of every school — classroom teachers.

A problem inherent to the teaching profession is the tendency for teachers to "top out" or "plateau" in job mobility almost as soon as they enter the classroom. Except for a few school districts that have experimented with career ladders and lattices, teachers have limited career options. A teacher who desires the challenges of leadership, mobility, and expanded responsibility often is forced to leave teaching, either by exiting education completely or by opting for such non-classroom education roles as administration, supervision, or counseling. Many teachers who remain in the classroom are forced to repress their leadership needs.

Our best and most creative teachers should not be forced to leave the classroom in order to search for outlets for their leadership abilities. Numerous opportunities for leadership reside within the role of teaching, and these must be reinforced and nurtured. Teachers must be empowered with the knowledge and skills to serve in leadership roles and given the opportunity to lead from the role of teacher expert. Examples of potential school improvement leadership roles for teachers include designing and conducting inservice sessions, engaging in peer-coaching activities, serving as mentors for new teachers, actively participating in training prospective teachers, writing and refining curricula, actively participating in school-based management teams, conducting action research, serving as systemic change agents, creating professional growth plans, creating partnerships between the school and the community, and in all of these activities, serving as role models and advocates for systemic change and school improvement.

Two recent developments have provided a supportive climate for expanded teacher leadership opportunities: the emergence of professional development school (PDS) partnerships between universities and K-12 schools and the movement toward school-based management and decision making.

While specific PDS models vary greatly, the basic premise behind this movement has been the simultaneous renewal of teacher education and K-12 programs. Rather than the traditional fragmented approach of tinkering with individual components of school and teacher education reform, the boldest professional development schools are attempting a systemic approach to change that acknowledges the interdependence of university-based and school-based programs. Teacher interns are placed in PDS settings for intensive, long-term internships under the guidance of expert mentor teachers. University faculty work closely with these partnership schools in supporting internship experiences, leading school-based education courses and seminars for interns and experienced teachers, actively participating in school improvement teams, and engaging in applied research activities that address classroom and school problems and issues.

In addition to serving as mentors to teacher interns, experienced expert teachers share their expertise in school-based university courses and seminars, provide leadership on school improvement teams, and play key roles in applied research activities. The PDS is viewed as an active community of learners that includes students, interns, novice and experienced teachers, administrators and other school personnel, and university faculty. Examples of PDS's that include many of these characteristics are described in Linda Darling-Hammond's recent book of PDS case studies (1994). In addition, the state of Maryland is proposing a redesign of teacher education programs that includes the PDS as a major component (Maryland Higher Education Commission 1992).

In recent years there have been numerous attempts to "restructure" schools to make them more responsive to changing needs. Several models have called for various forms of "school-based management," a term used to describe efforts to transfer resources and decision making from the central office to schools (Guthrie 1986). The assumption underlying this concept is that people who share in responsibilities and decisions will believe in what they are doing and will work more effectively toward common goals. This concept also testifies to the expertise of teachers and the need to put such talent to use in planning. Examples include restructuring efforts in Chicago, Miami, Buffalo, Louisville, Denver, Los Angeles, Philadelphia, Rochester, and Baltimore.

The success of school-based management (also known as "site-based management" or "collaborative decision making") is determined by the relationship between principals and their teachers, on the willingness of teachers to take responsibility for directing their own behavior, and on the amount of time teachers are willing to devote to working out problems and reaching consensus (Brandt 1989; Cawelti 1989; and Powell 1991). Approaches to school-based management are compatible with the notion of teacher leadership. In order to implement school-based management programs, it is essential to share with teachers the decision making and leadership related to teacher development and curriculum that traditionally have been the responsibility of central office personnel and principals. Issues related to the concern that teachers are ill-equipped for shared leadership (Diegmueller 1990; Elsberg 1991) can be addressed in teacher leadership preparation approaches suggested in this essay.

The recent interest in professional development schools and in site-based management provide a supportive climate for expanded teacher leadership opportunities. In the following sections, a model describing expanded teacher role options is presented, followed by suggestions for supporting teacher leadership roles.

Teacher Leadership Options

Teacher leadership can take many forms. Following are some leadership options. This is not meant to be an all-inclusive list, nor are the options mutually exclusive. Indeed, there is much overlap between categories. The key here is that teachers should be given the opportunity to experience leadership roles without being forced to leave the classroom permanently. Support for this approach may require some scheduling and role modification, and more will be said about this later in this essay.

Teacher as Preservice Teacher Educator. The emergence of Professional Development Schools as a vehicle for redesigning teacher education appears to offer new opportunities for teacher leadership in a variety of areas, including preservice teacher education. While specific PDS designs vary greatly, common features call for experienced teachers to serve as mentors for preservice teacher interns, to share expertise in seminars and education courses, and to play pivotal roles in blending theory and practice. The PDS often is compared to a teaching hospital, where state-of-the-art methods and research are modeled and skilled clinical faculty play key roles in mentoring and assessing the performance of future practitioners.

The potential for teacher leadership in preservice teacher education is expanding beyond the traditional role of supervision of student teachers. Whether as part of PDS partnerships or more traditional practicum designs, classroom teachers increasingly are becoming involved in methods classes as well as in hosting practicum experiences in their classrooms. They are in a unique position to apply theory to practice as teachers, mentors, and role models.

Partnerships with universities can lead to designing structures that provide leadership opportunities for teachers as well as for improving teacher education. The concept of the "clinical professorship" is not new but has taken on a fresh perspective in light of recent calls for reform of education and teacher education (Holmes Group 1986; Carnegie Forum on Education and the Economy 1986). Collaborative partnerships provide teachers and university professors with a unique vehicle to bridge theory and practice. They can establish a community of learners who model the melding of varied perspectives to more effectively address preservice teacher development and student achievement. Similarly, within site-based management teams, experienced teachers integrate their classroom experience with a more global understanding of school issues to bring a unique perspective to the future professional needs of preservice teachers. Teachers working in partnership with universities also provide outlets for leadership in such areas as mentoring, teacher-led inservice and staff development, and teacher research.

Teacher as Mentor of New Teachers. Experienced teachers have a key role to play in supporting the needs of beginning teachers. Mentor teachers can provide novices with guidance and structure in the context of a trusting relationship. Specific activities can include assisting new teachers in "learning the ropes" regarding school and system policies, practices, and politics, as well as assisting with specific classroom management and instructional needs. When school systems provide adequate mentor training, time, and financial resources, the teacher-as-mentor model provides an effective system for inducting new teachers into the profession.

The PDS model provides a structure for teachers to participate in the creation of a continuum for teacher preparation, induction, and continued development. This model can provide a framework in which veteran teachers can use their talents and vantage points to acclimate new teachers to the varied demands and opportunities available within the profession and to assist them in establishing and monitoring professional growth. It can establish a community of learners with an emphasis on a collegial, rather than a hierarchical, professional support system.

As members of site-based management teams, experienced teachers also have the opportunity to use their expertise in the development, implementation, and evaluation of effective induction experiences and systems. Within the site-based management framework, teachers gain ownership of both the content and the results of new teacher mentoring and induction approaches.

Teacher as Researcher. Teachers work in a living laboratory. They constantly are faced with decisions between alternative courses of action. The teacher-researcher accepts the challenge of applying the questions of applied social science to everyday problems and decisions. Activities include observing problems that emerge in everyday classroom situations, gathering data about the problems and alternative solutions, formulating hypotheses about potential solutions, gathering data to test and retest the hypotheses, drawing tentative conclusions, and suggesting and evaluating courses of action. A research orientation to teaching and learning raises the potential for continuous teacher renewal and school improvement.

In addition, a teacher-as-researcher approach could provide the basis for collaborative field-based research between schools and universities. The teacher researcher with a thorough knowledge of the classroom could be in a position to identify significant issues and questions to be examined. This orientation enables teachers to become both consumers and producers of research.

Once again, the PDS model could provide the framework for a continuing dialogue between classroom teachers and university faculty. The opportunity to establish collegial relationships when teachers and professors engage in collaborative work can lead to the identification of research agendas of mutual concern.

The site-based management model provides experienced teachers with the opportunity to provide data necessary for team members to be informed decision makers. It also serves as a vehicle for teachers to interject classroom perspectives into the formulation of issues to be addressed by the management team.

Teacher as Organizational Leader. Opportunities for leadership in professional associations provide an excellent outlet for teachers' need for satisfaction by providing recognition for their expertise and leadership. Moreover, professional organizations would benefit from the perspectives of large numbers of classroom teachers. Opportunities such as these should be encouraged by school systems, and support should be provided in the form of release time and financial assistance for travel. The PDS model could provide effective substitute teachers without increasing the financial burden for the school system.

Teacher as Staff Developer. Teacher-led staff development often is the most effective format for school-based inservice activities (Howey et al. 1981). Teacher leadership can include working with peers to identify school and individual teacher growth needs, identifying available resources to assist in meeting those needs, and when appropriate, delivering the inservice or professional growth activity.

There is a great deal of talent in the ranks of teachers, but too often this talent goes unrecognized and unrewarded. Teacher leadership in staff development activities provides opportunities for talented teachers to share their expertise with others and to gain well-deserved recognition (Marks 1983). In addition, site-based management, which incorporates expert teachers as leaders in staff development, creates a mechanism for teachers to develop pride and ownership in the professional development of their colleagues.

Teacher as Peer Coach. The role of the teacher as peer coach is to provide assistance to other teachers in the context of a supportive, helping relationship (Joyce and Showers 1982). A peer-coaching model can serve to resolve a dilemma often faced by principals: the conflict between their responsibilities for personnel evaluation and staff development. Principals are expected to represent the interests of the school system in evaluating teachers for purposes of contract renewal, tenure, and related personnel matters. In order to fulfill the staff development function, it is necessary for principals to build trust with faculty. Teachers must have confidence that the supervisor is there to help, not to "snoopervise."

Some principals possess the management and interpersonal skills to effectively play both the evaluation and staff development roles, but that is a rare combination. An alternative approach is to separate the functions, with the principal maintaining responsibility for management and the teachers working with their peers to support teacher development. PDS and site-based management teams create structures that provide opportunities for teachers to engage in peer-coaching activities as part of their professional responsibility.

Teacher as Curriculum Developer. Teachers have an important role to play as curriculum developers. Participation in curriculum writing workshops can tap their expertise and experience during the process of developing new curriculum materials. Within school-based management models, teams may rely on the teacher expertise available within their individual schools. Moreover, within the PDS model, experienced teachers engage in research activities and inquiry that can direct and evaluate curriculum development.

Not only is the product likely to be better if teachers are directly involved in this process, but the probability of implementation also is greatly enhanced. Teachers who have an investment in curriculum writing are more likely to use the products of their efforts and to encourage their peers to do so. Furthermore, teachers involved in management teams are positioned to address curriculum needs from the dual perspective of the classroom and the school.

Other Leadership Activities. Additional leadership opportunities may emerge as teachers consult with school system personnel, community leaders, and university faculty regarding classroom learning and student achievement. For example, teachers may serve as models for and coaches of university professors who re-enter the classroom to refresh and enhance their instructional skills; they might help prepare their peers, parents, or community leaders for reform efforts; or they might become leaders in site-based management initiatives.

The PDS model can serve as an effective vehicle for nurturing teacher leaders. In addition to the specific leadership roles mentioned earlier, the PDS can provide a framework for what Senge (1990) calls a "learning organization," where all participants constantly engage in processing new information, re-examining assumptions, and adapting practices to meet the needs of the organization. If the PDS is successful in building and maintaining such an open and dynamic climate, there will be many opportunities for teachers to assume leadership roles.

Organizational Support

The key to implementing a teacher leadership model is an organizational commitment to empowering teachers for leadership opportunities. While some implementation problems exist, an organization with a commitment to this approach can identify reasonable solutions. Following are some suggested strategies.

Empowering Teachers Through Training and Development. School systems should encourage teachers to develop the expertise necessary to assume leadership roles. This includes identifying teachers with interest and potential for leadership and providing them with the necessary support and training. Alternatives include university coursework, self-study, conferences, workshops, and perhaps most important, opportunities to try new ideas. Partnerships between school systems, universities, and communities can provide effective vehicles for empowering teachers through training and development.

A master's degree program to support teacher leadership has been established at Johns Hopkins University. This program is designed to prepare teachers for leadership roles in school improvement and in optimizing student learning. Throughout the program, course assignments provide opportunities to apply theory, concepts, and strategies to classroom and school settings.

Common themes that are integrated across all courses in the program include career-long professional development, the systemic change process, the design and evaluation of supportive environments for diverse student populations, classroom and school-based research, multicultural education, values, school and community relations, group dynamics, problem synthesis approach, and advanced instructional strategies. Within this program, teachers view themselves as change agents and social scientists who are responsible for continually examining, enhancing, and disseminating the knowledge base in teaching and learning.

In addition, partnership master's degree programs have been established between Johns Hopkins and local school systems to address specific leadership needs. An example of this is the Teacher Leadership Program established in partnership with Howard County Public Schools. This is a customized program that prepares teachers for leadership roles in school improvement efforts and incorporates the competencies reflected in the job descriptions for team teachers and department heads.

Another example is a Mathematics and Science Elementary Education Master's Degree Program developed collaboratively between

Johns Hopkins and the Montgomery County Public Schools. This program has been designed to enhance the mathematics and science background of elementary school teachers and to prepare them for future leadership roles in the school system. The program begins with the integrated study of advanced instructional strategies and the role of teacher as researcher. This framework serves as the foundation for integrated courses in content and advanced instructional strategies. Woven throughout the program are the themes of systemic change, reflective practice, effective human relations practices, presentation skills, and working with diverse student populations. Within this unique partnership, students create and implement staff-development experiences that meet school system needs.

With a similar purpose but addressing a different point in the teacher career cycle, Johns Hopkins has infused elements of teacher leadership in its Master of Arts in Teaching Program for preservice teachers. In this program, preservice teachers examine the teacher career cycle (Fessler and Christensen 1992), explore systemic change, conduct field-based research, and engage in reflective practice. From the beginning of their preparation, preservice teachers learn to assume professional responsibility for the students in their classes, for the wider school community, for their school system, and for their profession.

One caution noted in the literature concerning the preparation or encouragement of teacher leaders is the need to provide genuine outlets for the talents that are nurtured in this process (Smylie and Denny 1990; Wasley 1991; Wilson 1993). Teacher leaders need to become valued members of the school reform process if education is to benefit from their development. The establishment of partnerships that develop teacher leaders and create opportunities for them to use their talents in school reform efforts institutionalize the value of the teacher leader.

Team Teaching. Team teaching options provide opportunities for teachers to work and plan together in ways that maximize individual strengths. Open communication, planning, and cooperation are essential to effective teaching teams. The climate created by such activities may facilitate natural outlets for teacher leadership opportunities in such areas as curriculum development, peer coaching, and mentoring.

While team teaching traditionally takes the form of teacher-teacher collaboration, alternative models are emerging in the context of school-university partnerships. For example, mentor teachers and preservice interns may engage in teaming activities. Instructional teams may be enlarged to include university faculty and peer coaches for teachers and interns. The dynamics of these and similar configurations provide opportunities for teachers to experience natural leadership outlets for peer coaching, mentoring, action research, and new curriculum directions.

Career Ladders, Lattices, and Stages. A key feature of career ladders is the differentiation of teacher roles to provide opportunities for teacher leadership. Numerous examples appeared in the 1950s and 1960s (Christensen 1987) and have surfaced again in recent years (Jandura and Burke 1989). Such models provide for differentiated roles for teachers as they move up a ladder of responsibility and leadership. A fresh approach offered by Christensen, McDonnell, and Price (1988) advocates a "career lattice," which differentiates roles for specific activities and projects without committing to a one-directional "up-the-ladder" concept. Similarly, Huberman's (1993) models of teacher career trajectories present a series of options or paths that take the teacher in a variety of directions.

Building on previous models and their own research, Fessler and Christensen propose a Teacher Career Cycle model that "progresses through stages not in a lock-step, linear fashion, but rather in a dynamic manner reflecting responses to the personal and organizational environmental factors" (1992, p. 35). In this model, teachers move in and out of stages in response to environmental influences from personal and organizational dimensions. Supportive conditions for a variety of options can assist the teacher in experiencing a rewarding career progression. Such approaches provide specific strategies for empowering teachers for leadership.

Modest adaptations of role structures that provide opportunities for teacher leadership include the creation of such positions as team leaders, grade-level leaders, and chairs of staff development committees.

Flexible Employment Patterns. The notion of flexibility in employment patterns offers additional support for teacher leadership opportunities. One example of this would be summer curriculum writing teams, where teachers engage in planning and writing curricula that they will be using. Other examples include teacher internships in leadership positions and sabbaticals to enable teachers to gain new leadership skills.

One rather innovative option that deserves special mention is the temporary assignment of teachers to work as resource specialists in teacher centers. Both the Howard County Teacher Center in Maryland and the Regional Staff Development Center in Kenosha, Wisconsin, have used this approach. Teachers are "loaned" to the center to work with other teachers in curriculum and instruction improvement projects. After a specified period of time (one or two years) these individuals return to their schools, where their roles as teacher leaders continue.

Partnerships such as teacher leadership programs and professional development schools provide an opportunity for teachers to connect to university teacher education programs. Within such programs, teachers can become clinical faculty members who bring a valuable perspective to classroom and field instruction. Such affiliations also give universities the opportunity to discover and employ the talents of classroom teachers and to offer them adjunct positions. The professional development school can provide flexibility for the teacher to engage in professional activities beyond the classroom.

Summary

Providing teachers with leadership opportunities supports such current reform activities as professional development schools, school-based management, school-university partnerships, and teacher empowerment.

Teachers are in a position to provide leadership in such areas as preservice teacher education, mentoring, research, professional organizations, staff development and inservice, peer coaching, and curriculum development. Empowering teachers for such leadership roles provides outlets for teachers' needs for satisfaction and brings valuable expertise to the problems of school improvement.

The ideas presented in this essay are offered as a challenge to school and university-based educators. Effective leaders should use all of the resources at their disposal to enhance teaching and learning in their schools. Empowering teachers for school leadership will increase the potential for school improvement.

References

Brandt, Ron. "On Teacher Empowerment: A Conversation with Ann Lieberman." *Educational Leadership* 46 (May 1989): 23-26.

Carnegie Forum on Education and the Economy. *A Nation Prepared: Teachers for the 21st Century.* Washington, D.C., 1986.

Cawelti, Gordon. "Key Elements of Site-Based Management." *Educational Leadership* 46 (May 1989): 46.

Christensen, J.C. "Roles of Teachers and Administrators." In *Establishing Career Ladders in Teaching*, edited by P. Burden. Springfield, Ill.: Charles C. Thomas, 1987.

Christensen, J.C.; McDonnell, J.H.; and Price, J.R. *Personalizing Staff Development: The Career Lattice Model.* Fastback 281. Bloomington, Ind.: Phi Delta Kappa Educational Foundation, 1988.

Darling-Hammond, Linda, ed. *Professional Development Schools: Schools for Developing a Profession.* New York: Teachers College Press, 1994.

Diegmueller, Karen. "Report Raps Shared-Decisionmaking Efforts in Los Angeles." *Education Week*, 21 November 1990, p. 5.

Elsberg, Ted. "Dade County, Florida: Three Years Later." *Education Week*, 3 April 1991.

Fessler R., and Christensen, J.C. *The Teacher Career Cycle.* Boston: Allyn and Bacon, 1992.

Guthrie, J.W. "School-Based Management: The Next Needed Education Reform." *Phi Delta Kappan* 68 (December 1986): 305-309.

Holmes Group. *Tomorrow's Teachers: A Report of the Holmes Group.* East Lansing, Mich., 1986.

Howey, K.R.; Bents, R.; and Corrigan, D., eds. *School-Focused Inservice: Descriptions and Discussions.* Reston, Va.: Association of Teacher Educators, 1981.

Huberman, M. *The Lives of Teachers.* New York: Teachers College Press, 1993.

Jandura, R., and Burke, P. *Differentiated Career Opportunities for Teachers.* Fastback 287. Bloomington, Ind.: Phi Delta Kappa Educational Foundation, 1989.

Joyce, B., and Showers, B. "The Coaching of Teaching." *Educational Leadership* 40 (October 1982): 4-8, 10.

Marks, M.B. "Teacher Leadership in Staff Development." *Educational Research Quarterly* 7, no. 4 (1983): 2-5.

Maryland Higher Education Commission. *Report and Recommendations of the Teacher Education Task Force.* Annapolis, 1992.

Powell, Neal J. "School-Based Management in Smaller Secondary Schools." *NASSP Bulletin* 75 (March 1991): 11-15.

Senge, P.M. *The Fifth Discipline: The Art and Practice of the Learning Organization.* New York: Doubleday Currency, 1990.

Smylie, M.A., and Denny, J.W. "Teacher Leadership: Tensions and Ambiguities in Organizational Perspective." *Educational Administrative Quarterly* 26, no. 3 (1990): 235-59.

Wasley, P.A. *Teachers Who Lead: The Rhetoric of Reform and the Realities of Practice.* New York: Teachers College Press, 1991.

Wilson, M. "The Search for Teacher Leaders." *Educational Leadership* 50 (March 1993): 24

THE DEVELOPMENT AND
SUSTENANCE OF
INSTRUCTIONAL LEADERSHIP

BY SAM J. YARGER
AND OKHEE LEE

*Sam J. Yarger is a professor and dean of the School of Education
at the University of Miami in Coral Gables, Florida. Okhee Lee is
an assistant professor of education at the University of Miami. Lee
would like to acknowledge the support of the National Academy of
Education and the Spencer Fellowship Program.*

Consider the cases of three teachers who completed an extensive
professional development program in mathematics or science education in elementary schools.[1]

Joanne had a pleasant personality and often volunteered or was
designated by others in the program as a spokesperson and class leader. She loved teaching mathematics and was particularly good at integrating mathematics with other subject areas. Joanne occasionally
had conducted workshops on mathematics education for her colleagues
at her school. When the school district asked the project directors
to recommend several teachers who could provide districtwide workshops for elementary school teachers in mathematics education, Joanne
was one of them. The district mathematics supervisors valued her
work and offered her the position as a districtwide resource teacher
in elementary mathematics education. Working as a pair with another teacher from the same staff development program, Joanne loved
her work with teachers at the district level.

Jim was outgoing and full of energy, but he sometimes got in trouble
by expressing opinions and ideas different from the other teachers
in the program. He had held several different jobs before entering
teaching. Although suspicious of the education system in general,
he was devoted to children and cared about the school in which he
worked. He had been working as a union leader at his school for
several years. Near the end of the staff development program, he
became mathematics chairperson and oversaw issues of curriculum

and instruction in mathematics education. While teaching full time, he served as mathematics chairperson and union representative at the school.

Maria was a petite, rather reserved Hispanic teacher with a specialization in science. She had been one of a few key teachers at her school who had been organizing schoolwide programs for parents, predominantly low-socioeconomic Hispanics. Maria loved teaching children and did not want to move to other positions that did not involve teaching children. When the new principal asked Maria to be in charge of schoolwide programs for parents and teachers, she was torn between her desire to stay in the classroom and her commitment to parents and teachers at the school. She finally accepted the position and enjoyed her new assignment as an instructional leader at her school.

These three teachers were experienced and already held master's degrees in education. They sought opportunities for professional growth and career enhancement. They were among 22 elementary school teachers who enrolled in a professional development program that emphasized content, pedagogy, and instructional leadership in mathematics and science education for elementary schools. After completing the two-year program, the teachers were awarded a Specialist Degree in Education. These teachers currently are providing instructional leadership at their schools and school districts. However, their leadership roles differ for various reasons, including their backgrounds, personal characteristics, the schools they work in, and other factors.

What makes some teachers stand out as instructional leaders? What qualities are prerequisites to assuming leadership roles? What kinds of leadership training and experiences should be provided to develop their potential? Once teachers assume leadership roles, what should be done to support and maintain them in their new positions? These are the questions we will address in this essay.

Teacher Leadership and Education Reform

The topic of teachers as instructional leaders is not new but has become a key initiative in education reform. A number of programs focus specifically on promoting the instructional leadership of teachers. Many of these programs are supported from a variety of funding agencies; few are a regular "line item" in a school-district budget. This is an important point, because if teacher leadership roles are to be sustained and embedded in the structure of our education system, they must have regular, ongoing support.

An example is the Institute for Teacher Leadership, one part of the Puget Sound Educational Consortium, which is a school/university partnership between the University of Washington and 12 Seattle-area school districts.[2] This program began with a group of teachers working on action research to examine dimensions of teacher leadership and has expanded into other teacher-related activities, including publications and grant writing.

Another example is a program for the creation of instructional teacher leaders, a component of the Professionalism and Education Partnership in the school district of Pittsburgh, Pennsylvania.[3] Selected by a committee composed of teachers, principals, and district administrators, instructional leaders among the faculty are involved in making decisions about instruction, curriculum, assessment, and peer reviews at their schools.

Instructional leadership also is emphasized in intensive professional development programs in content areas. An example is the Educational Specialist Degree Program in mathematics and science education in elementary schools mentioned at the beginning of this essay. Other nationally recognized subject-matter collaboratives include the Urban Mathematics Collaboratives and the National Writing Project, both of which have established communities of experts and teachers from universities, schools, and the private sector.[4]

Some funding agencies require teachers to be trained as instructional leaders as part of a professional development program grant. The Teacher Enhancement Program at the National Science Foundation, for example, emphasizes not only the enhancement of participating teachers' knowledge of content and pedagogy, but also the ripple effects for other teachers who come in contact with program participants. The more prestigious the professional development program is, the more likely that participants will be pressured to take on instructional leadership roles when they return to their schools.[5]

The programs on instructional leadership and professional development mentioned above emphasize various approaches to education reform. Some respond to education reform initiatives within individual school districts. Others respond to particular education reform agendas advocated by external agencies. As a case in point, the three teachers at the start of this essay come from an extensive professional development program funded by the U.S. Department of Education's National Eisenhower Mathematics and Science Program, which advocates for teacher education reforms in mathematics and science.[6]

The limited professional literature on development programs describes at length the success stories of teacher enhancement in terms of content, instruction, and assessment. But this literature tends to provide idealized descriptions of instructional leadership roles by participant teachers. Indeed, there are many claims of what teachers can accomplish for themselves and for their colleagues. What is described less often is how to prepare potential teachers for leadership roles in the first place and how to sustain their roles. But before we address these issues, we need to define what we mean by instructional leadership.

Teacher Leadership Explained

There seems to be general agreement that the role of teachers as instructional leaders should be distinguished from the administrative behavior expected of principals.[7] While principals, by necessity, are concerned with the managerial issues of schools (budget, safety, personnel, etc.), teacher leaders tend to focus on issues of curriculum, instruction, and assessment. Teachers also are both more willing and more often permitted to participate in decisions about curriculum and instruction than about administrative matters.[8]

The emergence of teachers as instructional leaders has historical roots. Leadership traditionally has been perceived to reside with district or school administrators, where power flowed downward to the teachers. But that notion was challenged in the 1970s by Teacher Corps, a federally funded program that developed the notion of practicing teachers as "team leaders."[9] The Teacher Centers program, also federally funded, carried the idea of teacher leadership further in the early 1980s with the then-radical notion that teachers should be empowered to make decisions about and operate programs for their own professional development.[10] Subsequently, the education reform of the 1980s advocated viewing teaching as a profession and broader involvement of teachers in making decisions. These programs or movements sought to improve the quality of teaching by identifying exemplary teachers to serve as models for their peers.

The concept of teachers as instructional leaders has changed during the past 20 years.[11] Initial efforts focused on attracting and retaining high-quality teachers. The major issues involved the development of criteria for high-quality teachers, guidelines for their roles and responsibilities (usually developed by the state or the district), and incentive pay programs such as merit pay or career ladders. With distinctions such as "mentor teacher," "lead teacher," or "master teacher," a few selected teachers enjoyed recognition and tangible rewards. These efforts were never popular with teachers for various political reasons, and the *tangible* rewards were usually modest.

Currently, the emphasis appears to be on promoting the professionalization of all teachers. Major issues to be addressed include how to promote collegiality and thus the collaboration of teachers with teacher leaders, how to implement leadership activities in response to different needs of teachers in different contexts, and how to disseminate teacher-generated knowledge to the teaching profession and scholarly communities. It is still too early to assess the success, if any, of these current efforts.

Who is an instructional leader? Following are three definitions. First, based on interviews with a group of high school teachers who were recognized as teacher leaders by their colleagues, Wilson defined teacher leaders as: 1) risk takers and seekers of challenge and growth, 2) collaborators with and supporters of colleagues, and 3) role models for students and teachers.[12]

Rallis provided another definition, generated by curriculum coordinators from several school districts:

> An instructional leader is someone who speaks for teachers, establishes the direction of instruction, knows and interprets research findings, demonstrates and explains "best" practices, takes risks in instruction, works well with and supports teachers, encourages sharing, spreads a sense of where the school is headed instructionally, and helps teachers assess and evaluate their impact.[13]

Berry and Ginsberg offered another perspective:

> Lead teachers should be proficient classroom teachers. They should possess solid knowledge of subject matter, an understanding of child development and learning theory, an array of organizational and interpersonal skills, the ability to communicate effectively, and an understanding of public schooling in general and of their school in particular.[14]

Although different terms are used and different aspects of teacher leaders are emphasized, these definitions highlight some core components of teacher leadership. These components include: 1) commitment to classroom teaching and role-modeling for students and teachers; 2) expertise in subject matter and pedagogy; 3) specific personality characteristics, especially risk-taking; 4) well-developed

227

interpersonal skills for effective communication, collaboration, and support of colleagues; and 5) understanding of the contexts and the policies of the school and the school district.

Model of Teacher Leadership

Once a definition of teacher leadership is advanced, it becomes easier to discuss the three key issues in this essay: 1) how to identify potentially effective teacher leaders, 2) how to develop their potential for instructional leadership, and 3) how to sustain the teacher leader and the necessary environment for success. In order to discuss these issues, we propose a model of teacher leadership that consists of three clusters: personal characteristics, interpersonal skills, and institutional factors embedded in the school and district context. These clusters exist within the larger political, economic, and socio-cultural contexts of society.

Personal Characteristics. The most important factors for teacher leadership reside within the teachers themselves. Teacher leaders are, first, excellent teachers and role models for their students. But they also must serve as leaders for other teachers. The personal characteristics that define a teacher, while important, will not be possessed by each and every teacher leader at the same level. The more of these characteristics that are present, the more likely that the teacher leader will be successful. These characteristics include:

- High levels of expertise in subject matter and pedagogy.
- Willingness to take risks.
- Willingness to be responsible for one's own actions.
- Cognitive and affective flexibility.
- Sensitivity and receptivity to the thoughts and feelings of others.
- Persistence and patience.
- Orientation toward working with adults.
- Commitment to continuing professional growth.

Other personal characteristics are important, but those listed above represent what we have gleaned from the literature. It is important to note that, for the most part, personal characteristics cannot be taught. Rather, they must be viewed as characteristics to take into account when selecting prospective teacher leaders. The one exception may be "expertise in subject matter and pedagogy."

Interpersonal Skills. No one would dispute that a teacher of children needs highly developed interpersonal skills, but the skills necessary to deal with colleagues and other adults is quite different. Successful teacher leaders are:

- Effective oral communicators.
- Good listeners.
- Good group processors.
- Good mediators.
- Good negotiators.
- Culturally sophisticated.

A teacher's ability and motivation to work with colleagues distinguishes effective teachers of teachers from effective teachers of children. The success of teacher leadership depends largely on the cooperation and interaction between teacher leaders and their colleagues. Successful teacher leaders demonstrate the skills listed above because these skills allow them to collaborate with their colleagues on instructional improvement. These interpersonal skills, in interaction with personal characteristics, allow teacher leaders to earn the trust and respect of their peers and to guide and influence a colleague's instructional activities and decisions.

Special note should be taken of what we refer to as "cultural sophistication." If a teacher leader is to be successful, that teacher not only must possess an extraordinary amount of information about the "ins and outs" of how schools work, but they also must possess the ability to respond to situations in the schools in ways that demonstrate this knowledge. Culturally sophisticated teacher leaders know whom to talk to about difficult situations.

Finally, teacher leaders should understand how professional norms influence their interactions with other teachers. Teaching is characterized by isolation that limits interactions among colleagues.[15] Teaching also is characterized by norms of professional equality and autonomy. The structure of teacher leadership may complicate the professional relationships between teachers and teacher leaders. Teacher leadership forces teachers to open up their classrooms and interact with other teachers, thus breaking the isolation but also invading the "privacy" of the classroom. Teacher leadership also implies differentiated status, which may conflict with the norms of professional equality and autonomy.

Institutional Factors. Because teacher leaders must operate in a school and school district, there are institutional factors that influence success. Regardless of the personal characteristics and interpersonal skills that a prospective teacher leader might possess, if those who

229

make decisions in schools and school districts do not attend to these factors, it will be impossible for teacher leadership to emerge. While many institutional factors are important, the following are crucial:

- Administrative support and cooperation.
- Shared vision of effective schooling.
- Sufficient resources.
- Opportunity to lead.

Principals traditionally have made the decisions in the management of schools. Occasionally, they have even been leaders in the areas of curriculum design and instruction. The school is a social organization, and thus it creates structure to communicate expectations and requirements to teachers. Traditionally, control has been maintained over teachers by the use of rules and regulations, monitoring and supervising, and evaluation systems.[16] Obviously, the role of a teacher leader may interfere with the traditional relationship between principals and teachers, and so principals may not embrace teacher leadership enthusiastically. In some cases, principals may even be hostile to expanding the leadership role for teachers and may regard teacher leadership as a threat to their authority.[17] The "peer-nominated" teacher leaders in the Wilson study expressed a strong reservation about such conflicts with principals, and thus preferred to avoid risks.[18]

Even cooperative principals often find it difficult to accommodate teacher leaders because of the organizational and administrative constraints that operate in the school workplace.[19] It is not difficult to envision the road blocks a principal might encounter in providing a teacher leader with the time, resources, space, and flexibility needed to maximize the role.[20]

Identifying Potential Teacher Leaders

Berry and Ginsberg observed that research "provides no specific guidelines on how to identify potentially effective lead teachers."[21]

The model of teacher leadership presented earlier outlines criteria for the identification and selection of potential teacher leaders. All three clusters and their interactions should be considered. The question is how to assess these qualities. Unfortunately, there is no easy answer. Probably the most important point is that those charged with selecting potential teacher leaders should use information from many sources, including but not restricted to archival data, personal interviews, and the reports of others who know the candidates well.

Without doubt, the qualification of an applicant with regard to academic preparation and professional accomplishments can be gauged, to some degree, from transcripts and other records. Additionally, the applicant should be asked to provide statements concerning goals and plans for leadership roles. Finally (and, to some people, most importantly), the instructional practices of the applicants should be observed over a period of time.

In addition, an applicant must be respected and accepted by colleagues and supervisors. Information concerning the applicant's interpersonal skills and working relationships with colleagues and superiors can be obtained through teacher surveys, selected interviews, search committee reports, and letters of recommendation. Oral presentations to groups of teachers also can provide clear information about the applicant's communication and interpersonal skills. During either group or individual interviews, the applicant's understanding of issues related to public schooling can be obtained, including the needs and demands of the school and the school district, effective school policies, effective leadership strategies, and education reform.

Once the data are compiled, they can be compared to the selection criteria, which should establish the minimum standards of competence in major areas of teacher leadership. If the selection process is rigorous, fair, open, and consensus-based, then it will have helped all those involved to express their ideas, consider different perspectives, and develop a shared vision about effective schooling and teacher leadership. The implementation of a process based on high standards ensures the selection of the "best" teachers, sets the tone for serious tasks ahead, and establishes a process that will lead toward the accomplishment of those tasks.

Developing Teacher Leadership

Once potentially effective teacher leaders have been identified, the next task is to help them develop their potential. The literature provides little information on training for instructional leadership.[22] Obviously, the nature of the training will depend on the expected roles and responsibilities of teacher leaders, and the specific program should be designed to meet the particular needs of a school or district.

Perhaps a hint of what training programs might look like can be derived from examining the range of roles and responsibilities expected of teacher leaders. These include, but are not limited to: observing and coaching other teachers; mentoring new teachers;

developing and delivering workshops at the school or district level; selecting, adapting, and developing curriculum materials; making schoolwide or grade-level decisions about curriculum, instruction, and assessment; conducting peer reviews; appraising the performance of other teachers; selecting and hiring new teachers; interpreting and applying education research; and getting professionally involved, such as in teacher research and professional organizations.

The roles and responsibilities of teacher leaders vary depending on the program objectives emphasized in the school or district. Teacher leadership programs also may differ across subject areas, specializations such as special education or bilingual education, and grade levels. Thus training programs should be designed to respond to the expected roles and responsibilities that reflect these distinctions. In addition, program designs should consider issues of effective schooling and leadership, including the articulation of a shared vision, a needs assessment, a review of relevant literature, a survey of similar programs at other districts or institutions, the wisdom and practical knowledge of school personnel, and an examination of barriers and obstacles.

Once the objectives and designs of training programs are determined, the programs can be carried out reflecting the model of teacher leadership presented earlier:

Personal characteristics should be handled at the individual level. Leadership development may, at different times, be standardized, individualized, or a combination of both. In the standardized approach, the programs are offered for all teachers in a conventional format. In the individualized approach, the programs respond to the personal characteristics of individual teachers, each of whom have strengths and weaknesses. The goal should be the development of a conscientious teacher leader with many skills and requisite personal characteristics, as well as an understanding of his or her limitations.

Interpersonal skills are important because leaders, by nature, often are assertive and want to be in control, although this need not be offensive. Teacher leaders are in the delicate position of working with peers, serving as role models and guides. They cannot force their colleagues to accept them as leaders. Instead, they must earn respect and trust using genuine interactions and collaboration. For this purpose, training programs should emphasize the dynamics and realistic role expectations between teacher leaders and colleagues.[23] Such skills as listening, mediation, and negotiation should be part of the training program.

Institutional factors are important because teacher leaders also must learn how to work with their superiors. There should be a clear understanding by both the principal and teacher leaders concerning their respective roles. As Lieberman stated, two key questions should be resolved in this effort. First, to what extent should teacher leaders participate and take responsibility for decision making in the related issues of curriculum, instruction, and student learning? Second, to what extent should teacher leaders be provided with the resources and support necessary to carry out their work?[24]

Principals and teacher leaders should come to an understanding of shared leadership, the purpose of which is to help all members of the school community work toward the professionalization of teaching and increased student learning. In this shared leadership, the principal and teacher leaders both get involved in decision making, but their decisions fall largely into two different areas: administrative for the principal and instructional for teacher leaders.[25]

Sustaining the Teacher Leadership Structure

Often, once a program is in place, the initial enthusiasm and support dwindle, the program becomes stagnant, and sooner or later it is replaced by another new program. Although there are success stories of teacher leadership programs, the literature is silent on what makes programs successful and, more important, what makes them last. To make matters more complicated, teacher leadership is a fairly recent phenomenon. A great deal of effort has been placed on designing and implementing diverse programs across contexts, but little attention has been given to the evaluation of programs.

The most enduring reform occurs when the participants are committed to its cause. Throughout the implementation of programs, teacher leaders will face many obstacles and difficulties. Orchestration of programs will inevitably require trials and errors. Teacher leaders should learn from mistakes, be willing to explore new ideas, and be flexible with alternatives. Most important, teacher leaders should engage in professional growth themselves in order to continually develop their requisite personal characteristics, and to help other teachers grow as well.

At the start of any collaborative work among teachers, there is an inherent risk of being "exposed" after years spent behind the closed door of one's classroom. Teacher leadership involves an even greater risk because teachers may perceive teacher leaders as evaluators or another layer of administrators. Instead of promoting collaboration and shared decision making, the situation could deepen the "we-they" tension that often exists between teachers and administrators.[26] This is one of the main reasons why effective teacher leaders must avoid administrative roles and, instead, rely on the skills they have learned in preparation for instructional leadership roles.

Teacher leaders can be effective only when there is genuine collaboration and interaction between themselves and their colleagues. Teachers will listen to one another, contribute extra time and energy, assist one another for their own and their colleagues' professional growth, and take initiative in decision making for school improvement. Teacher leaders, in particular, can provide the impetus for building the culture of collaboration by guiding such effort in the right direction, serving as role models, creating new professional norms and expectations, providing assistance for colleagues who need extra help, and serving as mediators between teachers and administrators.

At the very least, opening a dialogue among teachers concerning issues of curriculum and instruction is a significant step toward the professionalization of teaching. The culture of teacher collaboration and leadership can sustain itself, even when institutional conditions or policies impinge, simply because teachers come to value it as part of the teaching profession.[27]

Finally, teacher leadership requires some coherent reordering of the workplace of schools. This reordering helps to create a climate that encourages teacher collaboration and involves teachers in making decisions. The principal's willingness to share leadership with teacher leaders is a key to improving the climate of the workplace for emerging teacher leadership. Without a great deal of change in the workplace of schools, needed institutionalization of teacher leadership will not occur.[28]

Implications

The three cases presented at the beginning of this essay described teachers who had completed an extensive professional development program that emphasized subject-matter expertise and leadership development. These teachers currently are demonstrating instructional leadership in a variety of educational settings. Joanne serves as a districtwide resource teacher in elementary mathematics education; Jim is the mathematics chairperson and union representative at his school; and Maria is the coordinator of parent-teacher programs at her school. The roles of teacher leaders vary greatly, depending on the needs of specific schools and districts.

It is ironic that teachers often have been denied the opportunity to make decisions about instructional improvement when that is, in fact, their area of expertise. The development of teacher leadership is an attempt to alleviate that problem by promoting collaboration and professionalization in teaching. The use of teachers as leaders should lead to the development of higher standards, seen by teachers as coming from their colleagues. This factor, by itself, will enhance the likelihood that these higher standards will be accepted and thus achieved.

In this essay, we have attempted to propose a beginning step for a model of teacher leadership that considers those aspects of the role that we believe are critical. We used the model to discuss some of the issues that have not been adequately addressed in the literature: how to identify potentially effective teacher leaders, how to develop their potential, and how to support and maintain the instructional leadership structure. This model can provide an initial framework for program design and implementation by district administrators, principals, teachers, funding agencies, and teacher educators.

However, in the absence of conceptual frameworks for guiding program development and evaluation, teacher leadership programs will continue to be sporadic, idiosyncratic events. Concerted efforts for the explication of conceptual underpinnings, implementation processes, and evaluation strategies are needed to make teacher leadership a genuine reform initiative, rather than another fad in the history of education reform.

Footnotes

1. The cases of the teachers are all real, although the names are pseudonyms. For more information, see Gilbert J. Cuevas and Okhee Lee, *Final Report to the U.S. Department of Education: Mathematics and Science Resource Teacher Project, 1990-1993* (Coral Gables, Fla.: University of Miami, 1993).

2. Puget Sound Educational Consortium, *Teacher Leadership: Commitment and Challenge* (Seattle: Puget Sound Educational Consortium, University of Washington, 1988); and Puget Sound Educational Consortium, *Teacher Leadership: New Skills — New Opportunities* (Seattle: University of Washington, 1989).

3. David E. Engel, "Pittsburgh's Teacher-Administrator Partnership: A New Relationship," *Educational Leadership* 47 (1990): 44-45.

4. Judith Warren Little, "Teachers' Professional Development in a Climate of Educational Reform," *Educational Evaluation and Policy Analysis* 15 (1993): 129-51.

5. Little, op. cit., pp. 134-35; Ann Lieberman and Milbrey W. McLaughlin, "Networks for Educational Change: Powerful and Problematic," *Phi Delta Kappan* 73 (May 1992): 673-77.

6. Gilbert J. Cuevas and Okhee Lee, op. cit.

7. Ann Lieberman, "Teachers and Principals: Turf, Tension, and New Tasks," *Phi Delta Kappan* 69 (May 1988): 648-53; and Sharon Rallis, "Room at the Top: Conditions for Effective School Leadership," *Phi Delta Kappan* 69 (May 1988): 643-47.

8. Mark A. Smylie, "Teacher Participation in School Decision Making: Assessing Willingness to Participate," *Educational Evaluation and Policy Analysis* 12 (1992): 53-67.

9. David D. Marsh, "Teacher Corps," in *Encyclopedia of Educational Research*, 5th ed., edited by Harold E. Mitzel (New York: Free Press, 1982).

10. Sam J. Yarger, "The Legacy of the Teacher Center," in *Changing School Culture Through Staff Development: The 1990 ASCD Yearbook*, edited by Bruce Joyce (Alexandria, Va.: Association for Supervision and Curriculum Development, 1990).

11. Barnett Berry and Rick Ginsberg, "Creating Lead Teachers: From Policy to Implementation," *Phi Delta Kappan* 71 (April 1990): 616-17; and William A. Firestone and James R. Pennell, "Teacher Commitment, Working Conditions, and Differential Incentive Policies," *Review of Educational Research* 63 (1993): 510-16.

12. Meena Wilson, "The Search for Teacher Leaders," *Educational Leadership* 50 (1993): 24-27.

13. Rallis, op. cit., p. 644.

14. Berry and Ginsberg, op. cit., p. 619.

15. Sharon Feiman-Nemser and Robert E. Floden, "The Cultures of Teaching," in *Handbook of Research on Teaching*, 3rd ed., edited by Merlin C. Wittrock (New York: Macmillan, 1986); Judith Warren Little, "The Persistence of Privacy: Autonomy and Initiative in Teachers' Professional Relations," *Teachers College Record* 91 (1990): 509-34; Mark A. Smylie, "Teachers' Reports of Their Interactions with Teacher Leaders Concerning Classroom Instruction," *Elementary School Journal* 93 (1992): 85-98; and Patricia A. Wasley, *Teachers Who Lead: The Rhetoric of Reform and the Realities of Practice* (New York: Teachers College Press, 1991).

16. Thomas J. Sergiovanni, "Why We Should Seek Substitutes for Leadership," *Educational Leadership* 49 (1992): 41-45.

17. Rallis, op. cit.; and Wasley, op. cit.

18. Wilson, op. cit.

19. Judith Warren Little, "The 'Mentor' Phenomenon and the Social Organization of Teaching," *Review of Research in Education* 16 (1990): 297-351; and Susan J. Rosenholtz, *Teachers' Workplace: The Social Organization of Schools* (New York: Longman, 1989).

20. Firestone and Pennell, op. cit., pp. 510-16.

236

21. Berry and Ginsberg, op. cit., p. 618.

22. Tom Bird and Judith W. Little, *From Teacher to Leader: Training and Support for Instructional Leadership by Teachers* (San Francisco: Far West Laboratory for Educational Research and Development, 1985).

23. Little, "The Persistence of Privacy," op. cit.

24. Lieberman, op. cit., p. 649.

25. Rallis, op. cit.

26. Wilson, op. cit.

27. Rosenholtz, op. cit.

28. Lieberman, op. cit., p. 652.

PART V
NURTURING TEACHER
LEADERSHIP IN SCHOOLS

TEACHER LEADERSHIP:
A FAILURE TO
CONCEPTUALIZE

BY MICHAEL FULLAN

Michael Fullan is dean of the Faculty of Education at the University of Toronto.

Teacher development has received increasing attention as a strategy for education reform for almost a decade. The results are not promising. Most attempts are at the level of rhetoric, are piecemeal, or are wrongheaded. Why is it that such an obvious, potentially powerful strategy fares so poorly at the very time that reform is so badly needed? I believe that there are two fundamental reasons that feed on each other to reinforce the status quo.

First, despite the rhetoric about teacher education in today's society, there does not seem to be a real belief or confidence that investing in teacher development will yield results. Perhaps deep down many leaders believe that teaching is not all that difficult. After all, most leaders have spent thousands of hours in the classroom and are at least armchair experts. And they know that scores of unqualified teachers are placed in classrooms every year and are required to learn on the job. Many teachers themselves do not value teacher development beyond an appreciation that the job is increasingly difficult and that somehow learning on the job is the way to survive.

Second, the strategies for teacher leadership that are used are superficial. They lack the deep, powerful conceptualization that is necessary to guide and connect their efforts. Thus such strategies are not convincing, and even when they are on the right track are not sustainable. They end up further reinforcing the subtle, unstated belief that major reform is not likely to succeed. The result is that teacher education and teacher leadership are not taken seriously. Teaching remains a weak profession in the eyes of the public and for many teachers themselves.

Yet there are glimmers of hope. Intuitively, the argument that quality teachers produce quality learning is compelling. And many

241

promising initiatives continue to be attempted. Two new goals have been added to the national educational goals in the United States. One focuses on parental involvement, the other on teacher development. The next decade will be critical.

These developments make the questions about the underlying purposes of teacher leadership absolutely crucial if we are to make the best use of this brief window of opportunity. I suggest in this essay that unless we develop a clearer and more powerful conceptualization to critique, learn from, and build on, we will engage in a series of false starts. It is one thing not to succeed. It is another not to know why we fail.

In sum, two fundamental problems − lack of confidence and lack of conceptualization − combine to reinforce the status quo. At the same time, the presence of negative and positive pressure points represents a potential avenue for success. In this essay I pursue this potential in two ways. First, I explain why existing efforts are falling short. Second, I outline the basis for a comprehensive conceptualization of teacher leadership for the future.

A Critique of Existing Efforts

The intent of this section is not to diminish current attempts at teacher leadership. On the contrary, many contain elements that will be essential for success. But it is necessary to understand some of the basic flaws if one is to achieve success through these developments.

The following paragraphs do not constitute a formal review of research, although virtually all the criticisms raised have empirical backing (see Fullan 1991, 1993; Goodlad 1990, 1994; Sarason 1993*a*, *b*). Rather, I shall use a variety of teacher development and teacher leadership strategies to illustrate the range and consistency of the problems. These include field-based teacher education initiatives; university-school partnerships, including professional development schools; various teacher leadership and teacher development strategies, such as formal teacher leadership roles, narrative, and autobiographies; site-based management; and state or national efforts to raise standards.

Field-based teacher education and teacher leadership programs (for example, mentors) are on the rise for both "push" and "pull" reasons. The "push" comes from the historical inadequacy of university-based teacher education. Long known for their theoretical irrelevance, lack of coherence, and superficiality, university-based teacher education programs have fallen increasingly into disrepute. The "pull" factor is that student teachers consistently report that time in schools is the most valuable component of their teacher education experience.

Superficially, both factors are true enough. The college of education component often is irrelevant, and practice teaching frequently is beneficial. The error comes in launching a whole new direction in the absence of critical need analysis. Thus England establishes a national policy that funds schools and school authorities directly as agents of initial teacher education with up to 80% of time spent in schools (United Kingdom 1993). Alternative certification programs, which are largely school-based, begin to flourish.

The point is not that these directions are without merit, but rather that they are partial solutions, superficially conceived. For example, there is overwhelming evidence that schools and school districts are conservative rather than innovative as systems, and that schools often are not particularly healthy organizations for the growth and development of their members. Why, then, would one think that increasing the amount of time in a conservative and unhealthy system would produce the innovative teachers we need for the future?

Schools as learning organizations are basically non-intellectual in the sense that the way they are organized, structurally and normatively, is not amenable to experimentation, critical reflection, continuous learning, assessment, or rethinking. This is not a criticism of teachers *per se*. But it is a fact that schools, by and large, are not reflective, learning places when it comes to their own continuous development. It would be a mistake to expect school-based teacher development to generate teacher leadership on a large scale.

Countering this one-sided solution has been the nominally balanced strategy of establishing university-school/district partnerships, often with professional development schools as a major platform. There are several problems with this concept. As with most bandwagons, the rhetoric outstrips the reality. Such partnerships frequently are narrowly conceived, affecting only a handful of schools and only a small part of the college of education. They tend to be confined "projects," rather than wider institutional reform strategies. The professional development schools become reified as PDS schools and experience considerable internal developmental difficulties, not to mention the gaps created between PDS project schools and other schools in the district (Duffy 1994). In most cases, despite the language of equal partnership, the focus is on the school side of the equation, not the changes needed in the university as an institution. University-school partnerships, touted as a powerful vehicle for edu-

243

cation reform, become yet another project. As my colleague Andy Hargreaves (in press) puts it:

> . . . innovative university-generated schemes of school-based teacher preparation often conspire to reduce the reflective component in teacher education still further. Schemes are concocted which lodge much of the day-to-day work of teacher preparation in schools, supervised by school-based mentors who also have regular teaching roles and who meet periodically with their students and each other in the university. In principle, such schemes integrate initial teacher preparation with inservice teacher development and even ongoing school improvement. In practice, however, reflection tends to be confined to classroom-based issues of improving individual instruction and rarely extends to critical, contextual reflection on school-wide issues that impede individual and collective improvement efforts in the long term.

The expansion and growth of various teacher leadership roles has been an enormous benefit to the individuals who hold these positions, but not to the profession as a whole. In some cases, the effect has been contrary to the intention. Many teacher-leader roles end up distancing those in the roles from other teachers. Judith Little (1990) found that lack of clarity and ambivalence on the part of teachers in "mentor" roles tended to produce a lower rate of direct teacher-to-teacher involvement of the very sort needed to make the role credible and effective. Smylie and Denny (1989) reported the same finding for the teacher leadership roles they studied.

Induction programs for beginning teachers under conditions of supervised mentoring also hold great promise; but aside from the fact that they are not widely available, they can become formalized and stultified without a compelling conceptualization. Even at their best, induction programs represent only one small piece of the solution. Similarly, narratives, autobiographies, and other methods of teacher reflection have been a great boon to personal introspection; but they suffer major limitations. Hargreaves (n.d.) has pointed out that "research on teachers' voice and teachers' knowledge is replete with studies of teachers who are caring, committed and child-centered." But such studies fail to connect with other realities on the job and other "voices" of a range of teachers, not to mention the voices of students, parents, and administrators.

Site-based management is yet another strategy aimed at broadening and increasing leadership at the school level among teachers, parents, and students. I recently reviewed the research on site-based or school-based decision making, and the findings are quite clear. In the majority of cases, the research shows that while there have been some changes in the participation in governance matters at the school level, there is no evidence of changes in the teaching-learning core of the school, nor in the development of collaborative leadership norms among teachers (Fullan 1993).

Finally, at the state and national levels, a number of jurisdictions are attempting to advance teaching and reform by codifying the knowledge base of teachers and establishing corresponding assessment methodologies to determine "what teachers should know and be able to do" (National Board 1993). I shall argue shortly that it is not sufficient to identify the knowledge base without a more basic understanding of the roles of teachers and teaching.

Clearly, the attention being paid to teacher leadership holds a great deal of promise, since there are so many avenues of development being pursued. What is lacking is a broader conceptualization to inform and with which to assess these developments. In the absence of such a framework, the various efforts are bound to fail. Ad hoc strategies dissipate efforts. There are no criteria on which to critique specific approaches. Particular strategies become ends in themselves. Teacher leadership for a few individuals becomes detached from the development of most teachers. Strategies become formalistic instead of organic. Specific successes are short-lived islands of hope. In sum, there is little chance that promising lines of development will intersect to create the fundamentally new working conditions necessary to teacher leadership on a continuous basis. For these reasons, an overarching conceptualization of where we should be heading and why is badly needed.

Toward a More Comprehensive Conceptualization of Teacher Leadership

Let us start indirectly. How many teachers out there are like Sarason's Mr. Hunkins and Mr. Triest?

> The first word that comes to mind is *uninteresting*. Not only were they uninterested in me (or any other student), but they did not seem interested in *anything*, including the subject matter. It is as if they came to class with a recipe (= lesson plan) that said "Do this first, that second, and that third, and if you follow instructions you will end up with a palatable dish you

will enjoy." There was nothing to enjoy! We were treated and felt like robots. (Sarason 1993*b*, p. 79)

How many teachers are "nonreading" professionals in the sense that they do not regularly read what is being said by the leading practitioners and researchers in their field? Equally bad, how many teachers uncritically accept what they read or hear because someone in authority has said it (Sarason 1993*b*).

How many teachers work predominantly in isolation and do not engage with colleagues in discussing and acting to solve problems of practice as a normal way of conducting business?

To be clear, I am not casting blame when I state the problems in this way. We know that the "system" is not characterized by conditions conducive to teacher development and has not rewarded teachers who have tried to break new ground. Later in this chapter, I will take up the matter of how to break this negative cycle.

The above questions contain the seeds, albeit negatively stated, of the kind of conceptualization that will be required to drive teacher leadership. I want now to talk about the nature of this conceptualization and the assumptions and actions required to get there, which also is part of the conceptualization.

The fundamental point is that a wholesale transformation of the teaching profession is needed. Teacher leadership is not for a few; it is for all. The vast majority of teachers must become new professionals of the sort described here. We cannot achieve quality learning for all, or nearly all, students until quality development is attained and sustained for all teachers. Six interrelated domains of commitment and knowledge will be required.

1. *Knowledge of teaching and learning.* The knowledge base for effective teaching and learning has increased dramatically over the past decade. Teachers need to understand how diverse, multi-ethnic students learn and develop, and they must be able to draw on a repertoire of teaching strategies to meet a wide range of individual needs. Teachers must be skilled in technology and international telecommunications. They must know their subject areas and how to teach these subjects in relation to other disciplines. They must master assessment and monitoring techniques for identifying a range of learning outcomes and be able to alter curriculum and instruction as needed.

2. *Knowledge of collegiality.* Compared to teachers of the past, today's teachers must be committed to, skilled at, and involved in collaborative work cultures inside and outside the school. While point one involves doing a better job in direct teaching/learning situations,

this point says that the former will not happen unless teachers assume direct responsibility for changing the norms of practice. The learning agenda and the learning conditions are two sides of the same coin. It is easy to specialize in one (by closing the classroom door) or the other (by becoming a professional committee member). But reforming pedagogy and reforming the norms of the profession are intimately related. Failure to recognize this interrelationship will produce superficial "restructuring" but little "reculturing" in teaching, learning, and professional collegiality (Fullan 1993).

Creating collaborative work cultures is incredibly complex. Yet this is a large part of the agenda for teacher leadership. This, as I have argued elsewhere, has implications for all teachers and principals (Fullan and Hargreaves 1991). With respect to principals, Clark and Astuto summarize it best:

> Viewing teachers as members of a professional community focuses attention on norms of collegiality and on the ethics of professional practice. This shift has implications for the work of principals. Sources of control are built into the processes of professional work and collaboration, not into the hierarchy of authority. Principals' actions that focus on stability, goal setting, regularity, accountability, intervention, control, and efficiency are either redundant, destructive of cooperation and a sense of community, or both. Alternative actions that support the professional community, the learning community, and the stakeholder community require more complex, professional expertise on the part of principals. Facilitating the working communities of a school requires actions that foster activity, the development of a professional community that incorporates diversity and difference, and the creation of a sense of individual efficacy and empowerment among students and staff members. (1994, pp. 517-18)

While the culture of the school is the immediate focus, part of this development also involves wider networks of teachers across schools, such as Ontario's Creating a Culture of Change initiative (Ontario Teachers' Federation 1994). It is true that the culture of the schools is changing, but the overriding and more powerful issue is that the culture of the teaching profession as a whole is changing.

3. *Knowledge of educational contexts.* Teacher leadership also means becoming expert not in the foundation courses in history, philosophy, and sociology, but in the specific knowledge, understanding, and skills of relating to and taking into account parents, communi-

ties, business, and social agencies. It means grappling with the questions of where one's community, state/province, and country are heading — all within the "givens" of increased multicultural, multiracial, multilingual existence. Becoming experts in these contexts is mind-expanding on the one hand, but quite specific in application on the other (see Zeichner 1993). It includes specific strategies for connecting parents to learning, for learning to teach for cultural diversity, for partnering with other educative agencies and institutions (such as early childhood programs, social agencies, businesses, colleges of education, etc.). In other words, teachers must critically reflect on the conditions and contexts of their work. Practicing positive politics means, for example, acting in politically legitimate ways to promote anti-racism, gender equity, cooperative learning, and so on. As Hargreaves concludes:

> Like it or not, teacher development is a political activity, especially so in the emerging postmodern world. Building more awareness, adeptness and acuity among teachers so they can pursue positive politics inside and beyond their schools for the benefit of their students, must therefore become a much more salient and explicit part of the teacher development agenda. (1994, p. 21)

Further, the teachers' new role places them in the midst of helping to forge what Goodlad (1994) calls "educative communities." This is not a matter of schools taking on functions that other institutions used to perform. Goodlad describes the starting point well:

> It is unreasonable to expect the schools to pick up the slack when families fall apart, religious institutions no longer attract the young, children are malnourished, drug addiction is rampant, prime-time television programs are vacuous and educationally bankrupt, and gang members, athletes, and narcissistic celebrities are the admired adolescent role models. (p. 225)

However, teachers of the future must be active, skilled players in helping to create new partnerships. To take one critical component of the relationship, we need parent development strategies (staff development for parents, so to speak) and teacher development strategies. Models that include both functions will be needed. In any scenario, teachers will have to be among the leaders in initiating and participating in these new developments. They must, in short, strive to become experts in context.

4. *Knowledge through continuous learning.* Teachers must lead the way in being learners throughout their careers. There is much

to learn, and it keeps changing. Improvement is a never-ending proposition. The intellectual and emotional habits of critical reflection and
action about one's "calling and daily work are the mark of a professional continuously engaged in self-improvement" (Goodlad 1994,
p. 38). Sarason states it even more forcefully:

> Unless you [as a teacher] take active responsibility for your
> professional development, unless you protect yourself against
> the insidious consequences of intellectual-professional loneli-
> ness, you reduce the satisfactions you will derive from your
> career. (1993b, p. 68)

Sarason has underscored the vital link between teacher continuous learning and student learning:

> Yes, we expect teachers to give their all to the growth and
> development of students. *But a teacher cannot sustain such giv-
> ing unless the conditions exist for the continued growth and de-
> velopment of the teacher.* (1993b, p. 62)

5. *Knowledge of the change process.* Teachers as experts in the
change process represent a major transformation because 1) change
is complex and extremely difficult, and 2) teachers and education
systems are known more for their capacity to resist change than for
their roles as agents of reform. Yet, it is clear that teachers are in
the midst of change all the time.

A good deal of knowledge of the change process is now available.
Much of it runs counter to traditional, rational models of planned
change. Teachers must know how to initiate change in spite of "the
system," how to understand and manage the "implementation dip,"
how to help create collaborative cultures and simultaneously manage
conflict, how to create shared visions over time through action, how
to plug into networks of ideas and resources, and how to hold their
own by practicing positive politics (Fullan 1993).

In other words, the teacher development curriculum of the future
must contain explicit education in the management of change, because
without it any sustained progress in the other domains of knowledge
will be impossible.

6. *Moral purpose.* Moral purpose — a front-and-center commitment
to making a difference in the lives of all students, especially the disadvantaged — must be integral to the conceptualization of teacher
leadership. Good teachers always have been driven by moral purpose,
but the image is one of lonely martyrs soldiering on against all odds.
I wish to make three additional observations. First, those small number

of teachers who believe that their high ideals and commitment are sufficient inevitably burn out, leaving no institutional residue for their efforts. Second, steps can and should be taken to articulate and push the moral purpose of all teachers. Third, pursuing moral purpose is a change theme, both in content (the substance of achieving moral purpose means making substantive changes) and in process (what you would have to do to create the conditions to accomplish the changes).

Teachers are in the business of helping to improve society. There is little danger that teachers will be smug about this lofty role, but they may be daunted. There is no need to be. It is a practical matter, although it requires teachers to think about what this means and to take it seriously. This is why Sarason (1993*b*) devotes a whole book advising would-be teachers to think and prepare carefully for what they are getting into and urges those who have a conventional image of an isolated teacher in an isolated classroom not to pursue teaching:

> Teaching is not and should not be for those unwilling or unable to be active agents of educational-institutional change. From the standpoint of the larger society, there is too much at stake to allow teachers to be passive participants in the dynamics and processes of change. (p. 19)

In summary, good intentions and even strong efforts will fail in the absence of a strong conceptualization that informs and is informed by actions. So far, teacher leadership strategies are not being guided by strong conceptualizations.

On Getting There from Here

The six domains of knowledge and commitment above are deeply interrelated. Provided that the overall mindset is maintained, development on several domains can be pursued simultaneously. There are two levels on which action is needed. One I will call the institutional strategy, the other the individual strategy. In the short run, I put more faith in the latter or, more accurately, in individual and small-group action as the route to institutional change.

The institutional strategy is employed when new programs are designed that deliberately incorporate the kind of conceptualization described in this essay. Thus any particular teacher development strategy should be put to the test of critically examining underlying conceptual assumptions in terms of the extent to which it contributes to the comprehensive agenda. A positive example is developed in Goodlad's (1994) conceptualization *and* corresponding sets of proposals and actions for simultaneously renewing teacher education and schools. In effect, comprehensive institutional strategies create a new teacher development curriculum, which links preservice education and continuous development of teachers, while at the same time engaging in the redesign of universities and schools. Much of this joint development consists of the critical processing of the education reform policies of the day. And much synergy is achieved among preservice and inservice education and education reform.

Also, at the institutional level, many of the stated objectives of new approaches to teacher development are on the right track. In practice, as I have argued, these initiatives are weak because they are not guided by a sound conceptualization. Failure to attain major objectives almost always can be traced to a failure to conceptualize how best to pursue the objectives in practice. Ideas of how to maximize implementation and impact are just as important as goals.

Individual and small-group action will turn out to be a more powerful strategy than relying on institutional action. Paradoxically, new actions by individuals (often, at least initially, in spite of the system) are the most likely route to institutional breakthroughs (Fullan 1993). This means that individual teachers must take responsibility for changing the conditions of learning. Sarason states it bluntly: "The field will not change unless and until teachers seek to create those conditions the absence of which is a source of dissatisfaction and the presence of which is a source of satisfaction" (1993*b*, p. 66).

In other words, individual teachers need to become aware that a large part of their role is to improve their profession. This obligation to bring about change can be effectively pursued only if teachers "know what they stand for, and why" (Sarason 1993*b*, p. 88) and work on the kind of image of the teacher presented in this essay. Knowing about the change process means knowing that there will be all kinds of barriers and that there will be many struggles along the way. Knowing about the change process also means knowing that the choice is between striving to create the conditions for personal intellectual growth necessary to make a difference in the lives of teachers and students versus being passive objects and perennial victims of change.

We also know that external and internal forces eventually must connect if there is to be institutional progress. If individuals and small groups of teachers do not push from the inside, there is no hope for such a connection.

I believe that one of the reasons educators are on the defensive is that their critics increasingly are using clear language and specific examples in their attacks, however unfair these attacks might be; while educators are responding with philosophical rationales. Generalized responses to specific charges are not credible. Rather, educators must be able to explain themselves and, indeed, must be proactive in the face of criticism. Teacher development, as conceptualized here, greatly increases the capacity of teachers to "explain themselves" and to develop the expertise and confidence to participate in public forums and to establish alliances.

None of this is to say that others will not be needed to get there from here. Educational administrators, university personnel, parents and communities, governments, and many others will be needed. However, we will not get there if we do not have stronger teachers helping to lead the way. There has never been a more urgent need for the teaching profession to come to the fore:

> No profession more than education provides as exciting an opportunity to understand the society in which we live: how it has changed, will change, should change. (Sarason 1993*b*, p. 138)

Unless teachers conceptualize their role in these terms, and work to make it happen, there is no chance for serious education reform. This is not a job for designated teacher leaders. It is a job for all teachers.

References

Clark, D.L., and Astuto, T.A. "Redirecting Reform: Challenges to Popular Assumptions About Teachers and Students." *Phi Delta Kappan* 75 (March 1994): 513-20.

Duffy, G. "Professional Development Schools and the Disempowerment of Teachers and Professors." *Phi Delta Kappan* 75 (April 1994): 596-601.

Fullan, M., with Stiegelbauer, S. *The New Meaning of Educational Change*. New York: Teachers College Press, 1991.

Fullan, M. *Change Forces: Probing the Depths of Educational Reform*. Bristol, Pa.: Falmer Press, 1993.

Fullan, M., and Hargreaves, A. *What's Worth Fighting for in Your School?* Toronto: Ontario Public School Teachers' Federation; Andover, Mass.: The Network; Buckingham, U.K.: Open University Press; Melbourne: Australian Council of Educational Administration, 1991.

Goodlad, J. *Teachers for Our Nation's Schools*. San Francisco: Jossey-Bass, 1990.

Goodlad, J. *Educational Renewal*. San Francisco: Jossey-Bass, 1994.

Hargreaves, A. "Development and Desire: A Postmodern Perspective." In *New Paradigms and Practices in Professional Development*, edited by T. Guskey and M. Huberman. New York: Teachers' College Press, 1994.

Hargreaves, A. "Towards a Social Geography of Teacher Education." In *Teacher Education in Industrialized Nations*, edited by N.K. Shimahara and I.Z. Holowinzky. New York: Garland, in press.

Hargreaves, A. "Dissonant Voices: Teachers and the Multiple Realities of Restructuring." Manuscript. Ontario Institute for Studies in Education, n.d.

Little, J.W. "The 'Mentor' Phenomenon and the Social Organization of Teaching." In *Review of Research in Education*, vol. 16, edited by C. Cazden. Washington, D.C.: American Educational Research Association, 1990.

National Board for Professional Teaching Standards. *What Teachers Should Know and Be Able to Do*. Detroit, 1993.

Ontario Teachers' Federation. *Creating a Culture of Change*. Toronto, 1994.

Sarason, S. *The Case for Change: Rethinking the Preparation of Educators*. San Francisco: Jossey-Bass, 1993. a

Sarason, S. *You Are Thinking of Teaching*. San Francisco: Jossey-Bass, 1993. b

Smylie, M.A., and Denny, J.W. "Teacher Leadership: Tensions and Ambiguities in Organizational Perspective." Paper presented at the annual meeting of the American Educational Research Association, San Francisco, 1989.

United Kingdom. *The Government's Proposals for the Reform of Initial Teacher Training*. London: Department of Education, 1993.

Zeichner, K. *Educating Teachers for Diversity*. East Lansing, Mich.: National Center for Research on Teacher Learning, 1993.

DRIFT, DETACHMENT, AND THE NEED FOR TEACHER LEADERSHIP

BY DANIEL L. DUKE

Daniel L. Duke is a professor of education in the Department of Educational Leadership and Policy Studies at the University of Virginia. The author is indebted to Bruce Bourget for his comments and suggestions regarding this paper.

The term *leadership* has been invoked so frequently by contemporary writers in such fields as business, public administration, personal development, and education that it is easy to conclude that the phenomenon is essential and ubiquitous. However, such a conclusion deserves reflection. In my view, people perceive leadership to be neither omnipresent nor absolutely necessary under all circumstances. For example, leadership may not be judged of critical importance when the task at hand is clear, when those involved possess the ability and willingness to accomplish it, and when no forces conspire to prevent the task from being accomplished. Collegiality, an understanding of what needs to be done, and a desire to do it may be quite sufficient for the job.

Sometimes, though, people lack clarity about what needs to be done, a condition I refer to as "drift." Even when the task is understood, they may be insufficiently motivated to accomplish it. "Detachment" is the term I apply to such a circumstance. The perceived need for leadership often is considered great in situations characterized by drift and detachment.* I believe these conditions can be found in a number of U.S. schools, particularly those in urban areas. This paper

---

*I regard the "perceived need for leadership" – or nLeadership – as a construct of equal or greater value than leadership itself. Ultimately, it is the circumstances for which leadership is regarded as vital that define the nature of leadership. The perceived need for leadership differs from David McClelland's nPower in that the need for leadership is considered to reside in the situation, not in the individual. A person perceiving the need for leadership does not necessarily have to provide it.

makes the case that leadership by teachers represents a promising antidote to drift and detachment.

Organizational Drift

Organizational drift can be described as a condition in which an organization is perceived to lack direction and coherence. Ambiguity surrounds the central concerns to be addressed, specific goals to be achieved, and values guiding the process (McCaskey 1982, pp. 1-8). Little relationship appears to exist between the efforts of individuals and units in the organization, a phenomenon that has been referred to as "loose coupling" (Weick 1979, p. 55). Those associated with and served by the organization lack a common conception of what is supposed to be accomplished (Smircich and Morgan 1991, p. 466).

Organizational drift is not considered to be a desirable state by many, if not most, students of organizations. Peters and Waterman (1982) found a clear sense of mission closely associated with organizational effectiveness in their study of Fortune 500 companies. Schein (1985) regards consensus of organizational goals and the means for achieving them to be a key to survival. Not only is such consensus critical to external adaptation, but it forms the basis for a strong organizational culture − a vital element of internal integration.

Some contemporary public schools can be characterized as adrift (Marshall and Tucker 1992, pp. 109-27). Educators are not always responsible for this condition, however. For example, efforts by states and school districts to develop core outcomes have run into stiff opposition from conservative groups that resent what they regard as the commingling of values and learning objectives. Guiding values such as equal opportunity and diversity that once served as rallying points have lost much of their potency in school systems that have become racially and socioeconomically homogeneous. Drift can be sensed in local debates over how to cut school expenses. In the absence of a clear sense of common purpose, such occasions often degenerate into rancorous competition among special interest groups.

When people do agree on the purpose of public schools, the level of generality sometimes is too great to guide practice in any useful way. Louis and Miles (1990) argue that this problem is greater for high schools than for elementary schools:

> One problem in high schools is the diversity of purposes and objectives. Yes, we all can agree that the goal is to educate stu-

256

dents — but in what, and for what? In elementary schools, achieving a unified view of what the schools should (and can) achieve is relatively easier. (p. 7)

Buzzwords predominate under conditions of drift. Almost everyone accepts the value, for example, of terms like *excellence, effectiveness, equity, efficiency, student achievement,* and *high expectations* as long as no effort is made to determine what specifically is meant by them. "School effectiveness," watchwords of the Eighties, serves as a good illustration. Virtually no one argued against the *idea* of school effectiveness; but when people began to specify what they meant by the phrase, differences emerged. Ron Edmonds (1982), for example, considered a school to be effective when it brought "an equal percentage of its highest and lowest social classes to minimum mastery" (p. 4). A Santa Clara County, California, project defined school effectiveness as a mean student achievement (for a school) on third- and sixth-grade standardized tests of basic skills that matched or exceeded prediction (based on statewide discrepancy bands) for three consecutive years (Duke 1987, p. 24). Others adopted definitions of school effectiveness derived from research-based correlates of student achievement, such as high expectations and student time on task (Duke 1987, pp. 72-74).

In a well-argued indictment of current educational practice that has captured the interest of the Clinton Administration, Marshall and Tucker (1992, pp. 109-27) contend that continued failure by our schools to clarify what students should know and be able to do when they leave high school will spell economic and social decline for the United States. They warn that agreement on the mission for public schools must not be based on minimal expectations:

> Our task is to shift the whole curve of American educational performance radically upward, and at the same time to close substantially the gap between the bottom an ˙ ᴊe top of the curve.
>
> Given the standard we must meet, the use of dropout rates and scores on standardized tests of basic skills to measure the success of our schools is an insidious form of unintended fraud. Just getting kids in school will not be enough to match our competitors. Just mastering the basic skills . . . will condemn these students to Third World wages at best and unemployment at worst. Minimum competency is institutionalized mediocrity. (p. 82)

While critics of public schools register alarm over what they perceive as organizational drift, many of those working in schools express a quite different view. In an irony worthy of O. Henry, public school teachers frequently decry the abundance of school and district goals, instructional objectives, and policy mandates they are expected to achieve (Cohn 1992, p. 126; Duke 1984, pp. 58-73). Schools and school districts around the country have devoted countless hours to developing mission statements, school improvement plans, and curriculum guidelines. States have added additional expectations and responsibilities. It would be difficult to find a moderate to large school system without some form of vision statement and set of student expectations.

How can it be that critics of public schools do not consider these potential sources of direction to constitute an adequate antidote to drift? Why do teachers themselves often find school goals, mission statements, improvement plans, instructional objectives, and the like to be burdensome and meaningless? Following a discussion of detachment, a second troubling condition of many schools, I will make an effort to answer these questions.

Teacher Detachment

Detachment refers to situations from which individuals withdraw psychologically while remaining physically present. No longer fully engaged, they are said to "go through the motions," doing just enough to get by. The symptoms of detachment vary. Under certain circumstances, stress and burnout may be indicators. At other times, denial of evidence of diminishing effectiveness, depersonalization of blame, excuse-making, and feelings of helplessness and hopelessness may be associated with detachment. To outsiders, those who are detached appear to care very little about what they are doing. However, the irony is that they actually may care too much. Detachment in the face of overwhelming challenges can be a coping mechanism.

Evidence of detachment on the part of many contemporary teachers abounds. In the *Metropolitan Life Survey of the American Teacher 1989*, 46% of the 2,000 teachers nationwide who were interviewed did not feel respected in today's society. One in three said they would not advise a young person to pursue a career in teaching. Believing they face increasingly serious societal problems, 38% did not feel that teachers should be held accountable for the academic success or failure of their students. It is heartening, of course, to note that most teachers do not share such negative feelings. Still, the percentage of teachers harboring concerns about their work is hardly inconsequential. The fact that these teachers often are concentrated in urban schools bodes ill for the future of many of our nation's neediest students.

Dworkin (1987) has studied teacher burnout in one urban area — Houston. One out of every five teachers in the district was likely to report burnout at some point (p. 63). The likelihood increased if the teacher was young, white, middle class in origin, and assigned to a school with a large minority population. Pines and Aronson (1988, p. 101) report that bureaucratic organizations promote three causes of burnout: 1) overload, 2) lack of autonomy, and 3) lack of rewards. Teachers have complained of all three (Duke 1984). Louis (1992) was justified, it appears, in assuming that "working conditions and career opportunities affect the degree to which teachers are actively engaged with teaching and strive to create exciting learning environments in their classrooms" (pp. 139-40).

After spending a year as a part-time teacher aide in an inner-city elementary school, I discovered that teachers frequently live with the awareness that they are not meeting and cannot meet, given the sheer numbers of at-risk students, the needs of many of their students (Duke 1986b). Such a realization hardly enhances an individual's feelings of self-efficacy or commitment to teaching. Those who do not give up the struggle entirely adopt a triage-style mentality, focusing their time and energy on students most likely to benefit from their limited efforts.

Indirect confirmation of these observations was found in a study of how teachers in six states dealt with students to whom they had given a low grade (Duke and Gansneder 1991). The likelihood that a student experiencing academic difficulty would receive special assistance from his or her teacher actually declined after the student received a low grade! It appeared that many teachers simply gave up. When some offered help, their interventions often entailed relatively small investments of time and energy (such as phone calls home or referrals elsewhere). My colleague and I were left with the nagging impression that large numbers of teachers knew how to do a better job than they currently were doing. The key to school improvement would seem to have less to do with giving teachers new knowledge than with fostering conditions in which they are moved to use the knowledge they already possess.

A Matter of Meaning and Leadership

The argument to this point is ripe with paradox. Schools are perceived to lack direction despite an abundance of directives. Teachers who care a great deal about young people feel compelled to disengage from their work. The surfeit of commitments, in an ironic twist, contributes to diminished commitment. In this section I try to understand how such paradoxes can exist.

In order to do so, it is necessary to appreciate the importance of *meaning* in people's lives. Meaning refers to that which makes lives seem significant and worthwhile. Meaning, according to psychotherapists, is associated with the feeling that life has purpose and coherence (Frankl 1969; Yalom 1980). As one of life's driving forces, the search for meaning does not cease at the workplace door (Bolman and Deal 1991, p. 269). When people are unsure that their work lives have meaning, despair and alienation can result. Obviously, such feelings can have adverse effects on organizational effectiveness.

According to Yalom (1980), two important sources of meaning for many people are personal growth and involvement in causes that transcend individual welfare. For teachers, work has the potential to address both of these sources of meaning. However, drift and detachment reduce the likelihood that teaching will be perceived as meaningful.

Let us first consider drift. While many non-educators criticize schools for lacking clear direction, focus, and a sense of mission, teachers often feel that their work is too prescribed and circumscribed. Upon reflection, these observations are not as contradictory as they appear. Directives do not necessarily imply direction. Quite the opposite in some instances. In fact, directives may proliferate when those in authority are unclear about what to do. Goals, objectives, and planning documents sometimes seem to form a bureaucratic mirage, creating the impression of direction where none exists. Many teachers, as well as the general public, feel like passengers on a ship commanded by a captain without a map or destination who, nonetheless, keeps reporting the distance covered each day.

In their effort to update William H. Whyte's study of "organization man," Leinberger and Tucker (1991) studied the beliefs of contemporary workers. Of this group, they concluded,

> It is . . . critical to their sense of well-being and identity that
> these new-style workers know why they are working. They want
> what they do to matter; they want their work to have meaning

260

and purpose beyond facile ascriptions of abstract creativity and certainly beyond a status that is derived from their position in hierarchy. In short, they seek meaning. (p. 404)

The desire for meaningful work, of course, is nothing new for teachers. If many teachers fail to find meaning in official statements of purpose and related efforts to provide direction, it may be due, in part, to their perception that directives lack authenticity. Teachers are sensitive to the fact that many attempts to provide direction are politically motivated or come from people with little understanding of the daily challenges of teaching. Even when they are invited to help set the direction, teachers may be suspicious. Involvement in decision making, they have come to realize, is not the same as influence (Duke, Showers, and Imber 1980). While they may be asked to provide input and attend advisory meetings, teachers frequently feel that decisions regarding what schools are to accomplish are made elsewhere. As long as teachers believe that efforts to provide direction for schools reflect views other than their own, they are likely to consider schools to be adrift.

Just as involvement is not necessarily the same as influence, so responsibility does not equal authority. Today's teachers would be the first to acknowledge that they have been asked to assume an increasing number of responsibilities as a consequence of budget cuts, role expansion, inclusion, new curriculum mandates, and other factors. Unfortunately, in many cases, they have not been accorded additional authority commensurate with these new responsibilities. Such circumstances are unlikely to promote greater commitment on the part of teachers.

Detachment is the opposite of commitment. It can result from the sheer magnitude of responsibilities as well as lack of authority. Pines and Aronson (1988, p. 101) note that overload often is tied directly to the failure of work to provide a sense of meaning. This is so because "overload puts people in situations in which failure is built in. If they comply with the bureaucratic demand for quantity . . . they fail the demand for quality service" (p. 104). Situations of this kind may arise because what is meaningful for teachers differs from what is meaningful for administrators. While administrators may judge the importance of their work in terms of accomplishing school goals and raising test score averages, teachers are more likely to derive meaning from their relationships with students and the perception that individuals have grown as a result of their time in class (Duke 1986*b*).

Dworkin defines commitment as "an affective attachment . . . to a person, object, role, or setting such that the probability of perseverance and continuance of a relationship to that person, object, role, or setting is enhanced" (1987, p. 30). Organizational commitment on the part of teachers is unlikely to result when teachers are expected to serve excessive numbers of students, handle too wide a range of needs, or accomplish too many objectives. The meaningfulness of an individual's work can hardly be enhanced by the knowledge that the needs of many clients are going unmet. Detachment in the face of such feelings, while regrettable and costly, is understandable. What, then, can be done to combat drift and detachment in schools where they are problems? These conditions warrant leadership in general and teacher leadership in particular. The reasoning goes as follows. Drift and detachment are organizational problems rooted in the individual's desire for meaning. Leadership is a catalyst for meaning. Smircich and Morgan (1991) maintain, for example, that,

> The actions and utterances of leaders guide the attention of those involved in a situation in ways that are consciously or unconsciously designed to shape the meaning of the situation. The actions and utterances draw attention to particular aspects of the overall flow of experience, transforming what may be complex and ambiguous into something more discrete and vested with a specific pattern of meaning. (p. 464)

In my aesthetic theory of leadership (Duke 1986a), I similarly hold that leadership helps bring meaning to the relationship between individuals and greater entities, such as communities, organizations, and nations. The theory is based on the notion that leadership can be understood as an attribution or a perception. As such, when the term *leadership* is used, it may reveal a great deal about what the person using it believes and regards as meaningful. In contemporary Western society, the perception of leadership frequently is associated with certain properties, including fit, originality, direction, and engagement. The last two constitute the antitheses of drift and detachment. In the presence of leadership, for instance, individuals often sense movement and purpose. "Direction is more than a course to follow. It is a path *together* with a reason for traveling it" (Duke 1986a, p. 15).

While a sense of direction often enables people to regard their actions as meaningful, it is not easily achieved on an organizational basis. Direction concerns intended outcomes, and people frequently

262

value different outcomes. Burns (1978) has written of the challenge of getting people to transcend their personal beliefs and commit to a common course of action. He refers to this process as transforming leadership and characterizes it thus:

> [Transforming] leadership occurs when one or more persons engage with others in such a way that leaders and followers raise one another to higher levels of motivation and morality. Their purposes, which might have started out as separate but related . . . become fused. (p. 20)

Later, Burns provides additional explanation. The function of leadership, he contends, is "to *engage* followers, not merely to activate them, to commingle needs and aspirations and goals in a common enterprise" (p. 461).

It is significant that Burns considers engagement to be a key element of leadership, going so far as to underscore the verb "engage" when he uses it. While Burns focuses on the relationship between leadership and engagement, Yalom (1980) writes of the connection between engagement and meaning. He has noted that the search for meaning may be so daunting at times that it cannot be pursued directly. Under such circumstances, meaning is best developed indirectly as a byproduct of engagement.

Engagement may be thought of as wholehearted participation or committed activity. With capable and credible leadership, individuals are willing to engage themselves even when they are unsure of the direction or ultimate purpose of the engagement. Through engagement, they subsequently can realize or discover direction and purpose (Duke 1986a, pp. 16-17).

Bolman and Deal (1991) recognize different types of leadership, each associated with a distinct framework for understanding organizations. They contend that symbolic leadership — the form of leadership most closely associated with meaning — is important when other forms, such as structural, human resource, and political leadership, fail to "contain the dark forces of ambiguity" (p. 439). Symbolic leadership, they claim, helps bring "order, meaning, and predictability out of chaos and confusion" (p. 439).

For present purposes, what is most valuable about Bolman and Deal's work is not their effort to differentiate types of leadership, but the idea that attempts by leaders to enhance meaning are more important under certain circumstances than under others. People in organizations experience different needs at different times. The perceived need for organizational leadership may vary depending on such factors as adequacy of resources and environmental circumstances. Sergiovanni (1992) notes that schools may need "strong and direct instructional leadership" when they are "in trouble" (p. xi). The importance of such leadership declines, he argues, when problems subside. The position taken in this paper is that drift and detachment constitute two troubling conditions that frequently are considered to necessitate leadership. The matrix in Figure 1 illustrates these needs.

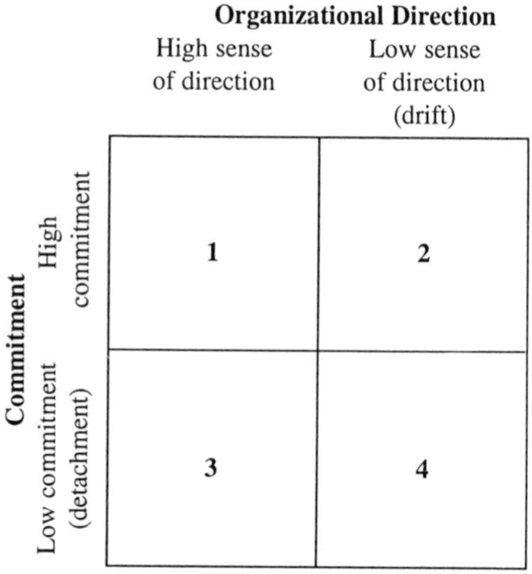

Organizational Direction

	High sense of direction	Low sense of direction (drift)
High commitment	1	2
Low commitment (detachment)	3	4

Commitment

Figure 1. The need for leadership.

Where both direction and commitment are present (Cell 1), the perceived need for leadership is least great. A greater perceived need for leadership characterizes situations in which either direction (Cell 2) or commitment (Cell 3) is absent. The greatest perceived need for leadership is associated with the absence of both direction and commitment (Cell 4). It is this situation, I believe, that describes a substantial number of schools in the United States, especially those in urban areas.

The second position taken in this paper is that the problems of drift and detachment in American schools can be addressed successfully by teacher leadership. This position is not intended to devalue the contributions of school administrators, parents, students, policy makers, and other citizens interested in public schools. It simply represents the belief that teachers are in the best position to deal with drift and detachment. In addition, their motivation to do so may be greater

264

than that of many groups. Administrators, students, parents, and politicians come and go. Their dedication to improving conditions in schools typically is limited by their tenure in office or period of school attendance. Teachers, of all the groups mentioned above, are most likely to remain for relatively long periods of time in a particular school. Furthermore, it is the school, rather than the school district or some other organizational entity, that is reported to have the greatest potential to serve as a source of direction and commitment for teachers (Grant 1988; Louis and Miles 1990). The fact that teachers have a vested interest in school improvement only strengthens the argument for teacher leadership. These reasons help explain, in part, why many of the recent proposals for restructuring public schools include calls for teacher empowerment and shared decision making (Marshall and Tucker 1992, p. 86).

The Promise of Teacher Leadership

This section explores some of the ways that teacher leadership can reduce the problems of drift and detachment in schools. It should be underscored that these two problems often may be linked. When teachers feel detached, they are less likely to regard efforts to establish direction in a positive light. When they believe schools lack direction, they are less inclined to feel a sense of commitment. Where both drift and detachment are present, therefore, it may be necessary to address them together (Pasmore and Fagans 1992, p. 394).

Mission statements, school visions, lists of intended learning outcomes, and sets of professional performance standards all have the potential to provide schools with a sense of direction. However, if these sources of guidance do not make sense to teachers or if teachers lack the knowledge, skills, resources, or opportunity to move in the desired direction, frustration rather than inspiration may result. In the past, teachers frequently were enjoined by others to pursue ambitious goals despite inadequate training, skimpy resources, and a variety of policy constraints. When teachers help determine school direction, problems such as these can be confronted directly.

In *Horace's School* (1992), Sizer writes about how a redesign committee of secondary teachers at fictitious Franklin High and Middle Schools plays a leadership role in charting a future course for its schools. The committee's report contains a number of recommendations for school improvement, ranging from agreement on a set of central beliefs about education to new forms of student assessment and a curriculum winnowed of superficial content. While the report

265

characterizes the committee's recommendations as "compromises," it would be hard to view them as anything but visionary. Sizer's account illustrates how the value of teacher leadership can derive, in part, from its capacity to recognize and respond to practical problems without abandoning idealism.

The teacher leadership in *Horace's School* is not just a figment of Sizer's imagination. When Prestine and Bowen (1993) studied four "restructuring" schools that were members of Sizer's Coalition of Essential Schools, they found substantial evidence of teacher leadership. The leadership often was "subtle, quiet and behind the scenes" (p. 308). It became manifest during "critical incidents" when issues or problems arose to threaten restructuring efforts. On such occasions, teachers in schools where restructuring was proceeding well invariably exercised initiative to maintain focus and keep people actively involved.

Wasley (1992) has written about a teacher-run elementary school in the Southwest that illustrates the potential of teacher leadership. Determined to find better ways to serve their 700 students, most of whom were Hispanic and poor, teachers at Aguilar Elementary School worked closely with their principal. As one teacher put it:

> For two years, the staff worked together to develop a mission statement and goals. We started our early intervention program which has a lot of pieces to it — peer tutoring, adult tutoring, summer school. We stopped pulling some kids out for remedial help. (p. 216)

Another teacher provided further detail:

> We just started doing all this stuff. No one told us to. We talked a lot about who we were, what our kids were, what our philosophy is, and then more ideas came up to the top. We all felt that we wanted multi-aged grouping and we wanted a more experience-oriented curriculum. And we wanted our kids to feel comfortable in a large school. (p. 216)

When Aguilar's principal took another job, the faculty was so committed to the direction they had charted for the school that they proposed not hiring a new principal. It seems no one wanted to risk bringing in someone who might not support their new initiatives. Instead, they asked for and received permission to establish a team management structure consisting of four teachers — a facilitator responsible for day-to-day operations and three coordinators for staff evaluations, building and grounds, and academics. When Wasley visited Aguilar a year after the implementation of team management, she found that teachers, parents, and the central administration were pleased with the results. Teachers acknowledged, though, that leadership can be stressful. As one teacher said:

> The thing is, that it's a different kind of stress than fighting with the principal, fighting with the system, always being told you have to do something when you know philosophically it is wrong.

Aguilar Elementary is not an isolated case. Contemporary examples of teacher leadership are plentiful. Teachers are participating in school-based management and serving on restructuring committees. As of 1993, four states already had, and at least 12 states were considering, charter school legislation that empowers groups of teachers to design and run schools under contract with a public sponsor. Teacher unions have moved beyond bread-and-butter issues to confront schools' need for direction. The Chicago teachers' union and the board of education are collaborating on the development of "learning-outcome standards" for students. In Rochester, New York, the union and the school board have negotiated an agreement where teachers assume collective responsibility for an innovative set of "principles for achieving schools."

When teachers help to establish a sense of direction or purpose for their school, they are less likely to experience feelings of detachment. However, direction is not achieved easily. Today's schools are highly politicized settings in which various special interest groups compete for influence over the course schools will take. Rather than challenging these groups, school officials often opt for appeasement and accommodation, agreeing to take on new, and sometimes incompatible, responsibilities without dropping existing ones. Currently, for example, efforts are under way to make schools centers for integrated student services ranging from health care to social welfare. The cost of trying to be all things to all people often is loss of focus and confusion.

It is safe to assume that most teachers have more to do than time to do it. Such is the nature of a profession such as teaching. Few members of the teaching profession accomplish everything that is expected or that could be done to help students. Mission and vision statements, target outcomes, and other sources of direction can help teachers when choices must be made concerning how to allocate their scarce time and energy. A sense of direction enables teachers to focus, thereby increasing the likelihood that they will experience success. Success, in turn, can be a key to commitment. Teachers who feel they are not accomplishing important goals are less likely to feel committed.

Focus is not the only ingredient in meaningful work. Balance also is important. Prolonged focus on particular goals may contribute to feelings of stagnation and reduced effectiveness. Earlier, the point was made that meaning derives from feelings of personal growth as well as involvement in causes that transcend personal welfare. Balance relates to the distribution of energy between activities that help move an entity, like a school, in a desired direction (focus) and activities that contribute to an individual's personal and professional development. Vroom (1960) noted years ago that participation in organizational activities was most meaningful when combined with efforts to increase individuals' skills and abilities.

In recent years teachers, both individually and collectively, have sought greater control over their own professional development. In Washington State, for example, the Washington Education Association has led an effort to reform teacher evaluation, de-emphasizing annual summative evaluations of teaching performance for competent professionals and creating greater opportunities for teachers to set meaningful growth goals. Similar efforts have been undertaken in school districts around the United States (Duke 1990). Teachers in Santa Cruz, California, have chosen to replace the meaningless annual ritual of teacher evaluation with peer observation and coaching, despite the fact that the change requires more work (Krovetz and Cohick 1993).

Teachers also have begun to play a larger role in staff development and school improvement efforts. Wasley (1991), in an excellent study of teacher leadership, found teachers mentoring other teachers, engaging in problem solving at the school and district level, and designing inservice programs. While teacher leaders have been in schools for a long time, Wasley notes that their roles in the past tended to concentrate on matters of organizational maintenance and efficiency. In recent years, however, teacher leaders have found themselves in the vanguard of efforts to change schools.

A team of researchers studying teacher leadership and school improvement found that considerable time may be needed for teachers to adjust to their new roles (Clift et al. 1992). Before "consensus on the value and importance of teacher leadership for school-wide initiatives" had been achieved, teachers experienced role ambiguity and periods of "overload and conflict" (p. 904).

The promise of teacher leadership is that teaching will become more meaningful to thousands of teachers in situations where they are unclear about school priorities or concerned about the direction in which schools seem to be moving. Education policy makers finally have begun to realize that direction and purpose must be embraced and internalized, not dictated and enforced. Administrators have recognized that teachers cannot be compelled to be committed. Through opportunities for teachers to exercise leadership and share authority, administrators are fostering conditions likely to reduce feelings of detachment.

Impediments to Teacher Leadership

While teacher leadership offers a way to escape drift and detachment, the journey is not likely to be smooth. Impediments can be found within teachers as well as the organizational structures in which they work. Wasley (1991) maintains that these impediments have a paradoxical quality: "those conditions that provided support [for teacher leadership] also were constraints" (p. 137). For example, teachers in her study were allocated time to undertake leadership activities, an important source of support. Unfortunately, they judged the amount of release time to be inadequate to the tasks of leadership. In another example of paradox, "teacher leaders loved the opportunity to collaborate with others, and yet felt lonely as their roles separated them from their colleagues" (p. 137).

Wasley, along with many other students of teacher leadership, tends to associate leadership with specific roles. Such a view all but ensures the feelings of separation noted by the teachers she studied. Leadership, however, is not the special province of particular roles. While certain roles carry with them the expectation of leadership, examples abound of individuals who are perceived to exercise leadership while occupying subordinate positions. In organizations such as schools, which consist of large numbers of professionals, the most desirable form of leadership, in fact, actually may be that which is not limited to particular roles but instead derives from expertise and experience.

In order to expand the parameters of teacher leadership beyond designated "leader" roles, teachers must be willing to abandon "crab-bucket cultures." Anyone who has gone crabbing knows that it is unnecessary to cap a crab bucket because as soon as one crab tries to scuttle out, the others drag it back down. Some faculties function the same way, actively resisting the efforts of any member to press

269

beyond normal practice. Teacher leadership hardly can thrive in such circumstances.

The traditional emphasis on individual rather than collective accountability in schools also has served as a deterrent to an expanded concept of teacher leadership. While teacher supervision, evaluation, and recognition typically have focused on individual teachers, many teachers know that education is a collective enterprise in which one's success is highly dependent on the efforts of others. A good model of collective leadership is the bomb detonation unit in the military. All members of these units are compelled to share leadership because each stands to suffer the consequences of poor performance. I believe that it is relatively useless to focus the evaluation of tenured teachers on the performance of individuals. The interests of students are better served when teachers regard the educational welfare of all students as their collective responsibility. The appropriate unit of accountability should be the grade-level cluster, department, or school — not the individual.

One reason why more progress has not been made in the development of models of collective accountability in schools probably is the tradition of lay control of schools. The incentive for teachers to be accountable is diminished when professional expertise and experience count for relatively little in the policymaking process. All too often, lay authorities intrude in matters that presumably are the domain of professionals and then insist that professionals be held accountable. The likelihood that teachers will embrace collective accountability for student learning is directly related to the extent to which teachers influence the formulation of policies related to curriculum, instruction, evaluation, and other professional aspects of schooling.

Lay boards, politicians, and special interest groups, of course, are not the only groups that exert control over public schools. School administrators are legally responsible for all that goes on in schools. Since most administrators once were teachers, it is understandable that many teachers associate leadership with leaving the classroom and entering the office. One way to promote teacher leadership, therefore, might be to reconceptualize the role of the school administrator. Schools could follow the lead of hospitals and hire business managers to handle all non-professional issues, thereby leaving decisions concerning the "professional core" of schooling to full-time teachers. Or they could emulate their counterparts in some European countries and appoint or elect "head teachers" to coordinate school operations and make decisions. Head teachers continue to teach while serving as administrators, thereby reinforcing the idea that teaching and leadership are not mutually exclusive.

It should be remembered that these suggestions for ways to overcome obstacles to teacher leadership do not apply to schools where teachers already possess a clear sense of direction and are committed to following it. As indicated earlier, such favorable circumstances may not necessitate teacher leadership. I have never understood why all public schools should be expected to adopt the same organizational model. It is common knowledge that different schools face different challenges. What evidence exists that the same type of leadership or organizational structure is universally appropriate? Public school systems should accept the fact that some schools may have a greater need for teacher leadership than others.

Conclusion

The argument in this paper derives from two basic beliefs. First, leadership is not ubiquitous. Second, leadership is more essential under some conditions than under others. Based on these beliefs, a case was made that certain schools, specifically those characterized by drift (lack of organizational direction) and detachment (lack of teacher commitment), were more in need of teacher leadership than other schools.

The emphasis on teacher leadership as an antidote to drift and detachment was based on an analysis of the nature of leadership and its relationship to meaning. This analysis can be summarized in terms of six propositions:

Proposition 1: Teachers are more likely to be committed to activities that they find personally or professionally meaningful.

Proposition 2: Meaningful activity is a function of focus and balance.

Proposition 3: Focus entails a clear sense of how to concentrate scarce time and energy in order to move in a desired direction.

Proposition 4: Balance involves the distribution of effort between the achievement of transcendent goals and individual development. Both are important sources of personal and professional meaning.

Proposition 5: Organizational leadership in schools is associated with efforts a) to enhance meaningful activity and b) to reduce meaningless activity.

271

Proposition 6: Teachers are an important source of leadership in schools because they are likely to understand which activities are meaningful and meaningless where teaching and learning are concerned.

References

Bolman, Lee G., and Deal, Terrence E. *Reframing Organizations: Artistry, Choice, and Leadership.* San Francisco: Jossey-Bass, 1991.

Burns, James MacGregor. *Leadership.* New York: Harper & Row, 1978.

Clift, Renee; Johnson, Marlene; Holland, Patricia; and Veal, Marylou. "Developing the Potential for Collaborative School Leadership." *American Educational Research Journal* 29 (Winter 1992): 877-908.

Cohn, Marilyn M. "How Teachers Perceive Teaching: Change Over Two Decades, 1964-1984." In *The Changing Contexts of Teaching,* The Ninety-first Yearbook of the National Society for the Study of Education, edited by Ann Lieberman. Chicago: University of Chicago Press, 1992.

Duke, Daniel L. *Teaching: The Imperiled Profession.* Albany: State University of New York Press, 1984.

Duke, Daniel L. "The Aesthetics of Leadership." *Educational Administration Quarterly* 21 (Winter 1986): 7-27. a

Duke, Daniel L. "Understanding What It Means To Be a Teacher." *Educational Leadership* 44 (October 1986): 26-32. b

Duke, Daniel L. *School Leadership and Instructional Improvement.* New York: Random House, 1987.

Duke, Daniel L. "Developing Teacher Evaluation Systems that Promote Professional Growth." *Journal of Personnel Evaluation in Education* 4 (1990): 131-44.

Duke, Daniel L., and Gansneder, Bruce. "The Identification of Effective Instructional Interventions for At-Risk Students." Presentation at the Annual Convention of the American Educational Research Association, 5 April 1991.

Duke, Daniel L.; Showers, Beverly; and Imber, Michael. "Teachers and Shared Decision Making: The Costs and Benefits of Involvement." *Educational Administration Quarterly* 16 (Winter 1980): 93-106.

Dworkin, Anthony Gary. *Teacher Burnout in the Public Schools.* Albany: State University of New York Press, 1987.

Edmonds, Ronald. "Programs of School Improvement: An Overview." *Educational Leadership* 40 (December 1982): 4-11.

Frankl, Viktor E. *The Will to Meaning.* New York: New American Library, 1969.

Grant, Gerald. *The World We Created at Hamilton High.* Cambridge, Mass.: Harvard University Press, 1988.

Krovetz, Martin, and Cohick, Donna. "Professional Collegiality Can Lead to School Change." *Phi Delta Kappan* 75 (December 1993): 331-33.

Leinberger, Paul, and Tucker, Bruce. *The New Individualists.* New York: Harper Collins, 1991.

Louis, Karen Seashore. "Restructuring and the Problem of Teachers' Work." In *The Changing Contexts of Teaching*, The Ninety-first Yearbook of the National Society for the Study of Education, edited by Ann Lieberman. Chicago: University of Chicago Press, 1992.

Louis, Karen Seashore, and Miles, Matthew B. *Improving the Urban High School.* New York: Teachers College Press, 1990.

Marshall, Ray, and Tucker, Marc. *Thinking for a Living.* New York: Basic Books, 1992.

McCaskey, Michael B. *The Executive Challenge.* Boston: Pitman, 1982.

Metropolitan Life Survey of the American Teacher 1989. New York: Louis Harris and Associates, 1989.

Pasmore, William A., and Fagans, Mary R. "Participation, Individual Development, and Organizational Change: A Review and Synthesis." *Journal of Management* 18, no. 2 (1992): 375-97.

Peters, Thomas J., and Waterman, Robert H. *In Search of Excellence.* New York: Harper & Row, 1982.

Pines, Ayala, and Aronson, Elliot. *Career Burnout: Causes and Cures.* New York: Free Press, 1988.

Prestine, Nona A., and Bowen, Chuck. "Benchmarks and Change: Assessing Essential Schools Restructuring Efforts." *Educational Evaluation and Policy Analysis* 5 (Fall 1993): 298–319.

Schein, Edgar H. *Organizational Culture and Leadership.* San Francisco: Jossey-Bass, 1985.

Sergiovanni, Thomas J. *Moral Leadership.* San Francisco: Jossey-Bass, 1992.

Sizer, Theodore R. *Horace's School.* Boston: Houghton Mifflin, 1992.

Smircich, Linda, and Morgan, Gareth. "Leadership: The Management of Meaning." In *The Organizational Behavior Reader*, 5th ed., edited by David A. Kolb, Irwin M. Rubin, and Joyce S. Osland. Englewood Cliffs, N.J.: Prentice-Hall, 1991.

Vroom, Victor. *Some Personality Determinants of the Effects of Participation.* Englewood Cliffs, N.J.: Prentice-Hall, 1960.

Wasley, Patricia A. *Teachers Who Lead.* New York: Teachers College Press, 1991.

Wasley, Patricia A. "Teacher Leadership in a Teacher-Run School." In *The Changing Contexts of Teaching*, The Ninety-first Yearbook of the National Society for the Study of Education, edited by Ann Lieberman. Chicago: University of Chicago Press, 1992.

Weick, Karl E. *The Social Psychology of Organizing*, 2nd ed. Reading: Mass.: Addison-Wesley, 1979.

Yalom, Irvin D. *Existential Psychology.* New York: Basic Books, 1980.

TWO TEACHERS EXAMINE
THE POWER OF TEACHER
LEADERSHIP

BY VIVIAN TROEN
AND KATHERINE BOLES

Vivian Troen is a fourth-grade teacher at the Edward Devotion School in Brookline, Massachusetts; a part-time faculty member at Wheelock College; and the project director of the Learning/Teaching Collaborative. Katherine Boles is a part-time classroom teacher at the Edward Devotion School and a Visiting Scholar at Harvard University. Her study of the effect of the Learning/Teaching Collaborative on classroom teachers is funded by a Spencer Post-Doctoral Fellowship.

Teaching is not a profession that values or encourages leadership within its ranks. The hierarchical nature of public schools is based on the 19th century industrial model, with the consequent adversarial relationship of administration as management and teachers as labor. Like factory workers in the 1800s, teachers all have equal status. Leadership opportunities are extremely limited.

Recognizing the serious flaws in this traditional model, school reform reports of the late 1980s made compelling recommendations for teachers to provide leadership in restructuring the nation's schools. The reports emphasized the importance of creating new roles for teachers that acknowledged the centrality of classroom teaching and extended teachers' decision-making power into schoolwide leadership activities.

The 1986 report of the Carnegie Task Force on Teaching as a Profession, *A Nation Prepared*, went so far as to say that without teacher support, "any reforms will be short lived" and that "the key [to successful education reform] lies in creating a new profession . . . of well-educated teachers prepared to assume new powers and responsibilities to redesign schools for the future."

In the education community's fervor to find a quick fix to school ills, the phrase "teacher leadership" has emerged as a new buzzword.

It is tempting to ignore the fact that such teacher leadership roles — in curriculum, school improvement, and professional development — often are limited in scope and vision and subject to easy cancellation when budgets are cut.

School districts proudly point to examples of teacher leadership no matter how minimal the impact on day-to-day operations. That's somewhat like calling a banana republic a democracy if a few of its citizens are allowed to vote (with the bulk of the populace resentful of those who do vote) and the supreme power at the top of the administrative ladder watchful and suspicious lest this idea of participation spread and disrupt the status quo.

We would suggest that true teacher leadership enables practicing teachers to reform their work and provides a means for altering the hierarchical nature of schools. Our experience has proven to us that it is absolutely vital that teachers have the tools and the power to remake the profession. What is needed is a culture in which classroom teachers are fully empowered partners in shaping policy, creating curriculum, managing budgets, improving practice, and bringing added value toward the goal of improving education for children.

What makes it so difficult to institutionalize leadership roles for teachers?

The nature of teachers. Concerned with the problems of teaching and most interested in life in the classroom, teachers are reluctant to think of themselves as leaders. They view with some discomfort the idea of assuming quasi-administrative or expanded teaching functions. Also, experience has taught them that teacher leadership and risk-taking are not valued in the schools in which they work. As Roland Barth put it, "A teacher is like a mushroom. It thrives in the darkness, but when it sticks its neck out, its head immediately gets cut off."

The structure of schools. In most American schools there is an expectation of top-down mandates with little input from practitioners. This organizational structure makes it as inappropriate for a teacher to assume leadership as it is for an assembly-line worker to suggest how to improve the assembly line. Perhaps we should say as it *was* for an assembly-line worker; many automobiles today are built by teams, and auto workers are increasingly involved in restructuring their work. As an indicator of social change, teaching is less progressive than making cars.

The egalitarian ethic. If some teachers are leaders and others are not, how can teaching be egalitarian? When teacher leaders emerge and begin to affect policy and the larger domains of the school, they encounter resistance not just from the principal, but from other teachers who have been heard to say, "Just who does she think she is?" To introduce teacher leadership is to introduce status differences based on knowledge, skill, and initiative into a profession that has made no provision for them. Seeing some teachers do something new and different, getting attention and respect, intensifies feelings of turf-protection and powerlessness in others. And this brings up what is probably the most important obstacle of all to the institutionalization of teacher leadership.

The issue of power. Often left undiscussed in the reform dialogue surrounding the implementation of "shared decision making," "school-based management," and the "professionalization of teaching" is the issue of power. Decision-making power in schools is allocated carefully. Decisions about classroom policy — what to teach, how to use time, and how to assess progress — are made by teachers. But other decisions that affect teachers' work — scheduling, class placement, assignment of specialists, and the allocation of budget and materials — are made at higher levels of the school bureaucracy. The norm, in which teachers feel powerless to affect schoolwide policy, is widely accepted by teachers and administrators. This view of power as a "zero-sum game," in which a gain in one area requires a loss in another, makes it difficult for teacher leaders to emerge in schools. And where principals fear they will be relegated to being operational managers as a result of teachers taking on new leadership roles, they actively oppose such changes; and teacher leadership cannot succeed.

What must be done, then, in order to further the goal of institutionalizing teacher leadership?

Reform the workplace. Working in isolated classrooms and competing for scarce resources, teachers often eye each other suspiciously as they lead their children down school corridors. The "egg-crate" mold of the school, with its secretive and competitive aspects, must be broken. When a philosophy of collaboration and risk-taking replaces teacher isolation, teacher leadership will emerge. When teachers work in teams and teaching becomes a more public act, teachers will venture beyond the classroom. Teams can become a forum in which teachers can take risks with their teaching and expand their knowledge base.

The egalitarian ethic must be reconsidered, not rejected. There is much to be said for teachers being equal members of their profession. Currently, teachers are not at all equal. They live in competitive isolation, competing for the scarce resources available to them, knowing that some teachers have more access to these resources than others. If teaching were truly egalitarian, we would value each teacher's contribution to the education of children and be able to recognize teachers' individual areas of expertise and celebrate teachers' leadership initiatives.

If teachers are to assume leadership roles that will positively affect their practice, they need time for reflection and opportunities to conduct professional inquiry. What we are calling for cannot be accomplished at the end of a long day in the classroom. There must be a reorganization of time and work if teacher leadership is to succeed. Time in the work day must be restructured so that it can become a resource, not one more reason why teachers are unable to assume leadership.

Redefine the role of principal. Because principals are encouraged to be instructional leaders, they often feel threatened when asked to make room for teachers. Principal preparation programs must be restructured so that principals are charged with the mission of developing a community of leaders within their schools. They must be provided with strategies to facilitate teachers taking on leadership roles, and they must participate in teaching teachers how to be leaders. They need to provide teachers with both the reason and the opportunity, including time, to lead.

Principals must understand that their influence over classroom teaching will be enhanced, not diminished, by involving teachers in making decisions on matters of curriculum, instruction, scheduling, and budgets. Principals in schools must come to believe that power is not "zero-sum"; by sharing power with others, the quantity of power for each participant increases. Finally, the role of the principal, with its plethora of administrative tasks, should be redesigned so that principals have the time to become educational leaders in their own right.

Support the role of teacher as leader. The phrase "teacher leader" will remain no more than an oxymoron if the education community continues to treat it as such. Teachers themselves must advocate for the creation of leadership roles. Building on their expertise in teaching and learning and their understanding of the needs of children, teachers now must acquire leadership skills and an understanding of organizational theory and behavior in order to facilitate change.

Teachers must become resources for one another, and they must become accountable to each other for the work they do. No longer should teachers stand by helplessly as teacher colleagues "sink or swim" in their first few years in the classroom. No longer can teachers turn a blind eye to the teacher who is behaving unprofessionally or to those who are not working hard enough.

Similarly, school districts must evaluate principals on their ability to foster teacher leadership in their buildings and to provide incentives and rewards for teachers who take the lead on tasks or problems. Teacher unions must cultivate leadership among their members and take responsibility for educating teachers in the political and organizational aspects of their work. Federal and state policy makers must support and oversee rigorous, professional standards of practice.

Simultaneously, colleges of education must recognize the importance of teacher leadership and strengthen their commitment to teaching those skills as a required component of teacher education.

If we are to change the professional environment of the school, we also must develop external connections — fostering better relationships between professionals in schools and parents, colleges, state departments of education, federal agencies, and the business community. This can lay the groundwork for teacher leadership to become a powerful catalyst for the professionalization of teaching.

The Learning/Teaching Collaborative

Our experience with a college/school partnership that restructured teaching and learning in several Massachusetts schools indicated to us that teacher leadership can be defined in new ways. We will use examples from this collaborative to illustrate new directions in teacher leadership.

In 1987, the authors of this essay, together with Wheelock College faculty member Karen Worth, created the Learning/Teaching Collaborative, a partnership between the Boston and Brookline, Massachusetts, public schools and Wheelock and Simmons Colleges. The goal of this collaborative was to provide opportunities for teachers to assume new professional roles while remaining in the classroom. Administered by teachers, this team-teaching model sets out to alter the organization of instruction, mainstream special needs students, integrate bilingual students into regular classrooms, and create new professional roles for teachers. Four components provide the framework for the collaborative:

1. Team Teaching: Teachers, functioning as a team, share curriculum and children. Five hours per month are allocated for team meetings outside the school day. In addition, principals have arranged

common planning time for teachers so that teachers, their interns, and the college supervisor can meet on a regular basis.

2. School/University Collaboration: Graduate student interns from Wheelock College or Simmons College work full time in the teams during the entire school year. A school teacher and a college faculty member teach the Wheelock interns' graduate-level curriculum seminar together; other teachers present guest lectures on their particular areas of expertise; and a number of classroom teachers teach reading and math methods courses at the two colleges. A steering committee composed of college and school faculty representatives and administrators from each of the participating institutions governs the collaborative and meets four times per year. Subcommittees meet throughout the year to handle budget, recruitment of interns, professional development of teachers, parent involvement, and public relations.

3. Special Education Inclusion: In a number of the teams, special needs children are fully mainstreamed. Special education teachers are members of the teams; they consult with teachers and give some direct service to children.

4. Alternative Professional Time: Each classroom teacher is provided with a minimum of one day a week (six hours) away from teaching duties to assume an alternative role — curriculum writer, researcher, or student-teacher supervisor/college teacher. This "Alternative Professional Time" (APT) is facilitated by the full-time presence of teaching interns.

Effects of the Collaborative
on the Development of Teacher Leadership

An increasing number of teachers in the Learning/Teaching Collaborative have assumed leadership. Leadership roles were not formally designated by the collaborative; they emerged naturally from the work the teachers did together. Though the teachers generally gravitated toward other teachers with similar interests when they assumed their leadership roles, their behavior became entrepreneurial and their roles self-determined.

Three aspects of the collaborative are central to the development of teacher leadership.

Teaming and the equal-status work group. The experience of working together in the team has been the most challenging and the most worthwhile aspect of the collaborative for the teachers. Team teaching has eliminated teacher isolation. The collaborative has given the teachers a common frame of reference and a common language. Teachers talk about teaching and report feeling energized by team discussions. They take increased risks with curriculum and feel accountable to other team members for the work they do. They trust their colleagues and feel the collective latitude to take professional risks.

Time as a facilitating factor. A key feature of the collaborative is the allocation of a significant amount of professional time to be used by the teacher at his or her discretion. School reform reports of the 1980s contained repeated pleas for a reconceptualization of the school day so that teachers would have more time to accomplish their work and assume new roles. However, most reform experiments have been unable to institute blocks of time for these purposes.

By providing full-time graduate-student interns to work in classrooms, the collaborative has managed to fulfill the promise of creating more time for teachers. Not only are there two teachers in the classroom during most of the week, but the presence of the interns has provided the teachers with time during the week to pursue their own professional development through APT, the six hours a week away from classroom responsibilities.

All teachers have assumed new responsibilities to fill the time. They speak about how busy they are, but they do not complain about their inability to accomplish their work because of a lack of time. Nor do they describe feeling guilty about being away from their children or being unable to accomplish their primary role of classroom teacher, though they all have taken on additional professional roles.

Collaboration with the college and leverage beyond the classroom. The college connection has enabled teachers to expand their professional influence and gain leverage outside their schools without leaving classroom teaching. The teachers discovered that working in the collaborative gave them more clout than they had as individual teachers. Since it was understood that the teachers were instituting a specific program − one that had guidelines and roles − teachers found it easier to request alternative professional time and common planning time from their principals. Principals, recognizing that APT invigorated their veteran teachers, were willing to oblige.

Developing a New Paradigm for Teacher Leadership

Our work in the Learning/Teaching Collaborative has caused us to rethink the definition of teacher leadership. Traditional descriptions of teacher leaders portray teachers who have been chosen to

Our purpose in this essay is not to present the Learning/Teaching Collaborative as the "answer" to teacher leadership, but to offer it as one model for implementing a new leadership paradigm. Once we move beyond the unsuccessful paradigm that mimics the current hierarchical nature of schools, new possibilities open for us. All too often, teachers' reluctance to assume leadership is attributed to the norm of equality among teachers. We would suggest that it is possible to respect the norm of equality and develop even more powerful forms of teacher leadership. New leadership paradigms can emerge as teachers themselves begin to assess the prospects of teacher leadership.

Teachers involved in the collaborative know that they influence the creation of policy and are privy to the details of the organization's functioning. The collaborative has broadened their horizons beyond the school and has exposed them in new and meaningful ways to the world of theory. Instead of competing for scarce resources, they have begun to work collegially and advocate collectively for changes in their work. No longer isolated in "egg-crate schools," they demonstrate their strength in ways they would never have imagined just a few years ago. They have seen their practice reflected back to them through the interns' eyes. As they assume new leadership roles, they have deepened their understanding of policy, curriculum, and the value of research to practice. The collaborative has provided renewal and stimulation for veteran teachers; it has made teachers accountable to each other for the work they have done together; and it has caused them to inquire into their own practices.

What Do Teachers Do in the New World of Restructured Schools?

Teachers are assuming leadership in many new ways in schools and school districts around the country. The following examples support our contention that leadership by teachers must be central to any program of school reform:

- Teachers participate in the larger world of curriculum and pedagogy in new ways. They keep abreast of current research and assume a more powerful stance, affecting the development of curriculum at all levels from textbook publication to state-house policymaking to classroom teaching.
- Teachers agitate for the inclusion of technology and technological advances, and they have a clear vision of how technol-

ogy can improve teaching and learning. They understand that technology makes it possible for teachers to break out of their traditional isolation, communicating with outside experts and their peers about the instructional content and pedagogical issues that are the heart of their work.

- Teachers go beyond the role of teacher as "deliverer of knowledge." They create knowledge by working on research in their classrooms and across schools and communities. They believe that, as teachers, they have a responsibility for systematic research and inquiry directed at the improvement of their practice.
- Teachers read widely from the professional literature and speak knowledgeably about the most current ideas in education. They participate in high-level debates about education and express their ideas confidently, knowing that their ideas are based in practice and substantiated by research.
- Teachers play a central role in the development and the implementation of policy. Policy decisions are not beyond their purview — that is, made elsewhere and delivered to them for implementation.
- Teachers confront issues of how to implement change. They understand the change process and how to work within the system to accomplish their goals.
- Teachers write about what they do. They are aware that they have a responsibility to share what they know with the community, with other teachers, and with policy makers, because teachers have a great deal of knowledge about children and about school.
- Teachers hold themselves and their colleagues accountable for the work they do. They are aware of their responsibility to maintain high standards, and they recognize their obligation to play an important role in decisions that affect them, their children, and their schools.
- Teachers learn about adult development and its ramifications. They assume that mentoring is a part of their professional lives, and they are aware of the importance of their legacy to the next generation of school teachers.
- Teachers seek to open communication with individuals and institutions outside of schools. They work hard to break down the barriers that exist around their profession, so that those outside the profession understand what goes on inside. Teachers understand the power of building a constituency, and they recognize that parents and the community are important allies.

Currently there are pockets of such teacher leadership activities around the country. If these ideas continue to remain the exception, they will go no further than individual classrooms and school districts.

What is needed now is a national movement that assumes teacher leadership is a core value, not an accessory of school reform available to a few individuals. A forum for discussion and a vehicle for setting standards for teacher leadership already exists in the National Board for Professional Teaching Standards (NBPTS). The board is in the process of extending the definition of teacher leadership beyond traditional boundaries and examining some of the alternative forms that teacher leadership can take.

We urge the NBPTS to take into consideration three pivotal elements that our work in schools has shown to be fundamental to a new leadership paradigm: Leadership among teachers must be *entrepreneurial*, *experimental*, and *generative*. When teachers assume roles that interest them and then adapt those roles to fit their own particular interests and needs, they become entrepreneurs who further the cause of school reform. When teachers assume their new roles and then mold and shape them to suit their needs and the needs of their students, they experiment with new curricula and pedagogy and improve the education of children. Finally, when teachers work with new teachers, educate the next generation of teachers, or do research and write about their work with children, they assume a generative role that benefits not only themselves, but all of us. Our experience in the Learning/Teaching Collaborative has demonstrated that empowered teachers can create successful models to change today's schools.

THE PROBLEM WITH POWER
BY DANIEL A. HELLER

Daniel A. Heller is Supervisor of Instruction at Brattleboro Union High School in Brattleboro, Vermont.

Imagine this scene. Eleven adults are sitting around a table in a small conference room. Eight of these people are the public high school's elected Faculty Senate. The other three are building administrators. The task is to establish a working relationship for the smooth running of the school that will allow the institution to chart a course of change to help it meet the future effectively and productively through a system of shared governance.

"We need to know how decisions will be made," says a Senate member.

"That's right," says another. "Who will have the final say? If the faculty votes for something, then it should happen."

"Well, I don't know," responds an administrator. "What if the request is not reasonable? What happens then?"

"Let's cut to the chase. Does anyone have veto power here? If administrators have veto power, then how can this be a system of shared governance?" asks a Senate member.

The conversation goes on for many meetings over several days. One immediately notices that a significant element is missing. The discussion never turns to education, to students, to pedagogy. Basically, it boils down to one question: Who's in charge here? With all the changes facing American schools, I often wonder if education institutions can survive conversations such as these, which serve to polarize staffs around power issues and avoid the important work of preparing young people to enter society as productive, responsible adults.

"Empowerment," "leadership," and "shared governance" have become buzzwords in education; but without further thoughtful definition, they are empty phrases thrown about by people who have no clear direction. These concepts are in the same perilous position as so many good ideas before them; they risk being merely short-lived fads. To avoid losing these powerful ideas and to avoid perpetuating the cynicism of education reform, members of the education community must carefully define and articulate these concepts, pursue them thoroughly, and work them into the everyday fabric of the education enterprise so that we can get beyond them to engage in the primary tasks of education.

Power is a problematic term. More than any other word, this one produces the most difficulties, errors, misunderstandings, and negative feelings. If education professionals persist, as we often do, in defining power in terms of the ability to make others do what we want (Who's in charge here?), then we are in trouble. This is a reductive, negative view. However, escaping this tradition is easier said than done.

Recently, I have been deeply involved in a school going through a process of moving from relative autocracy to a system of shared governance. Unfortunately, since we have not yet worked through the power issue, one of the questions most often asked has been, "Who has veto power?" Even though we have been trying to create a new system, we have been asking old questions about the concept of power. Everybody has wanted to know who has the ability to control the actions of others — who ultimately makes the decisions? These are legitimate questions only if we are unwilling to reconceive the idea of power. However, if we do not redefine the concept, then there is little chance for reform.

These questions also are symptomatic of the legacy of distrust that has built up in education institutions. People are used to having little or no institutional power. In this light, schools may have to ask those questions and to work through the answers, but they also have to get beyond them. Both teachers and administrators need to see that power is realized through sharing. The concept of collaboration must replace the traditional view of power. Administrators who try to control everything in the increasingly complex social, political, and legal arena of public schools are foolish. Teachers who think that professionalism means having to answer to no one are equally misguided. Schools are big pies; everybody can have a piece.

So what is a useful definition of power? I propose that school personnel begin to see power as the ability to control oneself, not others. As teachers, we should empower students to take control of their lives. Similarly, schools must empower teachers to make decisions in their classrooms about what is best for their students. There exists a cliché about power that I have discovered to be largely true: The only thing you can do with power is give it away. The way to invigorate people, to make them true professionals, is to give them power as I have defined it — the power to control their own lives.

The traditional power holders in schools need to help others see that those in formerly powerless positions can and should make decisions about their work and their professional growth. Those who traditionally have been in power must provide the space, the moral support, and the means for this to happen. This applies to professional development, school governance, and teaching. But first, these traditional power holders must look into their own hearts and egos and see the benefits of sharing. Sharing does not mean giving everything away; it means collaborating, working together, and honoring and respecting the perceptions and talents of others. Above all, it means realizing that together we are more powerful than we are individually.

Of course, just offering to share power is not enough. People are not always ready to accept power. They have to be coached into the dialogue. The sharing of power is the kind of fundamental shift that requires a gradual implementation through training and discussion. People become used to a hierarchical structure, which can be comforting. Someone else is responsible. Someone else takes the blame, finds the money, obtains the permission, and has the headaches. When one assumes power over oneself, then all the problems of making decisions come, too. Power is responsibility.

Another problem is that people tend to recreate the past because they really do not know anything else. Vaclav Havel, playwright and president of the Czech Republic, calls this *pseudorenascence*, a false rebirth. One creates the illusion of progress and innovation, but really the old has simply taken on a new form with new players — a shifting, not a sharing, of power.

The shift that educators should be looking for is fundamental: changing the basic manner in which we do business with each other, with our students, and with ourselves. The concept of the "power over" must become the concept of the "power to," as educators begin to realize the power within themselves. The system should allow people to make decisions for optimizing resources and educational experiences. Education professionals should have the power to do what they need to do, not the power to control others. The key is trust.

Much of the history of education is littered with mistreatment of teachers by autocratic systems, pedagogical fads that become systems and are forced on classrooms, and poor salaries. It is little wonder that some teachers unions have developed an "us or them" attitude. Of course, many administrators approve of this labor-management division and relish their "power" as managers. I have always been appalled at this division between teachers and administrators. Don't we all have the same goal: to provide the best possible education for our children? Why aren't we all one professional association? The time has come to gain power over ourselves as secure professionals so that we can then share without fear, recognizing the power in collective action and responsibility. There is a history to work through. Working through and beyond it is vital to the survival of American education. We must create a new history and a new culture through behaviors that embrace collective action. We must learn to trust one another and to stop bickering over trivial matters. Professionals should not be in competition with one another. The education of America's youth is far too important to be sacrificed to power struggles between teachers and administrators. At no time in the conversation can we allow ourselves to lose sight of the primary mission of schools: the education of our children.

Once we determine our common goals, whatever they are in any particular school or community, then we have to allocate resources. I do not know of many schools that are overstaffed, but many have staffs that are poorly deployed. One merely has to look at the typical career ladder in education. Many excellent teachers become administrators and no longer use their teaching skills. Why should not excellent teachers become teachers of teachers, while others with the requisite organizational skills become administrators? Empowerment necessitates a system wherein each professional has room and resources to do what he or she does best and is rewarded accordingly.

Can we convert schools into education centers? Schools should be places where people celebrate learning and personal growth. They should be places where people respect one another's talents and share those talents to the betterment of all. Creating such centers would entail reciprocal agreements with institutions of higher learning for training student interns and providing inservice for professionals. Teachers could then conduct seminars and courses for student interns, becoming adjunct faculty for the colleges. Thus we could utilize and validate teaching skills. The school would benefit from the interns by gaining more help for individualized instruction, more service on committees and local projects, and an influx of ideas and energy. Ideally, the result would be a wonderful swirl of educational activity.

In fact, I believe that there should be no non-teaching positions. One of the tragedies of the education system at present is the need for teachers to leave the classroom in order to climb the career ladder. Would it not be better for every member of the professional staff to teach at least some time each year? One forgets the difficulties of teaching once having left the classroom. Most teachers have noticed recent major changes in student characteristics and legal demands on their teaching performance. Being out of the classroom reduces both the understanding of these issues and sympathy for those who deal with them. How can supervisors offer constructive criticism without firsthand experience of the issues? How can their work be credible? If we value the job of educating children, then we should model the behaviors necessary for success, thus once again sharing in the full enterprise of education.

If all educators were also teachers, then we would better remember the excitement of learning and the fear of ignorance, the boredom resulting from being talked at and the joy of discovery. We might better sympathize with our students and be more sensitive to their needs and feelings. We also might model habits of life-long learning. Students would see us asking each other questions, training one another, and experimenting and failing and trying again without guilt or shame. Students might become partners with teachers and administrators in the quest for answers to complex questions. We could take risks together, pooling our human resources for success.

If the ultimate power is power over oneself, then how can this be achieved? First, schools must redefine the process of professional growth and evaluation, because empowerment includes responsibility, in this case responsibility for one's professional growth. If educators are to be true professionals, then they must embrace supervision as a growth experience, not as a factory-type inspection. Teacher evaluation, which has been shown to be fairly useless as a means for improving instruction, must be reconfigured as a helpful process, leading teachers to invest themselves in professional growth. Professionals must grow intellectually throughout their careers. However, for that to happen, school systems must be willing to provide the means, time, and space for that growth to occur. Above all, they must trust the professional teachers. I believe that the process of supervision and evaluation is a natural opening for shared governance. All members of the institution should own a piece of this process, have something to say about it, have some control over it. These members include students, teachers, administrators, board members, and parents.

The evaluation process can take place on a number of levels. The first is peer to peer. As teachers embrace the professional value of continuous growth, then the need for direct supervision by administrators becomes less necessary. Why should a teacher having trouble controlling a class ask for help from an administrator, when that teacher can ask a peer across the hall to observe his classes and offer advice? Here is a new form of power, the power to choose where your help will come from and the form it will take. Again, this does not just happen; the school must establish a norm of peer supervision.

Similarly, why pay expensive experts to come to schools for inservice days when teachers might better talk to each other, sharing what they are learning in courses, workshops, and professional reading? A good peer supervision program creates a state of continuous inservice. As teachers become familiar and comfortable with controlling their professional growth, they will see the benefits in improved instruction, an open flow of ideas, and shared governance through shared ownership of professional growth. And students will see teachers modeling the acceptability of asking for help and learning from one another.

Once teachers learn and the institution accepts that they can teach each other and that they have a great deal of expertise, then they can begin to make larger decisions. For instance, if a number of teachers have, through observing each other's classes and working together, discovered a weakness in the curriculum, then they are in a position to do something about it. They have, if you will, the power to act, which they have achieved through applying their expertise in an environment that honors that expertise. Once the institution has achieved this stage, power and leadership are simply floating publicly for anyone to tap into, when and if she or he can. I have seen the culture of a group of teachers changed by this process. Teachers became the experts on teaching that they should be. Their work and ideas gained a new dignity, and they felt a new investment in their careers. They were empowered to control themselves. Schools must capture this spirit of power if we are to reform our schools into what they could and should be. From this point, we can move easily to the larger issues of leadership.

The system I have described has definite implications for the administrator. This role necessarily will change as schools move away from traditional definitions of power. Schools are not factories. We do not manufacture identical products. We cannot control our raw material, and we cannot control the market into which we release our students. Schools are human enterprises; and the idea of productivity, while a useful analogy, is ultimately incorrect. Certainly we want to make the best use of the limited time that we have with our students. However, efficiency cannot replace the need to take time with individuals, to get to know our students as people, and to help each student to develop his or her unique qualities.

Administrators must help teachers to model independent thinking and problem solving for their students. To do this, the administrator must see his or her role as a supporter of, rather than the controller of teachers. Teachers should not have to ask permission to try new ideas, methods, or materials. Instead, they should share their plans with their administrators in order to fine-tune them and determine how the administrator might assist with funding, time, or observational feedback. In a sense, we must reverse the hierarchy. Administrators need to work for teachers, who themselves need to work for students. If teachers are to meet students' needs, then shouldn't administrators be meeting teachers' needs?

Schools are service organizations, and one can conceive of the various roles within them in terms of service. The job of the administrator is to create an environment that allows teachers to perform to the best of their ability. To this end, they need to find out what teachers need in terms of time, materials, training, and space. Administrators bring their own knowledge to this task, as well as the information they have received directly from teachers, from students, and from general or specific observation. Teachers serve the needs of students. They also bring their knowledge to the task, plus what they find out from the students themselves (such as learning styles, learning problems, interests, and the like), from the community, and from professional associations. Finally, all branches of the school, from student to school board, exist to serve one another in the joint enterprise of creating the best educational experience possible.

An illustration of this empowerment, trust, and service may be useful. Recently, I found myself in the position of having to evaluate the band director in the high school where I work. I had never observed a music class before and knew little about music in general. By training I am a secondary English teacher and instructional supervisor. But when the structure of the school in which I teach and supervise shifted, I was suddenly charged with evaluating the music programs.

The teacher and I sat down in September to discuss our plans for his evaluation. We had no trouble with my observing his generic teaching skills. But the teacher wanted more. At his request, we included several other components in the evaluation process. First, he would invite a professional music teacher from a nearby university to observe his teaching and write something for me to include in the summary evaluation. Second, the teacher developed a questionnaire for his students, so we could include student perceptions in the evaluation. Finally, he arranged to have some of his classes videotaped so that we could watch the tapes together and critique his classes. What began as a contractual obligation, the evaluation of the band instructor, became a process tailored to this teacher's needs and goals. Because we trusted each other and because I allowed the teacher to control the development of the process by giving up the absolute control traditionally associated with the supervisor's role, the results were of much greater value than they otherwise might have been.

But do teachers have to be evaluated at all? I suppose they do, but not through a process of obligatory and cursory inspection. Certainly, it is to a teacher's advantage to have performance reviews in his or her personnel record; and these should be done by qualified, credible evaluators. However, I do not see the need for an evaluation every year. In fact, evaluation can be intimidating, suppressing the teacher's willingness to take risks. On the other hand, supervision that is seen as formative and growth-oriented, as opposed to summative and evaluative, can be useful.

As long as the hiring process is imperfect, we will need a system that provides a fair method of documenting inferior work as grounds for dismissal. However, that purpose should not constrain the supervision system. Projects conceived in negativity are destined to be negative and confining, rather than liberating. Why not conceive the process as a liberating and growth-oriented one?

I work in a school system that requires teacher evaluation every three years. In the two alternate years, called supervision years, teachers develop goal statements to work toward throughout the year. There is no formal evaluation during this phase, thus encouraging growth and experimentation. The only documentation that goes into the permanent record is the original goal statement and a summary paragraph by the teacher recounting the year's activities toward achieving those goals. I actually saw one teacher's statement, which said, "Much of what I tried failed, and much of what I learned I learned too late to help my students this year." That kind of candid statement is a tribute to the risk and honesty this program encourages. To me, this is professional empowerment.

This "risk-free" supervision program has produced some terrific results with respect to teachers' professional growth and control over their professional lives. One teacher developed an evaluation procedure for himself, which included student questionnaires and peer review. He could experiment with this idea during his supervision year, and then actually put the process he had developed into practice for his evaluation year. Other teachers have kept logs of their work, particularly with new curricula, or diaries of projects such as organizing a student overseas trip. These logs became resource manuals for other teachers.

One of the most interesting supervision plans that teachers have used is the response journal. In this plan, the teacher keeps thoughts, reflections, and questions in a journal, which a supervisor reads periodically. The supervisor also writes thoughts and ideas in response to the entries. This creates a rich yet non-threatening professional dialogue. Once teachers are freed to develop their own professional growth plans, the only limit to the products is the imagination of the professionals involved. This type of system naturally encompasses the concepts of shared governance and leadership.

Over time, such a system can develop an atmosphere of trust, professional risk, and cooperation. Traditional power holders, such as administrators and school board members, learn to trust others and let go of complete control. Yet this still is not enough. All members of the organization also must demonstrate commitment. If only a few people come to meetings, develop meaningful goals, or take part in decisions, then there is no shared governance; and those doing the work will burn out. I believe lack of participation is partially historical. Who will believe that business can be done differently? For years, teachers have watched education fads come and go, while the power hierarchy remained virtually unaffected. Thus many teachers have had the negative experience of devoting time and energy to committee work that ended in disappointment. Why should anything be different?

My fear is that changing structures, with all the energy this takes, will not be enough. Unless we change attitudes, new structures will simply reproduce business as usual. Educators must develop new roles, new relationships, and new attitudes of trust and respect. We would see more progress toward renewed systems of shared governance and empowerment by changing our mindsets and leaving the structures alone than by simply changing structures without changing our thinking.

Groups of teachers, with the support of sensitive administrators, need to transform the system from within. By this I mean to work slowly, taking on small issues first to build credibility. For instance, teachers who have discovered weaknesses in the curriculum could proceed to correct them through experimentation and revision. What these professionals need is not direction but space and time to work. Perhaps they may need materials as well. Then administrators should get out of the way.

At the very heart of the process is trust. Not everyone will jump on board the new way of thinking. People are in different places in their lives and in their hearts. Some very fine teachers may prefer not to involve themselves beyond their classroom walls. The system must honor this. We cannot expect everybody to change suddenly. We must start small, keep at it, support change and empowerment, and bring people along as they are ready.

Another crucial ingredient in this type of reform is the school board. Laws differ from state to state but, generally, the board or some state body has the ultimate traditional power to control what transpires in schools: curriculum, pedagogy, funding, class size. Employees' efforts can be undone in an instant by the board's decisions. Therefore, boards should be informed at all steps of the change process, thus avoiding the suspicion that anyone is trying to sneak something by the board. In these reports, educators can show themselves as competent, caring, knowledgeable professionals. A constant flow of quality information is key. Educators must bring the board to the realization that the board's power increases as the power of individuals in the school increases. In other words, if they can help to maximize the potential of everyone in the school community, then they stand to gain as the ultimate leaders of that school community. The school board members are crucial players in establishing trust and confidence and taking risks for growth in the schools.

All of us together can break the cycle of mistrust and cynicism. We can increase teacher buy-in to an empowering system. If we believe in teachers as professionals, then we must treat them as such. A committee to study curriculum must have the power to make the changes it sees as necessary. This is one of the most difficult shifts for the administrator, to give up the control over and join forces with the professional staff. What is the point of all that talent, the rich resources that teachers contain and are, if they remain bottled up, unreleased? I am not suggesting that the administrator give up leadership, but that to lead often means to give others the space and authority to do what they do best, allowing them to share in the leadership, to become leaders themselves. Administrators must trust professionals to be professionals. The cynicism will not go away immediately, but it will go away as administrators build a track record of trust and shared decision making. Schools must see everyone, including students and parents, as leaders and potential leaders. The job of the administrator is to keep the process going, to keep all the balls in the air. This means coaching, supporting, helping, asking tough questions. The administrator has to provide the means for the process to thrive.

Issues of professionalism, shared governance, power, pedagogy, curriculum, all become subsets of the primary purpose of the school: to educate our children. A school should be a learning community. People should not be afraid to ask questions, to take risks, to help one another, and to support one another. This is a picture of shared governance. All members of the school community are leaders: students, teachers, paraprofessionals, secretaries, administrators, parents, custodians, food-service personnel, the business community, the board. Their collective power is, indeed, the ultimate power.

Rather than wasting time arguing over who can tell whom what to do, we should be grappling with the more important issues of how to help kids and mustering the resources at our disposal to bring our vision to reality.

THE NATIONAL BOARD FOR PROFESSIONAL TEACHING STANDARDS: TOWARD A COMMUNITY OF TEACHER LEADERS

BY JAMES A. KELLY

James A. Kelly is president and chief executive officer of the National Board for Professional Teaching Standards. He was elected the first president of NBPTS in 1987.

> *Teaching and leading are distinguishable occupations, but every great leader is clearly teaching — and every great teacher is leading.*
>
> — John W. Gardner

John Gardner tells a story about Woodrow Wilson when he was president of Princeton University. "How can I democratize this university," Wilson demanded, "if the faculty won't do what I ask?" (Gardner 1993, p. 25). Like many good anecdotes, this may be apocryphal. Nevertheless, it suits my purpose, for to me it signifies what is wrong with traditional efforts at school reform.

There is general agreement both within the education community and across the nation that America's schools are in need of strengthening. Our aspirations for education outstrip the current capacity of the education system and thus create major gaps between expectation and performance. We expect schools to enroll everyone, provide new services to the handicapped and to racial minority groups previously the victims of discrimination, offer instruction to millions for whom English is a new language, eradicate sex discrimination in the classroom, and adapt to technological change. Through it all, we expect schools continuously to improve student academic performance.

In their attempts to close the gap between expectation and performance, several very different but potentially complementary strategies have emerged. One is to "fix the kids": improve prenatal and early childhood services, attend more aggressively to children's health, address such problems of adolescence as teen pregnancy and youth violence, and improve skills training for young adults. A second is to "fix the standards": develop national standards for desired student outcomes and implement "consequential" tests of student progress (although precious little talk is heard about what to do with kids who "fail" the tests). A third is to "fix the schools": reorganize and restructure schools with more teacher collaboration and parent involvement (for example, programs developed by Ted Sizer, Jim Comer, and Henry Levin). A fourth is to "fix the technology": harness technology to educate kids in schools before the telecommunications revolution now under way offers more effective at-home learning opportunities at a fraction of the cost of schooling. Finally, we come to the teacher issue: "fix the teaching" by improving teacher education and state licensure practices and by implementing the new voluntary National Board Certification system being developed for accomplished teachers.

Unfortunately, efforts to employ these strategies to produce world-class schools for world-class students have met so far with only mixed success. I do not presume to make light of these efforts; they are serious initiatives undertaken by serious and intelligent men and women. I believe, however, that at least part of the answer lies in an understanding of the anecdote with which I opened this essay. Like Wilson's idea of democracy, they are all splendid notions that often have been imposed from above. Genuine, long-lasting school initiatives must derive from and involve teachers, for teachers are at the heart of education.

Historically, America's attitude toward its teachers has been ambivalent, perhaps even schizophrenic. On the one hand, we entrust them with our greatest resource, our children, and expect them to perform the daily classroom miracles I enumerated above. On the other hand, we pay them poorly and treat them with little or no respect. We pay lip-service to teaching as a profession; but in important ways we treat our teachers like "blue-collar" workers, cogs in a production machine who are told what to do and how to do it by "higher" authorities.

On reflection, I retract that statement. More and more factories are finding it cost-effective to create a climate in which all employees, regardless of their position or salary, are encouraged to participate in important decision-making activities. W. Edwards Deming and Tom Peters have preached the benefits of shared leadership for years. A recent issue of *Fortune* magazine highlighted the efforts of com-

300

panies committed to a total restructuring as they transform their traditional ideas about power and leadership. "Call it whatever you like: post-heroic leadership, servant leadership, distributed leadership, or, to suggest a tag, virtual leadership. But don't dismiss it as just another touchy-feely flavor of the month. It's real, it's radical, and it's challenging the very definition of corporate leadership for the 21st century. 'People realize now that they really must do it to survive,' says management guru Tom Peters" (Huey 1994, p. 42).

Meanwhile, the structure of the traditional school has been and continues to be hierarchical, with teachers quite firmly fixed on the bottom rung of a bureaucratic ladder designed almost a century ago. It is an all-too-frequently accepted truism that exemplary teachers who seek rewards for their efforts can most easily find those rewards by leaving the classroom. Moving "up" means moving out of teaching.

All too often, in visiting one school or another across the country, one is faced with a variation of one of the following three scenarios:

1. Maureen Jones is a third-grade teacher at Beatrix Potter Elementary School. Her first year at Potter was extremely difficult. Her colleagues, all veterans, volunteered no assistance; and she was too shy to ask for help. Besides, she didn't want anyone to know how inadequate to the task she felt. Overwhelmed by her responsibilities, she often considered resigning; but she needed the job and was unable to think of anything else in which she was either skilled or particularly interested. Now, after three years in the same school, she is less intimidated by both the workload and her students, though she admits that she does not especially enjoy teaching. She considers it fortunate that she has not been tapped to serve on any faculty committees since she has been at the school. Twice each year Maureen is observed by a supervisor, who arranges her visitation in advance. Maureen plans a special lesson for the event. Her supervisor meets briefly with her afterward, usually compliments her on her work, makes a few general observations ("I noticed a boy in the back of the room who didn't seem to be engaged"), and departs. Maureen is engaged to be married and plans to leave teaching after her marriage.

2. John Radcliffe has been teaching at Gertrude Ederle Junior High School for five years. During this time he has served on a faculty school-reorganization committee, advised the student newspaper, and won a "favorite teacher" award. On his own time, he is organizing a debating team that meets in his classroom after school. This will be his last year at Ederle. At

301

the recommendation of his principal, who told him that he has "leadership potential," Radcliffe prepared for the assistant-principal exam. He passed with flying colors. He has been given his first administrative assignment and will begin at the new school next fall.

3. Jeanne Folsom has been at Benjamin Franklin High School for six years. She has been asked by the seniors to give their graduation address. This year she is team teaching a humanities elective with a member of another department. The two teachers devoted some of the previous summer vacation to designing the course. Folsom heads the faculty curriculum committee and acts as mentor to a new teacher in her department. Recently, Folsom requested of her principal that she be permitted to teach three-fourths time in order to fulfill all her out-of-class commitments without short-changing her students and herself. Her request was denied. "The other teachers will resent it," was the explanation offered. Folsom has decided to withdraw from the curriculum committee and has asked the new teacher to find another mentor.

Not long ago, a visitor waiting for a meeting to begin was left to his own devices for a few moments in the faculty room of a large suburban high school. He wandered over to a large, crowded bulletin board that took up most of one wall. Under the heading "Professional Opportunities" was pinned a series of printed announcements of job openings in a variety of schools around the country. He searched in vain for a teaching position — not a single one was posted. The message was clear: teaching is not a respected, professional position. If you want to be considered a professional, leave teaching and move into administration.

Indeed, today's schools are faced with daunting problems; and today's teachers are expected to reach children who have experienced abuse and neglect, poverty, pregnancy, alcohol and drug addiction, violence, gangs, and persistent racism. These same children must be educated to succeed in an increasingly diverse and complex society and competitive global economy.

A special kind of teacher is required to meet these challenges. As Deborah Meier, principal of the Central Park East school in Harlem and a member of the NBPTS board of directors, points out:

> "Since we need a new kind of school to do a new kind of job, we need a new kind of teacher, too. The schools we need require different habits of work and habits of mind on the part

302

of teachers — a kind of professionalism within the classroom few teachers were expected to exhibit before. If teachers are not able to join in leading the changes, the changes will not take place. Politicians and policy makers at all levels may institute vast new legislated reforms; but without the understanding, support, and input of teachers, they will end up in the same dead end as such past reforms as "new math" or "open ed." For all the big brave talk they will be rhetorical and cosmetic, and after a time they will wither away. (Meier 1992, p. 594).

In his book *On Leadership*, John Gardner lists the attributes of the ideal leader. What a daunting list it is: physical vitality and stamina; intelligence and judgment-in-action; willingness to accept responsibilities; task competence; understanding of constituents and their needs; skill in dealing with people; capacity to motivate; courage, resolution, steadiness; capacity to win and hold trust; capacity to manage, decide priorities; adaptability, flexibility of approach. Gardner's list might well be headed "Qualities of an Exemplary Teacher." Those same behaviors that make for effective leaders are the prerequisites for our "new kind of teacher." We say that good teachers should be leaders, but in truth we do everything we can to discourage teachers from leading.

Recently I chaired a panel sponsored by the Charlotte-Mecklenberg schools. Our task was to identify the elements of a "world-class" school system and to establish a plan of action leading to lasting school reform. In our published recommendations is this description of a teacher's day:

> Punch a clock. Sign in and out of the building. Thirty minutes for lunch. Schedule bathroom breaks. No access to the school building unless the students are there. No private offices. No phones for private calls. No time to confer with colleagues. Handle bus duty, corridor duty, cafeteria duty and playground duty. Imagine asking lawyers, doctors, or college professors, for that matter, to put up with such conditions for one week, let alone a lifetime.
>
> Even alone in their classrooms, teachers are not in charge. Many are not free to shape their own curricula or choose their own instructional materials. They must suffer through days punctuated with loudspeaker announcements which suddenly disrupt instruction and put up with school schedules determined by strangers in central offices. Intentional or not, all this translates into no respect. (Murphy 1992, pp. 52-53)

The Genesis of NBPTS

Focusing its attention on these same critical issues, in 1986 the Carnegie Forum on Education and the Economy released *A Nation Prepared: Teachers for the 21st Century*, the report of its Task Force on Teaching as a Profession. The report called for sweeping changes in education policy to facilitate a rise in educational performance and achievement and the creation of a teaching profession equal to that task. It also spelled out the problem:

> The conditions under which teachers work are increasingly intolerable to people who qualify for jobs in the upper tiers of the American work force, the people who must now be attracted to teaching. Those people are, and tend to think of themselves, as professionals. Professional work is characterized by the assumption that the job of the professional is to bring special expertise and judgment to bear on the work at hand. Because their expertise and judgment is respected and they alone are presumed to have it, professionals enjoy a high degree of autonomy in carrying out their work. (Carnegie Forum 1986, p. 36).

Primary among the Carnegie Task Force recommendations was the formation of a National Board for Professional Teaching Standards to establish high and rigorous standards for what accomplished teachers should know and be able to do, to develop and operate a national voluntary system to assess and certify teachers who meet these standards, and to advance related education reforms for the purpose of improving student learning in American schools. The Task Force envisioned that this National Board Certification system would produce teachers who would provide active leadership in the redesign of the schools and help their colleagues to uphold high standards of learning and teaching. The National Board for Professional Teaching Standards was established in 1987 with a governing board of 63 members, the majority of whom are elementary and secondary school teachers.

Our vision is shaped by an image of teaching that is complex but grounded in knowledge that can be learned and applied by most teachers. We see teachers as informed and principled professionals who make thousands of small and large decisions influenced by a host of complicating factors. Like the anthropologist in the field or the scientist in the laboratory, what teachers do is guided by working hypotheses, educated guesses about the nature of what happens. These working hypotheses are constantly tested, revised, and revamped in the light of what is known about teaching and by teachers' own knowledge and experience.

Take, for example, one teacher, one student, and one lesson objective that presumably is unambiguous: teaching the concept of decimals. At any given moment during the lesson, the teacher weighs and acts on a shifting complex of information. What does that child already know? How must this new knowledge be linked to other concepts? What are the special strengths and weaknesses of the learner in abstract and linguistic reasoning? How well does he or she understand numbers and operations performed on them? What interests does he or she have that might be used in developing interesting problems? For example, could enthusiasm for baseball be used to transform the decimal concept into a question of batting averages? How is that one learner situated in the classroom or in the smaller group within that classroom? What material — be it a blackboard, an overhead, or some material to manipulate — can be used to demonstrate the concept? How will the knowledge be evaluated? What time of day is it? How long will the student's attention span last? What does the teacher do if the planned attack on the concept simply does not work?

And of course, each working hypothesis or decision is never made for only one learner at a time. The teacher makes decisions for 25 or more children simultaneously, weighing the best answers for the group. Amid this Babel of competing interests, the teacher is charged with selecting plausible solutions.

Such decision skills are not the hallmark of every occupation; rather, they are characteristics of a profession where practitioners make judgments by drawing on professional skills and knowledge learned from training and experience. The more one has the chance to hone these skills, the better they become. Thus professional experience becomes a critical component in developing and evaluating professional competence. Let us always remember that there is no single right answer to many of the most important questions in teaching.

Because they are professionals, teachers continually think about and learn from experience. As critical thinkers themselves, teachers are members of learning communities. They work in collaboration with other teachers in collegial settings to improve schoolwide learning. Teachers understand the environments from which their students come and are mindful of their students' many needs.

Such teachers — and there are hundreds of thousands of them in America's schools — embody the attributes of leadership that John

Gardner identified. These teachers are leaders and are capable of helping other teachers improve their teaching and leadership capacities.

Professional teaching standards derived from a view of teachers as leaders are most likely to be accepted if they come from an enterprise, such as the National Board, that is rooted in the teaching profession itself, yet incorporates in its deliberations the voices of all the other significant constituencies and stakeholders in education.

National Board Certification is an important step in the direction of strengthening America's teaching force. Until now, the teaching profession, unlike medicine, architecture, or accounting, has not codified the knowledge, skills, and dispositions that account for professional excellence. Consequently, certain misconceptions about what constitutes accomplished teaching continue to exist. Unfortunately, far too many Americans — school board members, administrators, and even many teachers — believe that any modestly educated person with some instinct for nurturing has the requisite qualifications to teach. While some educators focus on knowing one's subject, others argue for child-centered teaching, and still others for a "methods" approach. The reality is that all of these strategies have validity. However, even in combination, they do not encompass the breadth of a teacher's responsibilities. Accurately evaluating student needs and progress, translating complex material into language students will understand, exercising sound and principled professional judgment in the face of uncertainty, and acting effectively on such judgments also are necessary skills for an excellent teacher. The experienced, exemplary teacher also takes on the dual role of education ambassador and role model to the community by being available outside the classroom to parents and professional colleagues.

Until now, most attempts to recognize accomplished teachers have been characterized by limited teacher involvement in their origin and have not been based on high standards of professional practice. These efforts, as well as traditional "teacher of the year" awards, often decided from outside the profession, are greeted with considerable skepticism by teachers themselves. The absence of a credible and accepted method of recognizing outstanding teaching reinforces the notion that anyone with a fondness for children can teach — that the profession does not take itself or its responsibilities seriously. As we have seen, the authority structure of schools often places little faith in the expertise of teachers. Status — at least in terms of money and power to make decisions affecting classrooms — accrues to those who are farthest from the classroom. Little distinction is made between the first-year and the twentieth-year teacher. These factors combine to shape an image of the profession that is often frustrating to those who elect to venture into it and particularly discouraging to those with precisely the qualities America needs to strengthen its schools.

A system of National Board Certification that commands the respect of the profession and the public can make a critical difference in how communities view their teachers, in how teachers view themselves, and in how teachers improve their teaching practice throughout their careers.

National Board Certification differs from state licensing, sometimes called "state certification," in three critical ways. First, a state license is mandatory for teaching within its jurisdiction and indicates that the licensee satisfies entry-level requirements. In contrast, National Board Certification is voluntary and signifies highly accomplished teaching based on rigorous professional criteria. Second, state licensure requirements vary from state to state, whereas National Board Certification standards are uniform across the country. Finally, and most important, National Board Certification is developed by teachers for teachers, not established by those outside the profession. Such certification will be awarded to teachers who pass a series of performance-based assessments, involving activities both at the candidates' schools and at designated assessment centers.

The National Board Certification system now being developed involves three critical elements: 1) *standards*, establishing what accomplished teachers must know and be able to do and what accomplished teaching practice is; 2) *assessment*, evaluating teaching with a variety of performance measures tailored to the range of subjects taught and the students instructed; and 3) *professional development*, opportunities for teachers to reflect alone and with their colleagues on the elements of excellent teaching practice and to incorporate those elements into their own teaching.

National Board standards and assessments are based on a fundamental philosophical and policy framework expressed in five general propositions about excellent teaching:

- Teachers are ethically committed to growth and development of their students and are skilled at equitably helping all children learn.
- Teachers have command of the subjects they teach and know how to teach those subjects to all students.

- Teachers are responsible for managing and monitoring student learning.
- Teachers think systematically about their practice and learn and improve from experience.
- Teachers are members of adult learning communities.

These five propositions are explained at length in the National Board's policy statement, "What Teachers Should Know and Be Able to Do." This document can be obtained by writing to NBPTS Communications, 300 River Place, Suite 3600, Detroit, MI 48207.

To accommodate the diverse nature of the American teaching experience and the broad range of expertise and specialization expected of teachers, NBPTS is establishing standards in about 30 certification fields. The certification fields recognize the developmental levels of students, the subjects taught, and the contexts of teaching. Collectively, they will cover all K-12 teachers, including those who teach students with special needs. NBPTS standards committees are composed of highly experienced, outstanding professional educators; practicing classroom teachers make up the majority of and chair all standards committees. These committees are establishing standards that address both the unique characteristics of each certification field and the National Board's five-point statement.

In keeping with its vision of teaching as a highly skilled, collegial enterprise involving complex decision making, NBPTS has designed an assessment system that is performance-based and will employ a broad range of innovative assessment strategies. The current model for the assessment involves a series of exercises organized in two modules, one requiring a portfolio collected in a candidate's school setting and the second requiring data collected later at an assessment center. The school-site portfolio consists of reflective documentation of teaching and student learning and videotapes of classroom instruction. The assessment-center module focuses on structured interviews, simulations, written work, and assessments of knowledge of subject matter and content-specific pedagogy.

A Field Test Network (FTN) has been established to test the assessments, recruit initial candidates, and develop a variety of professional development models. The FTN is composed of 112 school districts and colleges and provides access to a nationally representative sample of approximately 7% of the nation's elementary and secondary school teachers. During the 1993-94 school year, several hundred teachers took part in a field test of the first two fields under development: Early Adolescence/English Language Arts and Early Adolescence/

Generalist. The full system of National Board Certification will be phased in over the next five years.

National Board Certification and the Teacher Leader: Some Issues and Dilemmas

I would like to return to the notion that for today's society, we need a new kind of school and a new kind of teacher. If this is correct, and I believe it is, we must create a professional and political climate conducive to the creation of this new kind of school and new kind of teacher.

The National Board for Professional Teaching Standards and its National Board Certification system can be a catalyst for creating new roles for teachers and for reorganizing schools. It can help teachers develop the tools they need to be empowered professionals. While teaching is portrayed all too often as the implementation of policy and curriculum developed by others — as following orders — the National Board advocates a role for teachers in which they are integrally involved in the analysis and construction of curriculum, in the coordination of instruction, in the professional development of staff, and in many other policy decisions fundamental to the creation of highly productive learning communities.

The National Board Certification process itself is designed to encourage professional collegiality and qualities of leadership. It supplies teachers with opportunities for self-renewal, which, as John Gardner would remind us, is a major prerequisite for meaningful change. The assessment requires that candidates demonstrate their ability to take risks, to solve problems, and to collaborate with their colleagues. Most important, it requires serious professional reflection.

Preparing for National Board Certification requires engaging in the kinds of activities, both alone and in a collegial setting, that lead to stronger teaching. The preparation of the school-site portfolio and the subsequent assessment-center exercises ensure that regardless of the outcome, teachers who have gone through the National Board Certification process have observed themselves in action, reflected on the rationale behind their classroom practice, and evaluated the degree to which their students have acquired specific skills. Moreover, collaborating with other candidates in preparing for the assessment encourages professional collegiality, while the feedback offered to all candidates should lead to stronger practice and increased insights.

Therefore, teachers certified by the National Board will be well-qualified to assume a variety of interesting and challenging leadership roles. These accomplished teachers also will be confident in observing their colleagues and equally confident in being observed; they will engage in substantive discussions about teaching; they will work with others in designing new courses and curricula; and they will understand how to undertake evaluation procedures. Furthermore, they will do these things as teachers who have not been compelled to leave the classroom in order to perform these roles.

A fair and rigorous National Board Certification system will offer school boards and administrators an objective means of identifying the strongest teachers and making full use of their knowledge and expertise. It can provide exemplary teachers with opportunities for advancement and the assumption of leadership roles without having to leave the classroom. It can motivate more teachers to engage in substantive professional-development activities and to work on improving their practice in order to advance. Most important, by demonstrating that teaching is a challenging professional endeavor that is treated with both respect and seriousness by its practitioners, by policy makers, and by the public at large, it can attack the twofold problem within America's education system: how to attract excellent teachers – teacher leaders – to the elementary and secondary schools and how to keep them in teaching once they are there.

However, along with its strengths, National Board Certification will offer a formidable array of challenges. New schools and new teachers presuppose new ways of thinking about education as a profession, and thus require serious and honest consideration by every segment of the education community and a willingness to make profound changes.

It is obvious that principals have a major role to play in the success or failure of a new school community of teacher leaders. For such a community to emerge, principals must accept the notion that treating teachers as if they were all the same is both inefficient and dispiriting. Working in concert with principals (teacher-principals or head teachers?), accomplished teachers should have the flexibility to assemble and reassemble school resources in response to their students' shifting educational needs. Many schools still are organized with little acknowledgment of the diversity that exists within the teacher work force. Making use of a system that identifies accomplished professionals in a fair and trustworthy manner can help free the schools from a structural straitjacket and enhance the likelihood that all school resources — time, people, money — are marshaled more effectively on behalf of student learning.

School districts and policy makers must take the responsibility to support and encourage principals who foster teacher leadership and are willing to uphold and support rigorous, objective, and professional standards of practice. Many principals, after all, were "promoted" out of the classroom because of their accomplishments as teachers.

Coming at a time when teacher preparation programs are reshaping their curricula, National Board Certification also can have a constructive effect on efforts to redesign teacher education. National Board standards that stress the interaction of subject matter knowledge and pedagogy will pose a special opportunity to many higher education institutions where different faculties claim responsibility for each of these bodies of knowledge.

With many initial candidates for National Board Certification coming from the current teaching force, there should emerge a new and growing market for preparing teachers for the National Board assessments. Institutions of higher education will be in a prime position to help practitioners evaluate their readiness for the National Board assessments and broaden and deepen their knowledge of the subjects they teach and the research on teaching. These institutions should consider the challenge of redesigning curricula to include the teaching of leadership skills and an understanding of organizational theory and education policy issues. They also should acquaint students with the activities and goals of NBPTS, National Board Certification, and the certification standards, so that students will be better prepared to apply for certification when eligible.

There is another issue we must address before we can expect to reap the benefits of a thriving community of teacher leaders. Teachers must be willing to take responsibility for creating and assuming their own leadership roles. Adam Urbanski, president of the Rochester Federation of Teachers and an NBPTS board member, asserts, "Teachers must be agents of change, not subjects of change." Sadly, in the current school culture, teachers too often are unwilling to assume roles that extend their responsibilities beyond basic classroom duties, even if these roles offer the possibility of additional autonomy or control over their professional environment.

In part through physical and psychic exhaustion, in part through simmering resentment, and in part through a long-standing conditioning that results in teachers seeing themselves as "subjects" rather than "agents," many teachers avoid opportunities for leadership in their schools, however meager those opportunities may be. For National Board Certification to realize its promise, teachers must be willing to take professional risks, to support and encourage one another, and to be genuinely collaborative. Many excellent teachers are isolated, practicing valuable skills in their classrooms that are not being shared with others. It is essential that they realize that by sharing their expertise with their colleagues they are not only increasing the potential for greater student learning, but they are moving toward greater professional empowerment.

In its own efforts to reach its goal of fostering increased student learning through a stronger and more professional teaching force, the National Board for Professional Teaching Standards consistently draws from a deep pool of America's accomplished teachers, who serve a variety of key functions within the organization. As board members, as members and chairs of standards committees, as teachers-in-residence, they offer their expertise, assume leadership positions, and above all keep the National Board from losing sight of its role as a significant, teacher-driven force for the improvement of America's schools.

Clearly, the positive impact of National Board-certified teachers in America's schools will take some years to realize and cannot be predicted with precision. Ultimately, this impact will be determined in part by the National Board's own work, but it also will depend on the actions of state and local authorities and on the decisions of individual teachers. While I believe the creation of a community of teacher-leaders will lead to dramatic and permanent changes in America's schools, it will require the dedicated efforts of all members of the education community to bring about those changes.

References

Carnegie Forum on Education and the Economy. *A Nation Prepared: Teachers for the 21st Century, The Report of the Task Force on Teaching as a Profession.* New York, 1986.

Gardner, John G. *On Leadership.* New York: Free Press, 1993.

Huey, John. "The New Post-Heroic Leadership." *Fortune* 129, no. 4 (21 February 1994): 42.

Meier, Deborah. "Reinventing Teaching." *Teachers College Record* 93, no. 4 (Summer 1992).

Murphy, John A. *The Charlotte Process: Reclaiming Our Legacy.* Charlotte, N.C.: Charlotte-Mecklenburg Public Schools, 1992.

National Board for Professional Teaching Standards. *Toward High and Rigorous Standards for the Teaching Profession*. 3rd ed. Detroit, 1991.